Contents

Preface

Our world often appears one of great sophistication and complexity. It is a world where five billion people struggle to survive, some with relative ease, some only with the greatest of difficulty and after enduring great hardship.

There is a need to understand the basic ways in which this enormous family works, their effects on each other and their effects on the environment. Today in our ever more complex world, where technology seems capable of overcoming all, there is still a vital need to work with the environment not against it. An increasing number of people find great personal satisfaction in understanding how the human race finds its way in the world, while many find it an indispensable part of their work.

This book is the second in a three volume series. It has two aims: (i) to show you the processes that shape our lives; and (ii) to show you how this knowledge can be put into action for the benefit both of mankind and the survival of the natural environment. So, whether you want to be a researcher, an engineer, help an international aid agency, become a planner, a farmer, an architect or a judge, if you are intending to be an environmental protester or simply have a love of understanding how things work, this is a book that will help fulfil these aims. The knowledge that we have gained and the help that we have received have been generously given by many people in both the developed and the developing world. To all these people who have become our friends we would like to express our sincere appreciation.

Brian Knapp, Simon Ross
and Duncan McCrae, 1989

Theme: Population, the uncertain resource

Chapter 1
The demographic transition

To the memory of Sarah, the wife of John Charlton who departed this life the 10th day of October 1790 aged 48 years.

Also the body of Mary Charlton their daughter who died the 20th day of November 1789 aged 9 years.

Also five of their children who died infants.

Headstone in a Durham graveyard

Introduction

Geography is about the patterns produced as people use their environment. In this first chapter we begin by studying the pattern of births, lives and deaths in the context of the resources that could support them (Fig. 1.1). We will look at the way the human family is developing. In subsequent chapters we shall examine more closely the particular characteristics that apply to the developing and the developed worlds.

Figure 1.1 A letter to The Times *in 1849 describing some of the conditions that had to be overcome in order to allow the demographic transition to get under way*

A SANITARY REMONSTRANCE

We print the following remonstrance just as it has reached us, and trust its publication will assist the unfortunate remonstrants:

THE EDITOR OF THE TIMES PAPER

Sur, – May we beg and beseach your proteck-shion and power, We are Sur, as it may be, livin in a Wilderniss, so far as the rest of London knows anything of us, or as the rich and great people care about. We live in muck and filthe. We sint got no priviz, no dust bins, no drains, no water-splies, and no drain or suer in the hole place. The suer Company, in Greek St., Soho Square, all great, rich and powerful men, take no notice watsomedevor of our cumplaints. The Stenche of a Gully-hole is disgustin. We all of us suffer, and numbers are ill, and if the Cholera comes Lord help us.

Praay e Sir com and see us, for we are livin like piggs, and it aint faire we should be so ill treted.

We are your respeckfull servents in Church Lane, Carrier St., and other corts.

(Source: *The Times,* 3 Oct. 1849)

Figure 1.2 Singapore's nation-hood is celebrated by this banner

People and their world

It is important to realise that we are part of a global ecosystem. This concept is central to the nature of populations, both at national and international levels. Some people see the world as a single global resource, arguing that anything we do in one country intimately affects all others; but on the scale of day to day existence most people look to the nation state as the best framework for decisions.

To survive and prosper, nations need to care for their resources and use them wisely. Nations also have to pay their way in the world, exporting and importing to the greatest benefit of their people. Some nations, such as Singapore, are very small and have extremely limited physical resources. Other countries, such as Indonesia, are able to call upon their own natural land resources to a much greater degree, being both self-sufficient in foodstuffs and able to exploit other natural resources such as oil.

Nations see the world not only from the point of view of resources but also from the viewpoint of their national identity. In some countries the concept of national identity is very strong in the public mind (Fig. 1.2); in others it is a weaker link, with the government able to influence the development of the country much less directly. It is the interplay of natural birth rates with both the resource base and the government policies that produces the complex population patterns we see today.

Population change

The calculation of population change is made by

$$Pi\ (r/100 + 1)n = Pf$$

where Pi is the initial population, r is the rate of change, n is the number of years in the projection and Pf is the final projected population.

There are several elements involved in changes to any population (Fig 1.3):

(i) the natural pattern of births, deaths and lifespan;

(ii) the effect of migration, either international or national;

(iii) government policies on population projections;

(iv) changes in the social norms of the population with regard to age of childbearing, family size, etc.; and

(v) external influences such as warfare, genocide and intergovernmental pressure.

Changes in the first element are entirely due to the improvement of medical facilities and diet, better housing, public health and more leisure time that accompany most social development; the other elements are under the potential control of governments to a greater extent.

Governments, through the use of the census figures, are able to gain a perspective on their population dynamics. How a government responds to the projections of change depends on

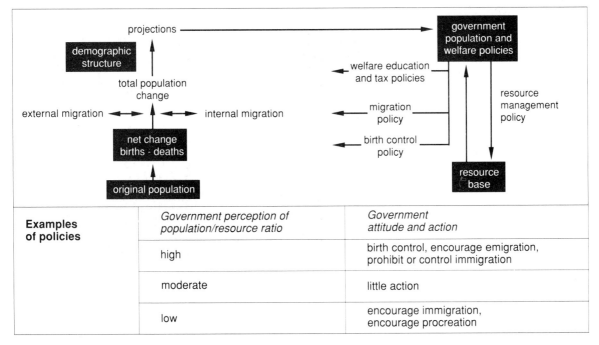

Examples of policies	Government perception of population/resource ratio	Government attitude and action
	high	birth control, encourage emigration, prohibit or control immigration
	moderate	little action
	low	encourage immigration, encourage procreation

Figure 1.3 The interaction between the factors controlling population dynamics

its perception of the population/resource ratio. If it believes that the ratio is poor, then a policy of birth control and emigration may be started; if the ratio is seen as only moderately adverse there may be little action, while if the ratio is seen as low, there might be encouragement of immigration and increasing family size. All of these types of responses can be seen in the world today.

The reason for children

People have to reproduce in order to survive as a species. Of course, few people see this need only in stark biological terms, but the necessity of reproduction is fundamental to the way people behave and their view of the human family.

Normally, biological necessity is translated into action for immediate or personal reasons. These vary sharply between the developed and developing world. In the developed world it may be for:

(i) the pleasure of having a child or children; or
(ii) emotional and personal support in old age.

In the developing world the pleasure of having

children is a bonus. Although you might find this hard to appreciate, children in the developing world are mainly born because:

(i) they quickly become cost effective, bringing more revenue into the household than they use: they provide extra hands on the farm when planting, weeding or harvesting need to be done; or they go out into urban areas to earn money; and
(ii) they are an insurance policy against becoming destitute in old age (Fig. 1.4).

Marriage is one way society organises itself to create some form of family stability (Fig. 1.5). Marriage does not occur in all societies; some societies are perfectly stable without marriage. But stability is important because children take a long time to bring up and the task of raising them requires an emotionally balanced input from men as well as women. Because most societies rely on marriage as the building block for families, having children has traditionally been acceptable only for married people. Although this is less rigidly adhered to than in the past, and in many developed countries something like a fifth of all babies are born out of wedlock, most people still think marriage *then* children is the correct way

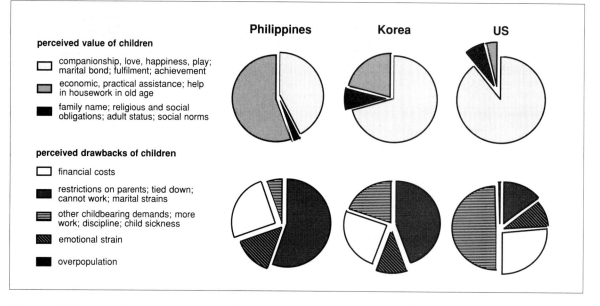

perceived value of children

☐ companionship, love, happiness, play; marital bond; fulfilment; achievement

▨ economic, practical assistance; help in housework in old age

■ family name; religious and social obligations; adult status; social norms

perceived drawbacks of children

☐ financial costs

▨ restrictions on parents; tied down; cannot work; marital strains

▤ other childbearing demands; more work; discipline; child sickness

▨ emotional strain

■ overpopulation

Philippines   Korea   US

Figure 1.4 Contrasts between the advantages and disadvantages of having children as expressed in a UN survey of sample countries

forward. Thus the number of children that are born to a family depends on:

> (i) the number of years after marriage that the woman remains fertile; and
> (ii) the spacing of children within this period.

In turn this influences the population growth as a whole.

> *As a group, discuss the role of marriage and its importance to society . What are the implications for state welfare of a breakdown in family life?*

In the developed world we have come to assume that people fall in love and then get married. This is, of course, a recent luxury permitted by affluence. In an environment where survival depends on having a family, marriage is not decided by choice but by necessity. Thus the arranged marriage so common in Africa and Asia today is a perfectly natural response to a practical situation. People who are working all day just to survive can spare little time for love – what they need is a reliable partner and children and love is a bonus. Under these circumstances it is totally understandable that parents should seek a match as advantageous as possible for their children.

Figure 1.5 Marriage, part of the social structure of communities. It is designed to add stability to the family unit

An Indian Worker

Charansingh is both fortunate and unfortunate. He is blessed with a family of five children, but the penalty is that they are all girls (Fig. 1.6). Each girl will have to be found a husband, for the arranged marriage is the way of life of most people in India. Although the dowry system is officially discouraged, the practicality of the matter is that a dowry will have to be found for each child. The husband's parents will expect it and will send him a list of the things they want. In total this will put Charansingh into debt for

Charansingh and his family

possibly the rest of his life, but he will have ensured the marriage of his daughters and thus he will have provided for their support into the future. The daughters and their children will become the shared responsibility of the husband's families as well as his. By such means is the welfare of society maintained.

Population and health

It is perfectly natural to try to improve the welfare and survival of the population. Improvements in health have been sought by every generation of people but it is over the last two centuries, and especially in the last few decades, that the most extraordinary advances have been made.

In the developed world the common infectious diseases that plagued previous generations have largely been eliminated by extensive vaccination and immunisation programmes. By this means, and by good sanitation and accurately understood nutrition, the infant mortality rate, for example, has been brought down to very low levels. Today, attention is focused on prolonging life and combating the remaining common forms of disease. Diseases of the circulatory system (particularly heart disease – 50 per cent of all deaths) and various forms of cancers (20 per cent of all deaths) are the most important. Both of these

are linked to lifestyle factors including lack of exercise, bad diet and smoking and are therefore difficult to combat without social education.

Think of a range of jobs that might make people more prone to disease. Are these jobs increasing or decreasing in number, and what can be done to lower the risk of disease?

Although there are probably around 500 million people in the developing world who suffer from malnutrition, the incidence of infant mortality in most developing countries has also dropped dramatically. However, the real problem with malnutrition is the way it causes permanent poor health, and therefore disability and lack of potential for earning a living. Thus more people are remaining alive, but their quality of life and earnings potential is far below a satisfactory level.

Death and disease for India's working children

Every year, Indian workers die prematurely in the shadow of the Taj Mahal, India's most famous monument, because the country still permits child labour.

In Ferozabad, a town near Agra, the site of the Taj Mahal, 50 000 children risk life and limb daily in the searing heat of its glass and bangle factories. Nationally, the Indian government estimates that there are some 17 million children working. The Indian Social Institute, based in New Delhi, says that the real figure could lie between 40 and 44 million.

During a spot check at factories in the town [there were] naked live wires on the floor and broken glass. Semi-clothed children worked in dimly lit and poorly ventilated rooms.

Besides risking accidental burns, children working in the glass factories suffer from lung diseases including silicosis. These arise when the children inhale large amounts of silica and soda ash dust, and fumes from kerosene

In another area of India, Tamil Nadu, children as young as six are woken before three in the morning, taken by bus to match factories in nearby Sivakasi, and work through till as late as seven in the evening.

'Employers find child labour cheap, flexible and docile.'

The Institute argues that child labour perpetuates the backwardness of the most disadvantaged people in India. 'Eighty per cent of working children are untouchables. Child labour ensures that they don't receive any education and remain illiterate. They are forced to remain in the unskilled sector.'

(Source: Paul Marriage and Kathleen Forrestier-Walker, *New Scientist*, 9 Oct. 1986)

The demographic transition

Whenever a man and a woman decide to have another child they are making a decision with implications for the whole world. This is because the growth of the world population depends on the balance between the millions of individual births and deaths. People make these decisions in the light of their own domestic circumstances and also within the general resource framework of the country they are living in. In this wider framework the attitudes of government can be crucial.

The rate of growth of population thus depends on:

(i) how individuals perceive their families (How many children do they want? Do they want to start a family when they are young or wait until they are older?); and

(ii) how each government sees the balance between the resources at its disposal and the population among whom resources must be shared. (For example, is fertility or birth control favoured? Are incentives given to have large families or small ones?)

Government control over family size varies widely from China, where one child per family has been stipulated as the norm, to countries such as Niger, where the government has so little relationship with the lives of the rural people that it plays no significant part in population decisions.

People also make decisions about their families based on their chances of survival. In many cases a strategy for survival is built into the social, religious and cultural norms. In this way the strategy is made most likely to succeed, although it is also made more difficult to alter in the light of revised circumstances.

Comment on the way at least one religion is designed to control the pattern of population. Suggest some of the recent changes in attitude that have made religious views more or less important.

The developed world

The family survival strategy has required considerable adaptation because the survival rate of children and the global resource base have been changing fast. Demographers have seen these changing strategies reflected in the structure of human families. The strategy appears to follow a consistent pattern which they have called the **demographic transition**. In the developed world the demographic transition is thought to have run its course and has occurred in four phases. (Fig. 1.6).

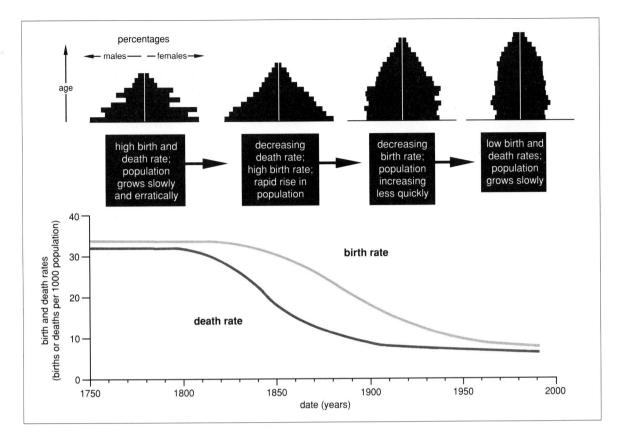

Figure 1.6 The demographic transition

Phase 1

In societies where the diet is poor, people have to work hard all the time and they have no effective medical facilities. Death rates are high and life expectancy short. Before the 1800s such a situation applied world-wide. Birth rates were relatively constant, but death rates fluctuated dramatically as a result of epidemics and famines, etc. Populations grew only slowly under these circumstances because, no matter how many children people had, they only just kept above the losses due to death from disease, malnutrition, accident, war or overwork. At no time and in no place did population increases exceed 0.1 per cent per annum.

Phase 2

From 1800 onward, those countries which became industrialised had medical and nutritional advances which transformed their societies.

In general, work loads declined, standards of personal health and nutrition went up, public health standards increased, and medical science became a reality. However, as death rates fell a rapid imbalance developed between the number of births and deaths. In order to survive, the concept of continuous child rearing had become a central and ingrained part of the culture and as the number of births matched more evenly the number of survivals, the population began to increase sharply.

During this period the populations of industrialised countries grew rapidly with growth rates of the order of 2 per cent a year. This resulted in populations doubling every 35 years or so. Indeed, without the large scale emigrations from Europe throughout the nineteenth century (which probably relieved the continent of 50 million people) some people are convinced that the demand for food may well have outstripped the supply systems available at that time (Fig. 1.7).

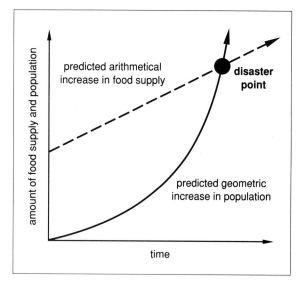

Figure 1.7 In the early years of the demographic transition, with rapid growth of population and little technological improvement in agriculture, some people believed that the world population would exceed the ability of the world to produce enough food. This prediction, known as the Malthusian prophecy, has formed the basis of many doom projections even up to the present day.This scenario is explained in detail in such books as The Limits to Growth. In practice, however, not only has technology made rapid advances, but populations have completed their transitions, leading to a lessening demand for food

Phase 3

It takes some decades for a cultural adjustment to be made to the changed situation with respect to death rates. Only then do people begin to have fewer children and change their concept of the family. After this the rate of growth of the population slows down. However, this adjustment takes many decades to work through because the children of the large families still have to go through the childbearing years.

Phase 4

By the 1930s the balance between births and deaths in the developed world was again becoming established, this time with both births and deaths at a low level. Since this time the death rate has remained more or less stable, with population changes produced by birth rate fluctuations due to social factors or migration.

In the developed world today the populations for countries that have not experienced large scale migration are in such a balance that the proportions of the populations are roughly the same in each age band up to the age of 60 – a unique state for any species. In the future, the populations of these countries will be determined solely by the birth rates. Death rates are already close to their lower limit, and in any case people live well beyond their childbearing years. Saving the lives of the elderly will not affect the population growth to any great degree. This means that fertility in these countries will fluctuate in response to cultural and economic pulls and pressures.

Figure. 1.8 Comparison between times for populations to double at current rates

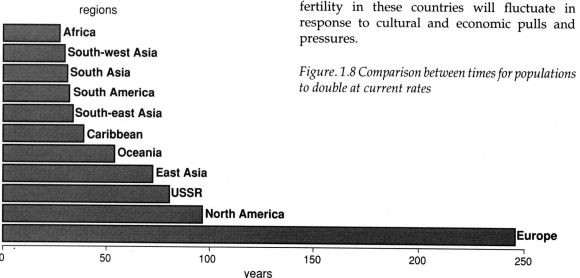

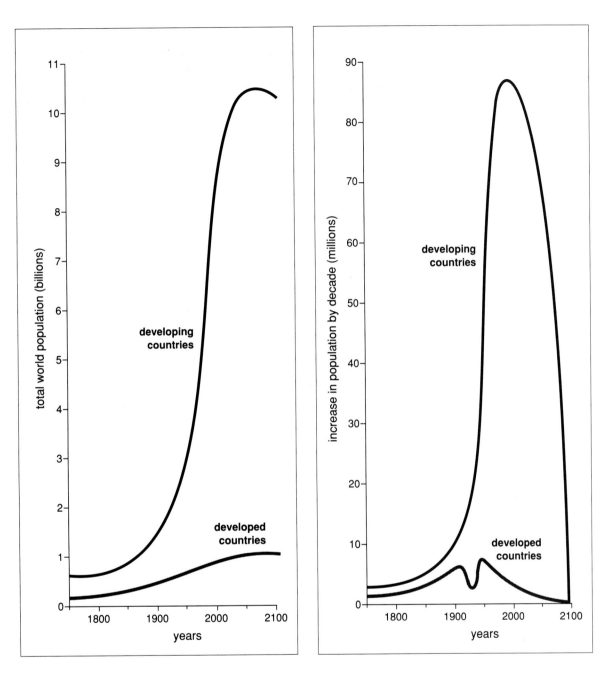

The transition since the 1960s

By the 1960s many of the developed world countries had completed their demographic transitions. The principal growth in the world population today is in the developing world (Figs 1.8, 1.9) and in countries such as the USA that have continued substantial immigration (see also Chapter 4).

Figure 1.9 The diagrams show how the population will expand as the demographic transition is completed. Several factors are involved, including the world total (a, above left), the rate of increase in numbers by decade (b, above right), and the change in the population structure of the developed and developing worlds because of their contrasts in infant mortality, family size and longer lives (c and d, overleaf)

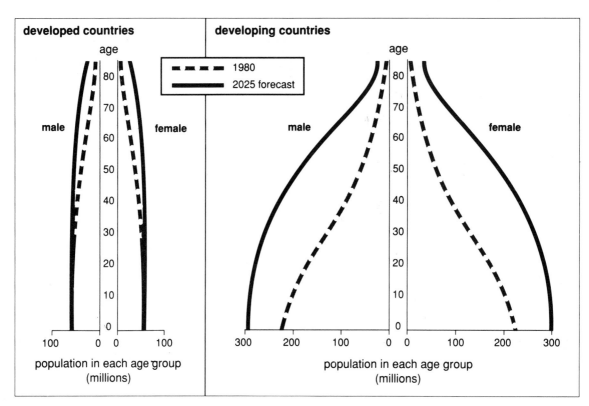

Figure 1.9(c) Changes in population structure

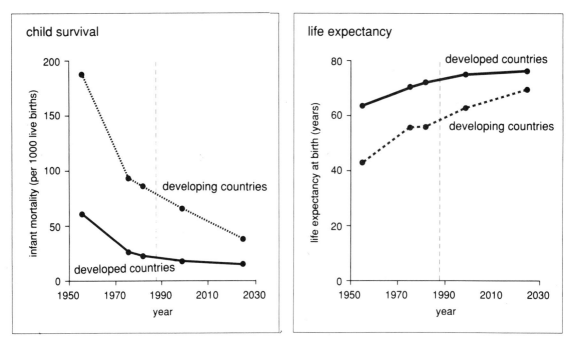

Figure 1.9(d) Past, present and forecast changes in child survival and life expectancy

The three quarters of the world population that live in the developing world mostly have a life-style strikingly different from that of people of the developed world. Death rates in the developing countries (except those like Ethiopia that are plagued by internal strife) have tumbled dramatically as medical aid and better nutrition have reached them (Fig. 1.10). Crude death rates for all developing countries are now 14 per 1000 in contrast to 9 per 1000 for the developed world. Because the decline in death rates has happened very quickly the imbalance between fertility rates and death rates has also been very dramatic. In some countries there is now a population increase of 4 per cent a year, leading to the population doubling every 16 years! In general the crude birth rate of the developed world stands at 3 per 1000 per annum as against the 17 per 1000 for the developing world. For zero population growth in a society of high mortality (life expectancy of 25 years – common in the developing world until recently) a family size of 5.2 children is required, giving a birth rate of about 40 per 1000. When life expectancy is beyond childbearing age (i.e. the developed world and increasingly the developing world) a birth rate of only 13.3 per cent is required, or a family size of 2.1 children. Even if the people in the developing world all decided to reduce their populations to nothing more than present replacement rates, there are a large proportion of couples who must still live through their reproductive years before zero growth will be achieved. It looks, therefore, as though a final world population stabilisation will not be achieved before the total reaches 8 to 10 billion, somewhere in the middle of the twenty-first century.

The unreliability of population projections is caused by the large numbers of variables that go into a population equation. For example, it is still not clear what really causes the population transition to be completed. Is it better economic conditions and pensions for the elderly so they do not have to be dependent on their children in old age? Is it the wish of adults to have greater independence and not be tied to their large families all their

Figure 1.10 *Help with nutrition, immunisation and other health-related programmes has reduced infant mortality and prolonged life. Here a Javanese baby is weighed. This helps the social worker to see when the nutrition level is too low*

lives? Is it the increased level of education that allows people better knowledge of contraception techniques and family planning? Is it the understanding by governments that rapid population growth hinders the development of their countries? How great a part does each factor play in the final equation? These are the crucial issues whose answers hold the key to effective future planning throughout the world.

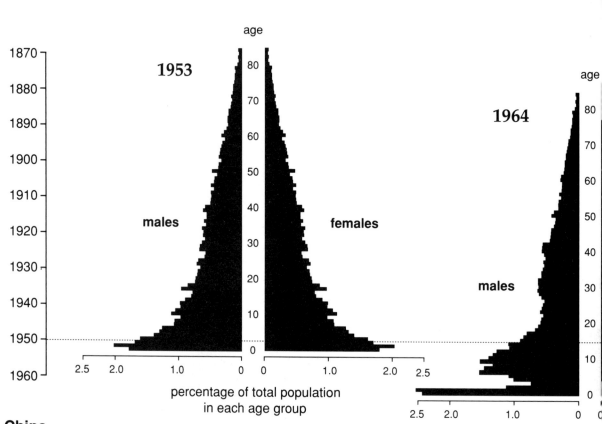

percentage of total population
in each age group

China

China has been an enigma since the communist revolution of 1949. It was not until 1982 that the first census for many years was released. In its pages we find one of the most extraordinary stories of the development of a nation.

Understanding the Chinese population structure requires an understanding of the nature of centrally planned economies and their all pervading role in society. Even such basic and private activities as procreation have been drastically influenced by state activities. Centrally planned economies are mostly dominated by Five Year Plans. These rigid dogmas do tend to cause rapid changes in direction because the only changes that can occur are between plans. In China each change of plan took on the scale of a revolution. Regular reverses of ideology were so drastic that they were even matched by fundamental fluctuations in the age groups within the country. The main changes that have occurred can be divided into four stages:

Stage 1

From 1949 to the start of the first Five Year Plan in 1953 the government was concerned to rebuild the country after the war, and there was a general impression that more workers were needed to rebuild society faster. At this time the government gave extra payment for every child born. Sterilisation and abortion were banned. As a result of natural recovery from the traumas of the war and this financial incentive there was rapid population growth. There was a net increase of 10 million people a year.

Stage 2

By 1954 China's population had reached 600 million, 10 per cent more than in 1949, and the effects were beginning to be felt. In 1956 the government introduced the first birth control programme. However, in 1958 there began the period of attempted rapid modernisation called the Great

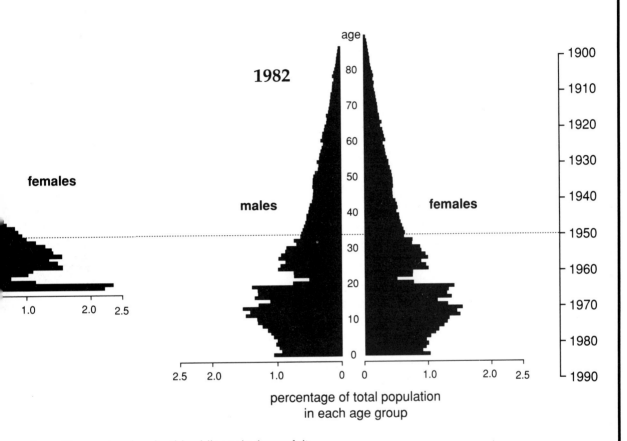

Population pyramids for China

1982

age
80
70
60
50
40
30
20
10
0

females

males

females

percentage of total population
in each age group

2.5 2.0 1.0 0 0 1.0 2.0 2.5

1.0 2.0 2.5

1900
1910
1920
1930
1940
1950
1960
1970
1980
1990

Leap Forward and under this philosophy it was felt there might be labour shortages and so births were again encouraged. But by 1962 the government had changed its mind: production was not rising, great famines had been caused by faulty planning and there was great cultural upheaval. So a new phase of birth control was begun in 1964.

Stage 3
Just as the birth control programme was beginning to have some effect the new upheaval – The Cultural Revolution – got underway. This period lasted from 1966 to 1971 and was a new period of high birth rate. The impact was felt again in food supply, housing, living standards and education.

Stage 4
In 1971 order was again restored after the chaos of the Cultural Revolution. A third family planning campaign was launched with the slogan 'Late, sparse, few'. In this period until 1979 the whole scheme relied on propaganda for success.

Stage 5
In 1979 the government decided it must act more decisively and the concept of 'only one child per family' was launched. The aim was to limit the population to a maximum of 1.2 billion by the end of the century.

Student enquiry 1A

The paths to transition

1. Using the information about France, compare the actual demographic changes with the transition model and explain why the changes were irregular.
2. Now refer to the three population pyramids for China together with a description of some aspects of its history. Use both pieces of information to construct a diagram showing the demographic transition.
3. China has experienced many turmoils in its recent history, and its population pyramid is unusually complex. Comment on the events which seem to have been the most important and why this might be so.
4. It has been said that governments have five courses of action open to alter the fertility rate: (i) persuade; (ii) manipulate services; (iii) change incentives; (iv) transform social institutions; and (v) coerce. Discuss how the information ofn China and France illustrates this suggestion.
5. 'If one were looking for a promising arena in which to demonstrate the possibilities of social engineering, one would not choose population.' Use the evidence from case studies in this chapter to comment on this statement.

———— Social factors affecting the transition: the case of France ————

At the beginning of the nineteenth century, France was one of the most populous of the European countries. However, during the century its population grew at a slower rate than that of neighbours such as the UK and Germany. As early as 1870, when France lost the Franco-Prussian War, some people in government began to associate low population growth with defeat, a feeling intensified after the defeat in the early years of the First World War. In the post-war period government resisted contraception and gave tax incentives for larger families, although the population growth was not affected because an increase was not seen as necessary by the population. However, after the Second World War there was a general feeling by the people, as well as the government, that an increase in population was required at least to allow the replacement of the people lost in the war. The baby boom occurred in most of the countries of Europe, but it was more sustained in France and heavily supported by government tax incentives. Nevertheless, social attitudes to marriage and children changed from the 1960s and the birth rate fell below replacement levels in 1974. The knowledge that the population was falling caused considerable consternation in government circles and further family allowances were introduced. In a poll conducted in 1978, it became clear that families regarded the extra cost of having the three children suggested by the government, as opposed to the two most people wanted, as too high. Important social factors influencing decisions also included the effect of persistent child bearing on the career of the mother, and the difficulty of returning to a reasonable part-time job after childbearing. It is now clear that the government simply cannot afford the large financial sums that would be needed to compensate women for their perceived losses. As a result the birth rate has fallen to 1.8 children per family.

Chapter 2
Controlling the population

Introduction

In this chapter we look more closely at how the demographic transition has caused a rapid increase in the world's population and the challenge this brings.

The challenge is to provide everyone with a satisfactory quality of life. This means ensuring that there is enough food, good health care, reasonable working conditions and enough money to buy some of the goods and services at present only available to a few. It can be argued that one way to help meet these goals is to help control the present population growth.

The population explosion

As was outlined in Chapter 1, in the developed world the demographic transition took about two centuries. For most of this time the improvements in nutrition and medical care that were being introduced in the developed world were not widely applied in the developing world.

As a result, while the developed countries completed their transition, and the national populations became much more stable, the developing world countries were left behind. Many of them still suffered from chronic epidemics and famines; natural controls which held the population steady.

The main changes in health and welfare for developing world countries came after the Second World War with organised attempts to spread the benefits of health care and food more widely. Organisations such as the World Heath Organisation (WHO) spearheaded a systematic world-wide attack on disease and malnutrition. Developed world countries began to donate increasingly large amounts of money as aid, and many people contributed to the funds of the voluntary organisations such as OXFAM. The results were spectacular. The infant mortality rate fell quickly and the average life expectancy began to rise. However, these swift changes had equally dramatic demographic consequences.

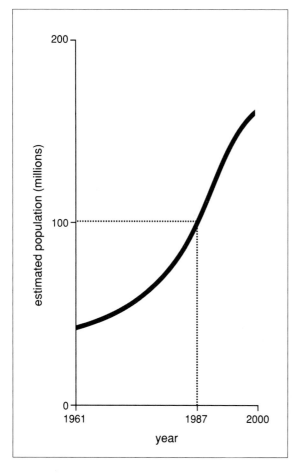

Figure 2.1 Nigeria's population growth

Matching resources to people

One of the main arguments for restricting populations is the threat of food shortages and exhaustion of resources. But the rate of increase in food supply has more than kept up with the population rise everywhere except in Africa, and the reason Africa is short of food is a short term combination of primitive techniques and political instability, not fundamental lack of resource.

Western methods used throughout the world would produce enough food for an estimated 33 billion people, even without future improvements to yields. The Food and Agriculture Organisation of the United Nations (FAO) can show that there is even less need to worry about resources and that the world is quite capable of feeding itself. Even if the whole world returned to a primitive kind of farming and stopped relying on artificial fertilisers the present population could still be comfortably fed.

People are inventing new methods of exploiting resources all the time and it can be argued that, as the oil runs out, alternative energy sources will be found, just as they have in the past. Nevertheless many people starve or suffer malnutrition and an even greater number are deprived of most of the benefits of advanced technology. In both cases this is because they cannot afford to buy the goods that are available.

When there are large numbers of people, basic resources can be spread too thinly. For example health care is harder to provide the greater the numbers that require it. Similarly, employment can only rise to match the wealth generated. A large population will find adequate employment progressively more difficult to provide.

People whose strategy had always been to have as large a family as possible because many of its members were bound to die, found more and more members surviving. And so a profound change in the world's population occurred – encapsulated in the popular term, **population explosion**.

The change from phase one to phase two of the demographic transition model occurred within a couple of decades. However, the large scale emigration that had taken the strain off Europe during its demographic transition no longer prevailed in the mid-twentieth century. Instead, the growing populations had to be accommodated within their national boundaries. Clearly, new solutions had to be considered if the rate of population increase were not to overwhelm the countries concerned (Fig. 2.1).

Pressure on resources

The present global soil resources are capable of supporting a growing world population. However, people also expect their quality of life to improve. For many this means an increase in money and material possessions. Yet, if it were possible to provide all the world's people with the extra income required to buy what they want, what would be the impact on the overall global resource base?

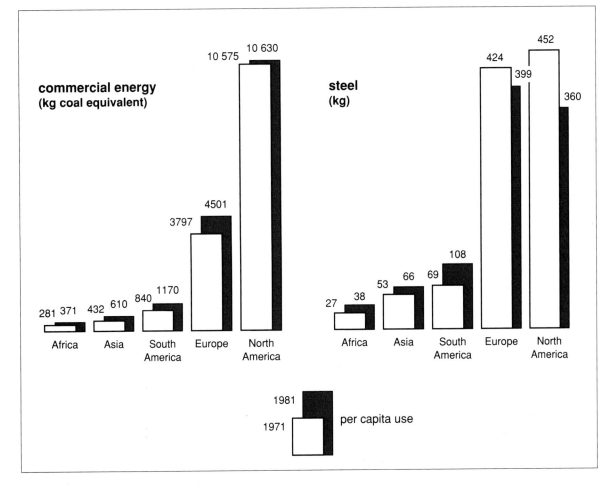

commercial energy
(kg coal equivalent)

steel
(kg)

per capita use
1981
1971

Figure 2.2 Global use of energy and steel are used here as indicators to show the potential demand for resources if all countries achieve the same economic status. The greatest impact will come as Asia's living standards rise

On average people in the developed world use up to forty times more raw materials than people in the developing world. Some of the resources are already exploited at levels close to the total available on Earth. It would not, for example, be possible to find all the raw materials required to provide each family in the world with a motor car – even if they could afford it. There are not sufficient resources for a continually expanding population demanding the current range of goods using the raw materials presently needed for manufacture. Figure 2.2 shows the way Africa, Asia and South America lag behind North America and Europe in the use of commercial energy, steel and newsprint. These are just some of the many resources that may run out quickly as demand rises. The impact of the use of timber on deforestation and soil degradation has already made world headlines (Fig. 2.3).

Many non-fuel minerals are currently transformed during manufacturing into products which are hard to recycle. Future generations will need major technological revolutions to find alternatives.

The demographic transition has not resulted in world starvation due to exceeding the carrying capacity of the land, but in the inability of large sectors of the population to get access to enough wealth to have a reasonable quality of life. In the sections that follow we shall consider various ways in which this objective can be met by manipulating the world's future population.

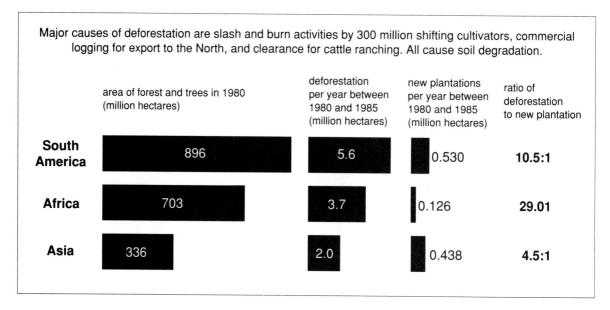

Major causes of deforestation are slash and burn activities by 300 million shifting cultivators, commercial logging for export to the North, and clearance for cattle ranching. All cause soil degradation.

	area of forest and trees in 1980 (million hectares)	deforestation per year between 1980 and 1985 (million hectares)	new plantations per year between 1980 and 1985 (million hectares)	ratio of deforestation to new plantation
South America	896	5.6	0.530	**10.5:1**
Africa	703	3.7	0.126	**29.01**
Asia	336	2.0	0.438	**4.5:1**

Figure 2.3 The rate of deforestation versus replanting in the tropical rainforests

New attitudes towards children

Large families fuel population explosions, but they also increase the health risk to the mothers (as childbirth is a major physical event) and thus increase the risk that many children will have to survive without a mother. Abandoned children are commonplace in many countries (Fig. 2.4). Many come from families where the mother has died and the father has not been able to cope alone.

Studies in India, where a high percentage of people are still in great poverty, *do* suggest significant reductions in family size in some areas. They show that the labour value of children and their security value for old age has declined even in rural villages where traditionally as many hands as possible were needed to work the land.

An analysis of fertility decline in nine villages 125 km from Bangalore in southern India, where the green revolution is well under way, showed that at least three factors were critical to reducing the economic value and increasing the economic costs of children:

    (i) the reduction in labour required following the introduction of the green revolution;

    (ii) increased availability of non-farm employment for those with some literacy and numeracy; and

    (iii) a recent increase in educational facilities.

Figure 2.4 Abandoned children on the streets can only survive by begging, by selling goods such as balloons or by operating food stalls

Figure 2.5 A school in a slum area of Calcutta. Even when parents are in poor circumstances, they have the education of their children as a priority and find money for books

Refer back to Figure 1.4 and comment on how close these changing perceptions in Indian villages are to the perceptions of people in the developed world.

There are other, more practical reasons. For example, the mud huts that used to need repairing after every monsoon are now made of brick. The water for household needs comes from tube wells instead of needing to be carried from a river. People also know that a job in administration (which requires a higher level of education) can only be achieved if their children to stay in school longer (Fig. 2.5). While they are in school children immediately become an economic handicap, so the fewer, the better. Thus increased awareness of better jobs in the future, coupled with less demand on the land has led to a reduction in fertility and one more step along the demographic transition.

Suggest how the better jobs that come with education can be of benefit to both parents and those left on the land.

Explain why people in many countries prefer boys to girls, even to the extent – on occasion – of killing the newly born girls. What would be the long term demographic result if such actions occurred on a large scale?

Safer birth in India

New Delhi: Birth and infant mortality rates have both fallen sharply in India, but diseases still kill nearly 10,000 Indian children every day, the UN Children's Fund said yesterday.

The Unicef report said that about 30 per cent of all cases of poverty-related diseases in the world could be found in India.

'By a crude reckoning, it could be said that more than a quarter of the problem of world poverty is to be found in just one country (India),' the report said. The Indian Government had still to provide safe drinking water to 46 per cent of its population, estimated by Unicef at about 759 million.

The report called for increased government efforts to reduce the incidence of child malnutrition, improve sanitation, and control such diseases as measles and polio.

(Source: *The Guardian*, 11 Dec. 1986)

Reducing infant mortality

The Indian studies show that economic improvement can lead to reduced fertility. Economic improvement can be produced either by providing people with more money directly, or by making certain that the economically active members of the family stay healthy and live long lives. In many parts of the world the chances of a higher income are still small, but the population growth can be curbed by giving parents the security that their children will survive. The problem of infant mortality has therefore to be tackled at the same time as birth control, for without better survival rates, people will not be persuaded to adopt a voluntary means of birth control. Although infant mortality is nowhere near as high as it was twenty years ago, it is a problem that has to be confronted by all countries (Table 2.1). Globally 40 000 children still die each day from common diseases.

Table 2.1 *Mortality during the first year of life (per thousand births) for selected developing world countries (left columns) and Western European countries (right columns)*

Country	Total	Country	Total
Nepal	173	Iceland	6.1
Bangladesh	146	Sweden	7.0
Lesotho	144	Switzerland	7.7
Haiti	144	Norway	7.9
Pakistan	141	Denmark	8.0
Senegal	127	Netherlands	8.4
Peru	115	France	9.0
Indonesia	111	Spain	9.6
Kenya	101	Eire	9.8
Mexico	82	UK	10.0
Sudan	81	W. Germany	10.3
Colombia	74	Belgium	10.9

High infant mortality rates place great strains on society in terms of:

(i) emotional strains on the family;

(ii) economic strains on the country because the sick and dying children have to be cared for; and

(iii) the continued pressure to have more children just in case those which have already been born die.

In the developing world most infant mortality stems from diseases caught by children who are already weak or to whom the medical facilities are not available. Most could be prevented by better personal hygiene and a more balanced diet. Many other deaths could be prevented by immunisation campaigns. It is now easier to educate people in preventative medicine by using TV, radio, schools, religious institutions and paramedics in the countryside. Put together, they allow a breakthrough in the health of small children. Just as a single cause cannot be ascribed to rates of mortality, neither can a single solution be adopted, because the causes are complex and often involve important cultural factors as the following examples show.

Egypt is one of several developing world countries that have dramatically improved their health by nationwide campaigns. Two simple methods are involved:

(i) mass immunisation against diphtheria, whooping cough, tetanus and polio; and

(ii) oral rehydration therapy (ORT) (sugar or rice, salt and water solutions) simply produced to replace the fluids and salts lost from the body during attacks of diarrhoea.

In Egypt diarrhoea killed 130 000 children under the age of two each year before the massive advertising campaign on TV with a slogan 'boil 200 centilitres of water, stir in the salts and give it to your beloved son'. The same message is written into the story lines of the soap operas most people watch.

The role of TV is particularly important because most women are illiterate. Within 2 years of the launch 90 per cent of mothers said they had heard of ORT and 80 per cent had tried it. Now infant mortality rate has been reduced by 200 per cent.

Egypt has taken on board all the new technology it can to prevent infant mortality from common diseases. It sees this as part of the birth control campaign that it must wage to try to halt the population explosion. But the same degree of success has not been experienced throughout the developing world for several reasons:

(i) the population in many countries is far more widely scattered than that of Egypt;

(ii) there is often a multiplicity of languages within one country and radio and TV do not reach all the people as effectively as is the case for Egypt;

(iii) many women are not taught properly about motherhood. Mothers still have their first children too early in life and do not leave enough time between pregnancies.

(iv) as they work over wood fires they do not realise that wood smoke causes anaemia by reducing the haemoglobin level, one of the main causes of children being born underweight. Underweight children have far less chance of survival than those of normal weight;

(v) personal hygiene is not effectively taught.

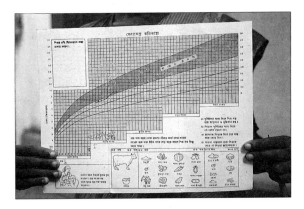

Figure 2.6(a) A diet sheet given to the poor in Calcutta to help get a correct feeding pattern for mothers and children; (b) a mother receives food supplement from the Calcutta Social Project to bring her diet in line with the requirements of good health

Ignorance is the main reason why so many children die. In Kerala state, India, for example, where literacy rates are the highest in the country, the rates of infant mortality are the lowest (Fig. 2.6).

The problem in getting some countries to develop a health care programme is that they still cling tenaciously to a system of administrative complexity inherited from the colonial days. So money goes on clerks and not on health care. India's infant mortality rate has only reduced from 129 per 1000 in 1947 to 105 per 1000 in 1986 – high even by the standards of the developing world.

It is easy to show that infant mortality is related to economic success as well as education. In Brazil, immunisation campaigns have been very successful, partly because infant mortality is being treated as an electoral issue. For some time, therefore, infant mortality has been on a downward trend. However, the recession of the 1980s and the foreign debt crisis have led to a reversal of the mortality trend. This is because the country has had to follow an austerity programme and in these circumstances the wages of the poor have gone down and they have not been able to afford to buy the right food for their children. Thus with increasing malnutrition, Brazil's infant mortality rate is again rising.

Altering cultural influences

Whereas it is easy to convince people of the benefits of a healthier population, and it is easier to show that smaller, healthy families are more likely to improve their quality of life, it is still difficult to convince many people that the size of their family ought to be limited. This is because, as part of a centuries old survival strategy, large families have been made a central part of many cultures. Thus it is often seen as a blessing to have large families and it is against the teaching of some religions to use methods of contraception.

Consider the role of religion in the population explosion. How, for example, do people resolve the conflict between some religious doctrines and smaller families?

Figure 2.7 Mummy, what's an uncle? (Source: *Earthscan*)

Better health care, without some form of reduction in the birth rate, will naturally lead to a booming population. This may or may not be a good thing. But if control is desired, a very powerful degree of coercion will have to be applied for a swift solution. China, for example, seeks to go rapidly towards the end of its demographic transition (see Chapter 1). In the cities it has instigated a programme of the one child family. This means that each family is only allowed to have one child (Fig. 2.7). This child is highly pampered by the state and the family given all manner of social benefits and tax relief. Then there is a great deal of social pressure not to have another child. Each community has a person employed to check potential mothers for pregnancy. If a woman who already has a child becomes pregnant, the whole community is notified. The woman and her husband are told they are letting down the policies of the community. Local elders visit daily with a view to forcing the woman to accept an abortion and this coercion can continue for many weeks. If, despite all this pressure, the woman still insists on having the child, the penalties are severe. Not only will the state tax the husband for having the child, but the child will not receive any state benefits, and those already given to the first born will be reduced.

> *Think about how a strongly coercive policy for birth control such as that employed in China would be received in a country such as Australia or Britain.*

This policy, which would be unworkable in many societies, has had a dramatic effect. It will put an end to the booming pattern of population by the middle of the next century, leaving China with less than 1.4 billion people. But such dramatic social restructuring also has inevitable drawbacks. China now has the largest and fastest growing elderly population in the developing world (see Chapter 3).

Who needs birth control?

As you will have detected from the discussion of China's solution, there are major problems resulting from a decision to go in for birth control on a large scale. The question arises: is a very tough birth control policy actually necessary (Fig. 2.8)?

This chapter has suggested that it is helpful to control national populations to allow their economies to match their resources. However, birth control and the reasons for pressing for global limits to population growth are much more complex.

When the UN met in 1984 to discuss the future of the world's population, they had as a backcloth the rapid rise in population which has brought the world family over the 5 billion mark. Most governments at the meeting favoured restraining population growth. They were worried that an increased number of people in the world would absorb all the benefits of economic growth in their own countries as well as in those with the increasing populations. However, there are several arguments that can be put forward for taking no birth control action.

The lesson of the population transition model presented in Chapter 1 is that the population will eventually attain its own stability. The biggest change comes when death rates fall. This has already happened, and there is evidence that birth rates are also now falling. There has already been a general decline in the rate of growth of global population since the early 1970s irrespective of the degree of coercion on birth control (Fig. 2.9). Is this a sure sign that economic improvements bring a reduced birth control in their wake? If so it may be sensible to wait for national economies to pick up in their own good time.

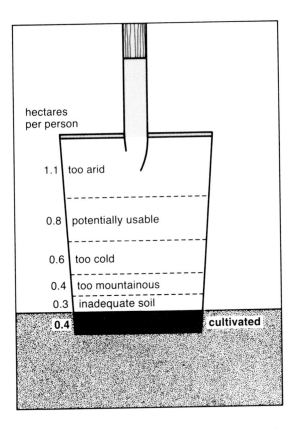

hectares
per person

1.1 too arid

0.8 potentially usable

0.6 too cold

0.4 too mountainous

0.3 inadequate soil

0.4 cultivated

*Figure 2.8 The case for and against booming popula-
tions can be seen in these three pieces of data. Rising
populations fuel the fear that there will be economic
and social decline. On the other hand the amount of the
global resource used to date is small. Set against all this
is the very real abuse that constantly reduces the
potential of the resources*

It can also be argued that more people on Earth
will help develop resources more effectively, and
give more brainpower to the development of
civilisation. The only thing that is wrong at the
moment is that too many people are under-used
and not helping the development of society
because they have not been educated and
allowed to achieve their potential.

The high population growth rates of some
countries are often blamed for their poverty and
famines. But there is little evidence to support
this. Many of the poorest countries have dramatically improved their standards of living. Africa's
ten richest countries have more or less the same
population growth rates as the poorest ten. Thus
it can be argued that although large populations

150 born every minute

The world population is
expected to pass the five billion
mark within the next few weeks,
a United Nations seminar in
London was told yesterday.

Every minute the world
population grows by 150; every
day by 220,000 and every year
by more than 80 million.

At this rate it would reach six
billion by the year 2,000, seven
billion by 2010 and eight billion
by 2022. Then, according to
the latest estimates, it would
become stable at about 10 billion in about a century or so
from now.

Mr Lester Brown, president
of the Worldwatch Institute,
told the opening session of a
three-day conference called
The State of World Population
1987, that the main challenge
facing the governments of most
Third World countries was how
to persuade their populations to
reduce birth rates while economic and social conditions
were declining.

If they failed, economic deterioration could eventually lead
to social disintegration of the
kind which undermined earlier
civilizations when population
demands became unsustain-
able, Mr Brown said.

(Source: The *Daily
Telegraph*, 14 May 1987)

eat more they also produce even more. This, of
course, is the basis for the traditionally large
peasant family.

Student enquiry 2A

Changing birth rates

1. Analyse the article 'Population booms. . .' and explain the diversity of factors that can influence population growth in a developing country.
2. Now study the graph of births in Britain since 1900 (A2). You will see that there are many fluctuations. Death rates are quite constant, so it is possible to use the birth rate variations to estimate the number of people entering the workforce in the future. Item A3 shows the annual change in the British workforce. Most people enter the workforce at age 16 and leave it again at age 65. This information can be used to draw a graph of the change in numbers of employable age. This has been done in A3. Using the graph A3 describe the pattern of future employment change in Britain. Identify the years when there may be higher than average employment and those years when it will be easier for people to find jobs.
3. There was a world recession between the mid-1970s and the mid-1980s. Was the change in Britain's potential workforce likely to have made the problem better or worse for Britain's government?
4. Suggest how the future changes can be used to plan for fuller employment.
5. How far would it be true to say that biology can be any government's secret curse and its secret ally?

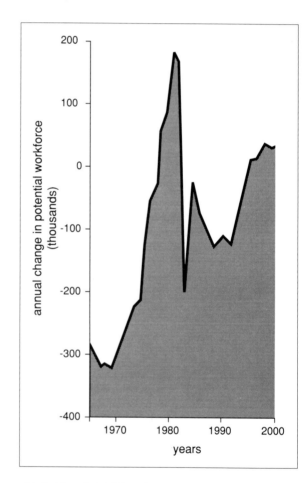

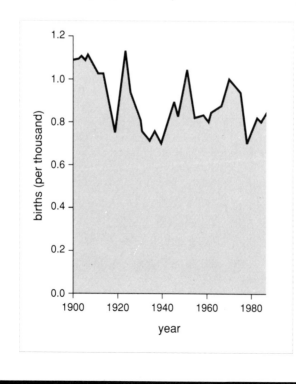

A2 (left) and A3 (above)
(Source: *New Scientist*, 3 Dec. 1987)

Population booms as Egypt debates need for control

The Reagan Administration's new line on population growth – that it has a neutral economic effect – can be assured of a sympathetic hearing in Egypt. Many of the country's politicians, planners and economists have said the same for years.

Unlike the United States, Egypt is in the front line to test the theory. It has a growth rate of 2.7 per cent, which, for now, means a million more every eight and a half months. The total population is 47 million: if the growth rate stays steady, this will double to 94 million by the year 2010. The country's habitable regions are about the size of the Netherlands.

Western analysts have, for a decade, pinpointed population growth as the most serious of Egypt's problems. Yet the last time the subject was publicly debated here, in the pages of the prestigious newspaper, *Al ahram*, the argument centred less on solutions than on whether a population problem existed

Gamal Abdel Nasser, in the 1950s, summed up an argument that is still fashionable. 'Instead of concentrating on birth control,' he said,'we would do better to concentrate on how to make use of our resources.'

'We live in and make use of only 4 per cent of the area of our country . . . if we direct our efforts to expanding the area in which we live instead of concentrating on how to reduce the population, we will soon find the solutions.'

Later he modified his views, and set up a nationwide family planning programme during the mid-sixties. Today, the comprehensive nature of the service is, on paper, impressive. The Egyptian Ministry of Health has 3100 health units offering family planning services: every village is within two miles of one. Facilities are also provided by private agencies, and by most of the country's 5000 pharmacies.

Since 1977, the US Agency for International Development has put $55 million into the family planning programme. US money has also backed a big advertising campaign to persuade Egyptians that 'small families are best.'

The programme is not working. In the 1970s, the growth rate reached a record 3 per cent, and then stabilised at 2.7 per cent. The average Egyptian woman is still producing between five and six babies: fewer in the cities, more in the countryside.

This is partly because Egypt is a conservative, traditional society, and traditionally babies have been welcomed. Women (mostly illiterate) fear that their husband will divorce them if they stop having babies. And even though Egypt's top religious dignitary, the Sheik of Al-Azhar, has pronounced (on being prompted) that birth control is not forbidden in the Koran, most simple Egyptians believe to control conception is to tamper with the will of God.

Economically, it makes sense to have large families, at least in the countryside. Children can work on the farm, look after elderly parents – and cost little, since the necessities of life are heavily subsidised by the Government.

The programme has provided plenty of light relief. A population programme in Minya, in upper Egypt – funded by the World Bank and the British Overseas Development Agency – was initially headed, on the Egyptian side, by an official who did not believe in birth control: later, it was found that lessons in hygiene to villagers had succeeded in raising population growth – by lowering the infant mortality.

Another scheme in upper Egypt involved paying incentives to clinics which distributed large numbers of contraceptive pills. Wily peasants did a deal with clinic attendants. Chopped up pills added to chicken feed, it turned out, significantly improved the weight of young birds.

Both Nasser and Sadat, fearing political unpopularity – and from conviction – chose not to make a priority of family planning. President Mubarak is prepared to speak out strongly on the subject, but has shown no initiative beyond planning a National Council for Population.

At least the president does not talk in stirring terms about colonising the desert: possibly because he has examined the record. Egyptians have shown little pioneering spirit, preferring (if they move from the village) to settle in the city.

The total amount of desert land reclaimed since Nasser's great projects during the 1960s is about 500 000 acres producing only 5 per cent of Egypt's agricultural output. Over-optimistic plans to reclaim two million acres by the end of the century would feed only an extra half million families.

More likely is a bigger food import bill, and huge strain on big city services and infrastructure. Egypt, once the granary for ancient empires, now imports more than half its food.

A1 (Source: *The Guardian*, 1984)

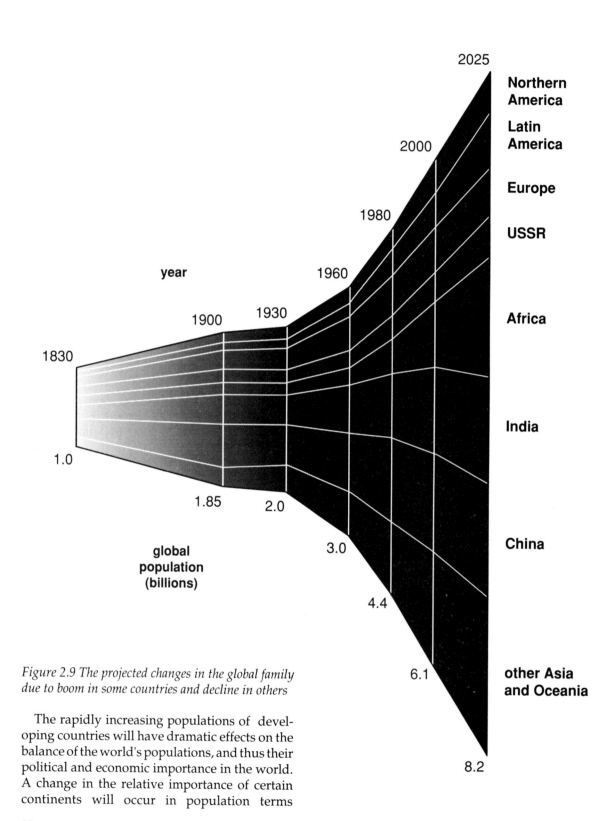

2025

Northern
America

Latin
America

2000

Europe

USSR

1980

year

1960

1900   1930

1830   Africa

1.0

India

1.85   2.0

global
population   3.0   China
(billions)

4.4

Figure 2.9 The projected changes in the global family   6.1   **other Asia**
due to boom in some countries and decline in others   **and Oceania**

The rapidly increasing populations of devel-
oping countries will have dramatic effects on the   8.2
balance of the world's populations, and thus their
political and economic importance in the world.
A change in the relative importance of certain
continents will occur in population terms

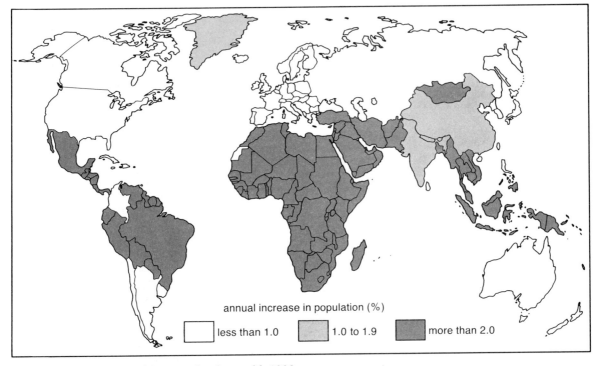

annual increase in population (%)

less than 1.0   1.0 to 1.9   more than 2.0

Fig. 2.10 Rates of natural increase for the world, 1990

(Fig. 2.9, Fig. 2.10). Europe, for example, will become a shrinking part of the global family, while Africa will form a much larger proportion.

> *Consider how the change in the number of Asian people living in Asia may have an impact on either Australia or Britain. List those factors that you feel are positive and negative from the developed world standpoint.*

Tanzania: no birth controls?

Tanzania shows us the classic debate between those who believe economic development is the key to population success and those who think population control is the key to economic success. The Tanzanian government's approach to population policy suggests that if the population is more effectively distributed, if the child and adult mortality rates are reduced by better health care and nutrition, and if food supplies are increased, there will be no need for birth control. The government promotes spacing of children purely to improve maternal and child health. In the words of a UN report: 'The government

has no intention of restricting its population in view of the vast amounts of uninhabited land still to be settled.'

Tanzanians view an effective population policy as part of a larger socio-economic policy whereby the higher population is accepted but deflected from the urban centres and resettled in effective village communities (the **ujamaa** policy). By contrast a planning document of the United States Government Aid Agency, USAID, warned that: 'Tanzania's high population growth rate negatively interacts with its moderate economic growth rate and food self-sufficiency objective. It also threatens the physical ecology in certain parts of the country and undermines all efforts to improve the levels of well-being of the population. Unless the current rate of population growth is arrested, Tanzania will find it difficult to sustain its current development achievements, let alone move towards self-sufficiency.'

At the moment Tanzania's population is growing with a net reproduction rate of 2.4 per cent, a figure that will take the country from the 17 million of the 1978 census through the 27 million estimated for 1990 to 37 million by 2000.

Student enquiry 2B

Forecasting Tanzania's way forward

It is very difficult to make forecasts of population and its impact on a country. In Tanzania the population is distributed very unevenly. Tanzania is still primarily an agricultural subsistence economy and thus the density of the population has to reflect the carrying capacity of the land.

1. The table shows regional statistics for Tanzania. Map B2 gives the administrative regions in Tanzania. Prepare two tracing overlays of the map. Use a suitable shading scheme to illustrate the pattern of population density on one overlay and growth rate on the other overlay.
2. B3 and B4 show the annual rainfall probability for the country. This is an indication of the carrying capacity of the land. Use B3 and the maps you constructed in Question 1 to assess the regions where the potential carrying capacity is matched by the population and its growth rate, and those which would seem to be heading for trouble. Display these conclusions on a map showing risk of overpopulation.
3. Assume you are in charge of Tanzania's future population policy. You decide on a policy of redistributing the population. By means of a map, indicate directions of redistribution that you would implement. Suggest some problems that redistribution might bring.

Table B1

Region	Map ref	Average density per square kilometre	Annual growth rate of population (per cent)	Rainfall probability index
Mwanza	1	73	2.9	2.2
Shinyanga	2	26	3.6	1.0
Mbeya	3	18	3.3	2.2
Tanga	4	39	2.7	2.2
West Lake	5	36	4.0	3.5
Dodoma	6	24	2.9	2.0
Morogoro	7	14	2.9	2.2
Arusha	8	11	3.9	2.0
Iringa	9	16	2.7	2.2
Kilimanjaro	10	68	3.0	3.0
Dar es Salaam	11	611	8.2	2.2
Tabora	12	11	4.5	1.0
Mtwara	13	46	2.0	1.0
Mara	14	33	2.6	2.2
Kigoma	15	17	2.9	2.2
Singida	16	12	2.7	2.0
Ruvuma	17	9	3.3	2.2
Lindi	18	8	2.1	1.5
Coast	19	16	1.7	2.2
Rukwa	20	7	4.6	1.0
Zanzibar	21	164	3.3	4.0
Pemba	22	209	2.1	4.0

(Source: *Journal of Developing Areas*, 1982)

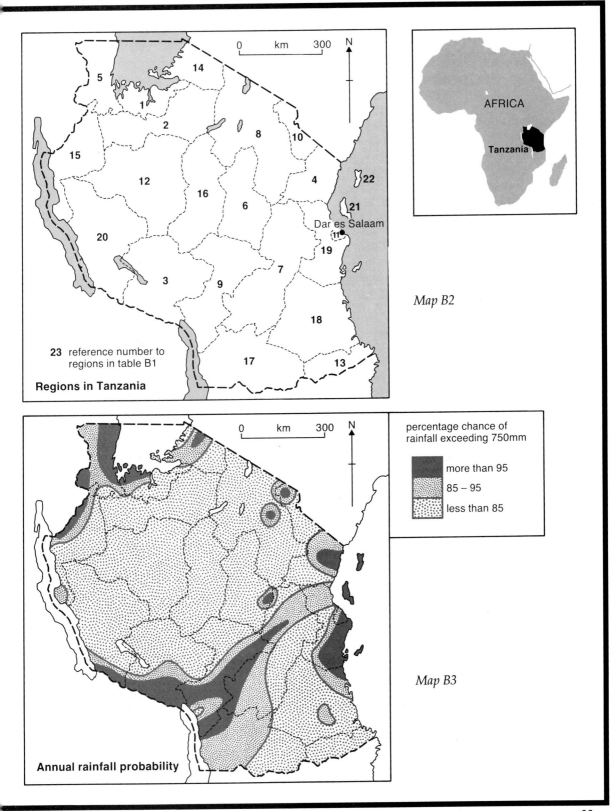

0   km   300   N

5

14

1

2

8

10

15

12

4

22

16

6

21

20

Dar es Salaam

11

19

3

9

7

18

23   reference number to regions in table B1

17

13

Regions in Tanzania

Map B2

AFRICA

Tanzania

0   km   300   N

percentage chance of rainfall exceeding 750mm

more than 95

85 – 95

less than 85

Map B3

Annual rainfall probability

... as Romania presses for procreation

Death squads are a hallmark of South American dictatorships. Now Romania's strong man, Nicolae Ceausescu, has created 'birth squads'. The squads visit married women in their homes to ask them why they are not having babies.

The squads are the latest twist in Ceausescu's campaign to increase the birth rate in his cold and hungry land. His aim is to cut the country's astronomically high abortion rate. Yet the country has the fourth highest birth rate in Europe.

A directive from the central committee of the Communist Party compels every woman of child-bearing age to undergo a monthly medical examination at work. If the test indicates a pregnancy, then failure to produce a child within nine months can result in charges being brought against the woman.

Harassment extends to financial penalties. Adults who are not married at the age of 25 must pay a special tax of up to 16 per cent of their wage. There are tax penalties too against childless couples who fail to provide a medical reason for not having children.

Economic pressures that Ceausescu has been unable to halt make many people reluctant to start a family. The country has one of the four lowest standards of living in Europe.

All basic foodstuffs are rationed in Romania. Since 1981, it has been an offence punishable by up to five years in prison to store more food than a typical family would eat in a month.

(Source: *New Scientist*, 25 Dec. 1986)

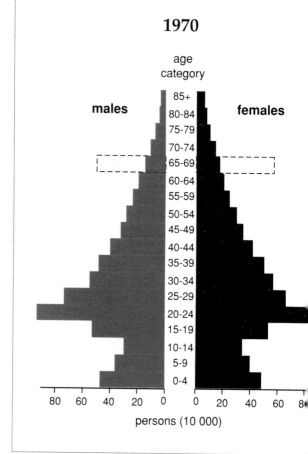

Reasons for promoting more children

Although public attention usually focuses on the ways to contain the populations of the developing world, in countries where the demographic transition has been completed there are now worries about internal population decline. The forecasted changes in population composition, with fewer young people and more elderly (see Chapter 3) have induced serious attempts to increase populations in some countries. In Romania the birth rate fell 30 per cent between 1975 and 1985 and abortions outnumbered live births. Faced with such drastic social changes, Romania has lowered the legal age for marriage to 15 years and added 16 per cent to the income tax on people who are still single at 25. The policy now is to push up the population as fast as possible.

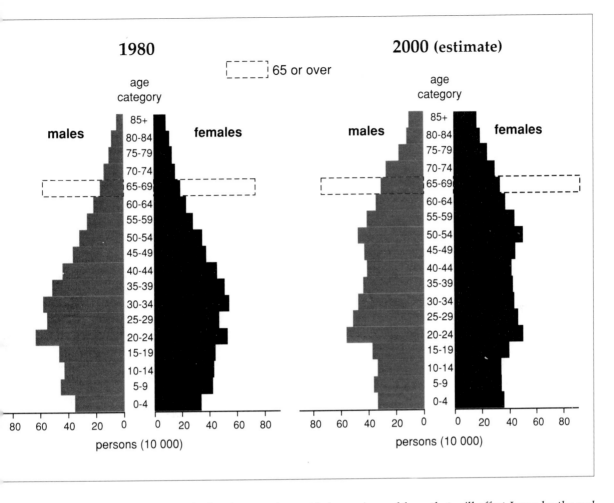

1980

2000 (estimate)

┌─────┐
└─────┘ 65 or over

Figure 2.11 *Population pyramids that forecast the rapid change in workforce that will affect Japan by the end of the century*

It is the change in ethnic balance which causes today's powerful countries the greatest concern both within their national borders as well as across the globe. This is because the people who have migrated from developing world countries to the developed world often retain their tendency to have large families. Indigenous people then begin to worry about maintaining their cultural identity and they see their whole civilisation as threatened. The higher birth rates of Muslims in the USSR will, for example, leave the Russians as a minority people.

The fact that the world population is still increasing matters not one jot in a situation of fear that there will not be sufficient people to maintain national identity. Such fears are strongly held in

such countries as West Germany and France. It is felt that a country that can support itself from its own population resource prospers and that one that requires guest workers from overseas is at a disadvantage.

In Japan, where the population boom is now over, there is still a large young population. There are plenty of hands to forward Japan's economic miracle at the moment (Fig. 2.8). But in the future this will not be so. Furthermore, in 50 years time there will be a thirteen fold increase in people of pensionable age and fewer people to earn the wealth to pay for it. An imbalance between young and old can be far more important to a country than the total number of people it contains as we shall see in Chapter 3.

Student Enquiry 2C

Can Europe survive a declining population?

Before you begin this enquiry look carefully through all of the information provided.

1. On a map of the EEC plot the birth surplus in 1964 and 1982 given in Table 2C1 as column charts. Describe the pattern and suggest some reasons for the variations observed.
2. In some developed world countries the population is increasing only because of the higher birth rate of the immigrants. As a group talk through some of the implications of this situation.
3. Suggest how you could achieve a balanced population programme that does not lead to a decline in standards for any sector of the community.

Norway, the land with everything, is fas

The treasury coffers are overflowing and the shop are full of the latest in fashion and high-tech.

This year, it finally triumphed in the Eurovision Song Contest, but Norway, seemingly the country with everything, is facing a critical shortage. It is running out of Norwegians.

Just to stay even, Norway needs 2.1 children for each family. At present the rate is 1.8 and according to official figures, on present trends, the population will go into absolute decline in 2021. Among a population of 4.1 million, 500 000 people are over retirement age and this figure is expected to double by the end of the century.

A government report last y suggested that it was 'too ficult' to have children in N way. It proposed extended ternity leave, increased c allowances, more nurs schools, and better housi While state-subsidised po sculptors, and Sami-lapp b carvers abound, young ad willing to take a governme assisted plunge into parenthe are thinner on the ground.

The Central Bureau of Sta tics recorded only 28 0 marriages in 1983, the low figure, for almost 50 years. the same year, more than 70 couples divorced. If pres trends continue, 27 per cen all Norwegian men and 20 cent of all women will be unm ried at the age of fifty.

Country	Birth surplus		Total fertility rate	
	1964	1982	1964	1982
Norway	8.2	2.4	3.0	1.7
Sweden	6.0	0.2	2.5	1.6
Finland	8.3	4.7	2.4	1.7
Denmark	7.8	-0.5	2.6	1.6
United Kingdom	7.5	1.1	2.9	1.8
Eire	10.9	10.9	4.1	3.0
Netherlands	13.0	3.8	3.2	1.5
Belgium	5.5	0.8	2.7	1.6
West Germany	7.7	-1.5	2.6	1.4
France	7.4	4.7	2.9	1.9
Switzerland	10.1	2.6	2.6	1.6
Austria	6.2	0.4	2.8	1.7
Portugal	13.2	5.9	3.1	2.2
Spain	13.6	6.0	3.0	2.0
Italy	10.3	1.6	2.6	1.6
Greece	n/a	5.2	2.3	2.1

Table 2C1

(n/a = not available)

ınning out of Norwegians

Norway has a word for married people who live ether, *sambo*. Unlike in ıtain, such couples qualify for same benefits as married ıples who have children. But State's liberal mindedness failed to produce the desired ults.

The Norwegian male does appear particularly shy, but Spring, when a young man's ıcy traditionally turns to ıughts of love, Norwegian ıps tend to grab a case of ıavit and head for a hut in mountains, or go reindeer ding.

It is at this point that large nbers of Norwegian women marriageable age may be ın making for the Green ınds, or embarking on interminable trans-Saharan overland expeditions.

The problems posed by a declining birth rate and an even older population have become a central issue in the general election campaign here.

Both the main parties have pledged to help people with young families, and are falling over each other to woo the pensioners, who have suffered in the past four years from a shortage of nursing homes and hospital beds, and increased health and service charges.

According to Mrs Mathilde Fortvedt, aged 75, chairman of the Hordaland branch of the Norwegian Pensioners Association, the association now has 115 000 members and is growing.

'We talk to the Government and we ask them for more help. We want more pension money. It is not enough.'

With no sign yet of a baby boom to match the oil boom, and with immigration low even by Scandinavian standards, the pensioners are coming to represent an ever-larger sector of the population. As a result, they are gaining political clout.

In one sense, they have time on their side. In Norway, the average life expectancy for women is three years greater than in Britain. Norwegian men live 2.5 years longer than their British contemporaries. Perhaps it is because they are conserving their energy.

(Source: *The Guardian*, 19 Aug. 1985)

Why has East Germany been the only industrialised country able to reverse the falling birth rate?

In 1975, both West and East Germany were in the same situation, with a number of deaths in the population that was greater than the number of births by 50 000 to 60 000. Ten years later, the Federal Republic of Germany has the oldest population in the world, while the German Democratic Republic has increased the number of births by one third, i.e. from 180 000 to 240 000 per annum. This is in spite of the fact that, in East Germany, contraception and voluntary terminations of pregnancy are both readily available, while family allowances are low – so that the reasons for this development must clearly be sought in the overall family policies implemented since 1976. These include the following measures:

- any birth, from the second child on, gives entitlement to a 'Baby Year' or year of parental leave with a statutory grant amounting to 70–80 per cent of salary,
- a grant, to the mother, of one month's additional salary for each birth;
- a rule forbidding the dismissal of a mother with a child under three;
- an additional day's leave per month for mothers to work at home;
- a 40 hour week (instead of $43^3/_4$ hours) on full pay;
- the setting up of day nurseries to meet over 70 per cent of requirements;
- the priority allocation of housing to households with a certain number of children;
- availability of loans at the time of marriage and at the birth of each child, so as to make possible either home ownership or the acquisition of household equipment.

Some of these provisions could certainly be transposed into those European countries which are suffering badly from a falling birth rate – but what governments would be prepared to pay for them, even at the cost of their own survival?

(Source: EEC briefing document)

Student Enquiry 2C concluded

Too many little Ahmeds

The recruitment ban (on foreign workers in Germany) was really directed against the Turks, who make up much the largest single group of foreign workers – about 1.6m, treble their 1970 number. They are also much the most obviously foreign. German housewives are apt to notice that Turks eat lamb and garlic where Germans eat pork and cabbage, and that their Turkish neighbours have, by German standards, an inordinate number of children (30 births per 1000 population compared with 10) who are swamping German schools.

What would happen if lots of them did pack their bags? The Social Democrat-governed city of Dusseldorf put its money where its conscience was and commissioned a study to discover the effects of a hypothetical exodus, over two or three years, of three quarters of its 36 500 foreign workers (out of a total population of 600 000). The study showed that public commuter transport and rubbish disposal services would probably collapse; that the city would suffer a massive loss in tax revenue and purchasing power; that construction and hospital services would be severely cut back; that many schools and nurseries would have to close, making a good number of (mostly German) teachers redundant; and that whole residential quarters of the city would become derelict; to say nothing of all the pizza parlours and kebab houses which would close their doors.

(Source: *The Economist*, 4 Feb. 1984)

EEC given warning on fall in birth rate

Britain and Denmark have the highest divorce rates in the EEC, a European Parliament report said yesterday.

The report also points out that social stresses and a falling birth rate will lead to a dramatic drop of 25 million in the population of Western Europe by the year 2050 'if present trends continue'.

It calls on the EEC Council of Ministers to adopt a 'dynamic policy of family support measures', including longer parental leave, more part-time work to ease the lot of working mothers, and a European policy on housing which helps first-time home owners and the elderly.

M Nicole Chouraqui, a French Gaullist MEP and author of the report, said the traditional family in Europe was under pressure as never before because of economic crisis and unemployment.

Divorce and separation were on the increase – nearly three divorces per 1000 inhabitants in Britain and Denmark – and the birth rate in the EEC had fallen by 30 per cent, a figure 'curiously reminiscent of the 1930s', the report said.

To maintain Europe's current population levels, a fertility rate of more than two children per woman was needed – which has been achieved only in Ireland where 2.74 children were born to each woman, compared to 1.77 in Britain and 1.30 in Denmark and West Germany.

According to the last full statistics available, those for 1983, the Catholic cultures of the EEC's newest members, Spain and Portugal, had the lowest divorce rate.

(Source: *The Times*, 23 Oct. 1986)

Chapter 3
Issues of an aging population

"... NOW LOOK HERE YOUNG MAN !"

Introduction

When societies reach the final phase of the demographic transition they experience a relatively static population with low birth and death rates. Such stable societies are the most successful economically and can take full advantage of this success to support and nurture their people. But although this stage in the demographic transition may sound idyllic, the way the transition is completed brings a whole set of problems. The issues raised have global implications, both for the developed world which is coping with them now, and for the developing world which will face the same problems in the years to come.

Perspectives on growing old

One of the most dramatic statistics in the UN demographic yearbook is the world's population over sixty, because it shows a population explosion stored up for the twenty-first century (Fig. 3.1, next page). It used to be said that a long life was 'three score years and ten'. Not any more. In 1950 just one person in 12 of the population was over 60; by 2050 that proportion will have risen to 1 in 7. The world's population is 'greying' fast. And the consequences of this are at least as far reaching as those produced by high birth rates.

Just imagine yourself as one of the billion old people who will be alive by the turn of the century. One of a billion who worry about a pension, who find it hard to keep warm, who can't quite remember things as well as before, who can't keep up with the queue and get jostled to the back by impatient youngsters. Imagine this and you start to see the range of problems old age brings to the community or, put another way, that the community brings to old age.

Consider the attitudes that the community has to its elderly, and try to explain how such attitudes have arisen.

The greying of the population, sometimes referred to as the 'granny boom' because women have a longer life expectancy than men, is just as much a product of development as the improvement in infant mortality.

Figure 3.1 (a) Older people playing golf. This is a sector of the population that is growing rapidly. They can no longer be regarded as a peripheral part of society without economic value. (b) The demographic pyramid for Britain's over 60s shows a strong tendency for women to outnumber men

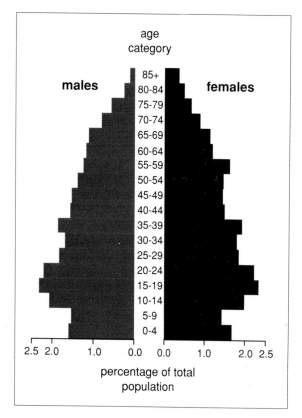

What are some of the social implications of an imbalance of sexes in the elderly population?

Supporting the elderly

Development has turned the population pyramid on its head. After centuries where the young far outnumbered the old, now the situation is going into reverse. Support for these people is almost a 'Catch 22 situation'. At the moment over one seventh of all government expenditure in Britain goes to pay state pensions. Because falling birth rates mean there will be fewer people to be taxed in the future, the amount of money available to share out as pensions will get smaller. Couple this with the increasing number of old people entitled to pensions and you will see that a shrinking cake will have to be shared among more and more. In the future pensions will get smaller, not bigger. Pensions may well drop to less than a third of the working wage and thus hit people really hard at a time when their heating and health care costs are increasing rapidly (Fig. 3.2).

Figure 3.2 There is an increasing need both for formal health care, as illustrated by this sheltered home, and also for informal community support for the elderly

Governments in many developed countries have already begun taking steps to try to reduce the pension burden by decoupling pensions from State benefit. They know they simply won't be able to find the money – and this will be true of communist and socialist governments just as much as conservative and republican ones. The welfare state is going to have an increasing burden, and the more governments can encourage the more wealthy people to look after their own pensions by taking out insurance schemes while they are in work the better, because it will leave a bigger fund for the less fortunate in society.

> *Discuss the concept that governments will no longer be able to support all the elderly. Try to suggest alternatives to private pensions and private health care.*

Impact on the young

The greying of the world has taken place so rapidly that governments have been taken by surprise. But more than this, people have also been taken by surprise. Now, both people and governments are awakening to the real problem ahead.

Some of the statistics worry people in the developed world. In France one in six French women has no children; in Germany the population is actually declining; in many developed countries increases in population are only being achieved because of the higher birth rates of the immigrant

Figure 3.3 The much vaunted two adults, two children policy of the 1960s and 70s (as shown by this board in Indonesia) might be useful for countries with high growth rates, but it would be too simple a statement for many developed world countries

communities. In Austria there is already one pensioner for every two workers paying tax.

In 1931, for every British person aged 75 or over there were 13 people aged between 45 and 64; in 1991 there will be fewer than 4. So the base of financial and social support for the elderly is shrinking.

The progress of development is making live births more certain, and parents are choosing to have fewer children. Thus, whereas it was common to have over ten children in Britain and other developed countries before the First World War, today it is more common to have one or two.

> *Examine the argument that people in the developed world are going to see a need for increased family sizes. Will they need the children for support in old age as much as they did in the past?*

Zero population growth requires more than two children per reproductive family because many people do not get married and some people are unable to have children (Fig. 3.3). Thus the 'two child family' ideal so readily expounded by national advertising campaigns of the 1960s and 1970s underestimates the requirements of the population; there need to be a lot of three child families if zero growth rather than decline is to be seen.

Figure 3.4 (a) The skills of many years have been acquired by normal retirement age. Furniture restoring, for example, is a craft that cannot be learned quickly and can be carried on well into retirement age; (b) a retired teacher invigilating an examination. This is a skilled task which benefits the students because the invigilator has time to care; it benefits the working teachers because it allows them to get on with other work, and it benefits the retired person because it gives him a valued and respected position, and a small supplementary income

This demographic change will also affect the developing world. Birth rates are falling in most of the world even though the concern is still how to feed the present population. The emphasis is still on birth control, but how far can this go? Can too severe a birth control programme store up trouble for later generations when the population greys?

Most people in the developing world do not get a pension. There is little prospect of them getting one unless they work for the government as an administrator or in the military. So a successful birth control campaign can leave people with fewer means of support in later life.

Impact on the old

A fundamental problem in the developed world is that, in the struggle to ensure people were extricated from the drudgery of the industrial revolution where they were worked to death, trades unions have ensured that most developed world governments pay state pensions to women over 60 and men over 65. However, this has had some unfortunate repercussions. The unions have had to argue that people are worked out by 60 or 65; that they need to retire. This was a dangerous ploy and it has led to the attitude that people are useless after 65. Patently this is untrue, but it has become an institutionalised fact. Further, it has led to the assumption that people wanted to leave work to find something better. Many people enjoy and have built their lives round their work. Is it right to assume they will also enjoy being divorced from something they have done all their lives?

The retirement problem has been further exacerbated by the apparent decline in employment. Thus there has been pressure from the young for the elderly to give way and let them have the jobs. However, it is only the less skilled jobs that can be transferred in this way (Fig. 3.4).

As skill becomes an ever more important part of a job will it be valid to assume that the young can readily replace the older members of the workforce? Suggest some areas where it would be true and some where it would not.

Figure 3.5 Retired people on an outing. In future more and more retired people will be taking active forms of leisure

The result of prolonging life and reducing the working years has been to produce a group of people whose middle age has been lengthened, but most of whom do not have the disposable income to enjoy their later years at much more than subsistence level. Many people are made dependents again when aged 60 or 65, whether they like it or not. And of course, most people do not like it. Why should they see their standard of living fall just at the moment when there may be more time to spend at leisure?

A lowering of income can be a frightening prospect and may well be the reason many elderly people so readily slip into a world of watching TV and simple games.

> *In what ways could it be argued that many countries demean their elderly?*

The facts about elderly people tell how their role has been misrepresented. At least three-quarters of old people in the developed world are almost free from any disabling disease and less than 1 in 20 suffer from any form of senility (Fig. 3.5). Doctors confirm that, in many cases, people are decrepit in old age because the earlier life they led was unhealthy rather than for any other reason.

In the developing world the chances of surviving to lead a useful and healthy old age are less bright than in the developed world because the poor conditions people suffer in their youth and young adulthood have already doomed their future. In the developed world many of the old people we see around were also born under conditions much harsher than we experience today. When you become a pensioner the people around you will not look as old as their counterparts today nor have the same debilitating diseases. They will be even more active and healthy than the older people today. If it is not obvious already, it will be blatantly obvious that retired people are capable of performing useful jobs. They are also capable of being retrained to other jobs – to many of which they are uniquely suited. It is simply a matter of society's attitudes.

> *Suggest a number of jobs that older people could train for, and for which they are readily suited. You should consider both those that require time and those that require skill.*
>
> *How would it help society if elderly people were trained for new jobs?*

Student enquiry 3A

Forecasting the needs of the elderly

1. The graph shows the actual and predicted elderly population in Britain until the year 2021. Describe the pattern shown.
2. The state has to provide elderly people with a basic pension. When will this provision be a particular burden on the state?

3. How would you use this information to argue for the apparently contradictory statements: (a) that there is no need to panic over the provision of more facilities for the elderly; and (b) that there is every need to provide for the elderly at once.

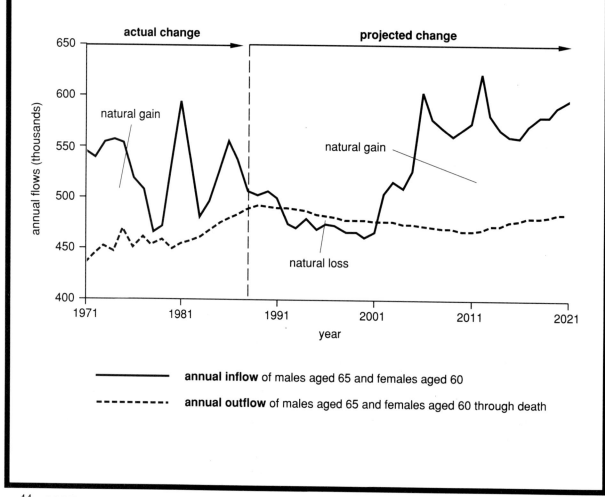

annual flows (thousands)

actual change

projected change

natural gain

natural gain

natural loss

year

——————— **annual inflow** of males aged 65 and females aged 60

- - - - - - - - - **annual outflow** of males aged 65 and females aged 60 through death

The greying of Japan

Japan has a unique demographic history. Between the two world wars people had large families, but during the Second World War many of the youth were killed. Then in the post-war years, when the country had to struggle to rebuild, people began to have smaller families. As a result their dependants were few: few parents, because the life expectancy in Japan was short, and few children because the birth rate had fallen. So there was plenty of surplus wealth to reinvest in the country to make more wealth. Only a little had to be set aside for dependants. But more recently the effects of these events have come into stark perspective, for most of the people who worked to rebuild the country are now nearing retirement age, and there are fewer people to replace them. There are now two job opportunities in Japan for every qualified school leaver!

It is a well known cliche within Japan that the older people retire too soon, live too long, have too small a pension, and have never learned to enjoy leisure (Fig. 3.6). From being 9 per cent of the population in 1980 the over 65s will be 21 per cent in 2025. This has meant that Japan is faced with the prospect of having to dismantle its system of lifetime employment in which employees worked for the same company and were given guaranteed rises for each year of service. Japan is greying so fast that, even with its huge trade surplus and wealth, the government fears that it will have too many people who have to be paid highly. It is a dilemma to which Japan has not yet found an answer.

The influence of senior citizens

Every **cohort** (age band) within the adult population has a proportion that are self supporting, and some who are dependent. In the developed world old age dependence has largely been transferred from the family to the state. However, being able to rely on the State is relatively recent. Before this people had to try to save the best way they could for their old age.

Many of the present senior citizens belong to generations who were brought up to save. Those

Figure 3.6 Reminiscing on working days, Tokyo

currently in the 55-64 cohort save 85 per cent more than the UK average and they represent 68 per cent of all those with savings of £10000 or more. Most of these savings are in building societies or government stocks which means that the money is readily accessible. Many of the older people also own their own homes outright, giving them an additional large disposable income. Today some of the senior citizens have nest eggs of substantial proportions.

Traditionally senior citizens have been regarded as having a low purchasing power. As evidence of this notice how few advertisements on the TV are directed towards the retired. But while the pressure on the State to provide basic services will increase, for a substantial minority of senior citizens life will not be difficult. The high wage earners of today will be wealthy senior citizens of tomorrow, and they will be able to exercise considerable political and economic power if they wish. Their market share will continue to grow because they have disposable incomes not consumed by the necessities of bringing up a family. At the same time they will not have to provide large amounts of money when they are ill, because the State health service will take care of them.

People reading the advertisement were asked to indicate, by ticks in the spaces provided, whether they thought the following features were very important or desirable:

1. That St Mary's Mead should reflect the true atmosphere and environment of a traditional Cotswold Village, through preserving natural trees and walkways, through full use of Cotswold Stone Facings and natural slate roofing and through a picturesque centrepiece of a Mill House and village pond.
2. That while designed for relaxed Village living, its location would, nevertheless, be on the very edge of a substantial and thriving Market Town, meaning that full and plentiful amenities such as shopping and cultural and relaxation activities should be on its doorstep and mostly within walking distance.
3. That its local position should include easy access for its residents to many nearby sporting and relaxation clubs and facilities, including Golf, Tennis, Fishing, Swimming and Bowls.
4. That the design and fitting of all its accommodation units should take into account fully the needs of more mature residents, including ease of care and maintenance, the latest in specially designed fully fitted kitchens and bathrooms, the highest standards of installation and economic, independently controlled central heating throughout.
5. That the luxury Cottage housing units should be designed to be capable of easy conversion into one-storey living if ever needed, through the provision of an extra shower room downstairs.
6. That Cable Television viewing installation points should be in all Apartments and Cottages, thereby extending considerably the degree of television programme choice and ensuring the best possible reception standards.

(Note: the name St Mary's Mead derives from a famous location in the Miss Marple books by Agatha Christie. It is intended to conjure nostalgic images of timeless, peaceful countryside surroundings in an age just after the Second World War)

Figure 3.7 (a) Extracts from an advertising campaign targeted at the older person typify the increasing market share occupied by the elderly; (b) it is giving rise to completely new locations for housing such as this expanding town near Phoenix, Arizona, USA

In the United States the senior citizens already wield considerable political power because many of them are substantial contributors to the political party funds. In all developed countries house builders and tourism operators have already begun to exploit these markets, providing specialised accommodation and specialised long term holidays to see people over the cold winter months(Fig. 3.7). Seasonal migration to the south coast of England or the Sun Belt region of the USA already occurs on a large scale; it is clear that there are far more economic opportunities for perceptive firms in the future.

How will China cope?

As we have seen in Chapters 1 and 2, China has attempted a massive restructuring of her population. While it can be argued that this will achieve the goal of reducing the total population, it will have a very great effect on the way society develops even in the medium term. The cartoon at the start of this chapter characterises the rapid change in the Chinese society. China now has the largest and fastest growing elderly population in the developing world.

The Chinese people have always lived much longer than other societies in the developing world; today they have 44 million elderly. By the end of the century there will be over 80 million elderly people, or about 11 per cent of the total population.

Despite the size of these numbers, there are no signs of panic in the Chinese government. Their lack of alarm – although not lack of concern – is because of the traditional support of the old as part of the family unit. The Chinese have also developed a flexible retirement policy, linked with youth unemployment (they have had to find 100 million jobs for those leaving school in 1978-82, for example!). In the past the withdrawal from the workforce of a healthy adult was regarded as unpatriotic because China was engaged in a great rebuilding programme; today it is put forward as an honour and a privilege.

At the moment pensions are generous in recognition of the part played by the elderly in the struggle to build up the nation. A pension of 50 per cent is given, and sometimes even up to 100 per cent of salary for people with a history of out-standing achievement. However, the Chinese government could not provide such pensions for all even today, and certainly not in the future. At present the people living in the countryside (four fifths of the population) are excluded – and thus the family structure of support is vital. But the policy does not take any chances: the family unit is strengthened by a virtual ban on rural/urban immigration and laws that require the young to care for the old. The marriage law requires children and grandchildren to take full responsibility for elderly family members. Only the old without children are eligible for welfare.

Consider how the Chinese norms of society could be applied in Britain. What would be the advantages and disadvantages of building a granny annex to the family house, for example?

Student enquiry 3B

Finding a role for the senior citizen

Study the following pieces of information

There are over ten million people in Britain of pensionable age.

Picasso, one of the world's celebrated artists wrote : 'We don't get older, we get riper.'

Older people find themselves unable to cope with 'normal' houses because 'normal' houses are built for the mythical young family of two parents and two children.

One pensioner wrote to a Sunday newspaper:
'We must prepare to do battle to maintain our independence. I am haunted by the fear that unless I can dispel the assumption that I am a senior citizen the following events may reasonably occur:
    (i) I shall have a gang of young thugs sent to my home to paint my kitchen instead of going to prison.
    (ii) I shall have patients from the local mental hospital drafted to dig my garden.
    (iii) I may be forced to go to 'suitable' entertainments, drink tea and wear a paper hat.
    (iv) I may receive vast boxes of assorted food to which I feel I am not entitled.
We pensioners are in a terrifying position. We are recipients. Hands off please. I am in charge of my life.'

For the purposes of adult education classes, 12 people are necessary to make a class viable. But when calculating this local authorities count pensioners as only half a person.

One in every two Americans regrets having retired.

1. Explain why most forecasters concentrate on the problems old people will cause to society.
2. Suggest ways in which pensioners may play an active and financially rewarding part in the national economies of the developed world.
3. Think about the locational requirements of the 'empty nesters' within an urban area. Try to suggest what the effect of this might be on the urban scene.
4. Attempt to plot the distribution of empty nesters on a map of your local area and then explain the distribution. (Estate agents will often provide information to help you do this.)

Paying for granny

The social affairs ministers of the OECD have just spent a glum couple of days in Paris. They have been contemplating the time when one person in five will be a pensioner, and one in ten over 75; when only three people of working age will have to earn the wealth to support each pensioner; when old age pensions will account for one fifth of national income. This geriatric nightmare is what the OECD predicts for the average industrial country in the year 2040.

Add to such numbers the extra burden of caring for the oldest old: Britain's health service spends ten times as much on the care of a patient over 75 as on one of working age.

Not just a burden

Terrifying though the prospect of granny power sounds, a bit of constructive thinking can make it more manageable. The elderly of tomorrow will not be the same as the elderly of today. Many of them will be richer, better educated and healthier than their parents and grandparents. Governments need to turn these qualities to their advantage.

Most state pension schemes were designed when being old was equated with needing state help. Now, some of the old are richer than their children. Wise governments will target help on the poorest old: such as long-term unemployed, who never contributed much to the (earnings related pensions) scheme, and lone parents, who spent years in unpensionable part-time jobs.

If the state pays less to wealthier old folk, a problem remains. Someone will still have to earn the output to pay the return on their private assets. You cannot, as it were, feed tomorrow's children with bread baked today.

One task that may fall increasingly to the young elderly is that of caring for their own parents. One study suggests that 84 per cent of those who reach the age of 60 in the early 1990s will have at least one child alive when they die.

(Source: *The Economist*, 9 July 1988)

It is estimated that one in ten units of all new private housing is now designed, built and sold exclusively to retired people. There is a market of between 250 000 and 400 000 and to satisfy this 20 000 units must be built each year. There is a large proportion of Britain's wealth locked up by the over 55s who are, in many cases, living in houses too big for their needs now that they are 'empty nesters' – their children having left home. And although many retired people are still active, there are also many who will need some form of social support in sheltered accommodation.

Figure 3.8 Older people such as this grandmother, in the countryside of Kenya, can still look forward to support from the extended family. But the support in a city slum has faded away. To be old in a city is not good news

Growing old in the slums of Kenya

Kenya has not taken the controlled road to development advocated by the Chinese. Given the nature of its complex tribal society and its colonial history it has adopted a system based on the western way of development. Although this has seen the wealth of many Kenyans increase substantially, it has resulted in widespread migration from the country to the city. In the country the elders were always the most respected members of society, the ones who made the rules and kept the society stable (Fig. 3.8), but as many people migrate to the cities families have become more fragmented and the traditional structure of society has broken down.

The people who crowd into the city slums try to earn enough money to be able to return to the countryside. So if you are poor and elderly in the slums you have, by definition, failed. And the elderly in the slums feel failures. Deprived of their natural family support in a society of slum dwellers, with no security, the elderly are perhaps the most disadvantaged of all the poor.

Mika Kerago is 84 and lives in the New Grogan slum area. His home is not much more than six feet square. There is no toilet, no electric light, and the nearest water is 300 m away.

If all this were not enough for one old man to bear, he literally never knows where his next meal is coming from and lives completely isolated from neighbours although they are only a few feet from his front door. But he sees nothing wrong in this. 'Why should my neighbours help me? They don't know me. They don't owe me anything. They have their own problems.'

Mama Ndoga lives 80 km north of Nairobi on the farm that belongs to the family. She is about 70. But she still thinks nothing of bringing a sack full of pineapples from the fields to help with the harvesting (Fig. 3.8). 'I do my bit, just like the rest', she says proudly. There is no retirement out in the countryside, but there is little abandonment either. The rush to the city may help some, but the elderly are rarely among them.

Theme: Migration

Chapter 4
Long distance migration

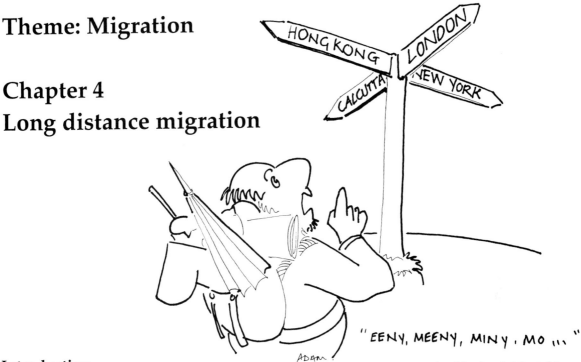

"EENY, MEENY, MINY, MO ..."

ADAM

Introduction

Migration is a deeply rooted cultural process, helped by people's unique ability to adapt to environments without evolution. Migration has been enormously important to the progress of the human species; it has allowed development of a global resource base and thus overcome the restrictions imposed by any one environment. The forces driving movement in the Stone Age are as real and as important today: they drive people from one country to another and between countryside and city in an unending search for a more fruitful existence.

Migration occurs when people perceive a distant environment to be more advantageous than the one they are in, and they have the means to reach it (Fig. 4.1). Migration is, therefore, intimately concerned with communications in its widest sense. All sorts of communications are involved – just as we might read about exotic countries in books which make us want to travel, so people who migrated in the past learned mainly of distant places through word of mouth.

People have walked vast distances to their promised land. The great trek of the Americans to the western states, for example, was accomplished by whole families who walked 5000 km on a journey of considerable hardship taking several months. They knew little of the world they were going to, only what they had gleaned from a few short newspaper articles and word of mouth. On the hearsay of a few dozen reports perhaps 350 000 people set out to walk to the west in the years between 1846 and 1852. Such is the power of the migratory urge.

Although many people choose to migrate, some unfortunate people are pushed from their environment by persecution of various kinds. This may take the form of political harassment or physical violence and threat to life. The Mormons, the Quakers, the Jews, and the Ethiopians are just some of the groups of people that have been more or less evicted from their homes; some were lucky and found new land which they could call their own; others could only flee to a land already occupied. These people are called **refugees**.

The history of migration

The peopling of the globe has been the result of 'waves' of movement over time. It is a historical process that has given us the present geographical distribution of people (Fig. 4.2).

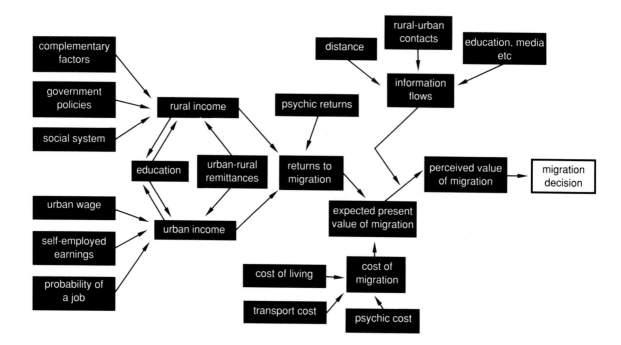

Figure 4.1 The complex reasons behind the decision to migrate

Much early migration was in the form of **slavery**. As strong nations exploited new lands they discovered that the indigenous populations were too sparsely distributed to be coerced into working effectively and so people were forcibly moved from areas of surplus to areas of deficit. This was true in the Roman and Grecian eras and also in the time of European colonisation. However, the European forced migrations were of greater significance because they employed improved ocean-worthy ships: thus new continents were colonised.

Europeans found tropical climates difficult to work in and thus resorted to the importation of people who were believed to be better adapted to the climate. The notorious slave trade between West Africa and the Americas is a classic example. Its result was to give America its foundation of racial mix in which people of African descent make up, for example, over 10 per cent of the total population of the USA (Fig. 4.3).

> *Slavery has had long term effects on the societies involved. Explain some of these effects, including the feeling for cultural roots, and the economic and social position former slave groups now find themselves in.*

When the slave trade was abolished the colonial powers replaced slavery with **indentured labourers**, mostly of Indian and Chinese origin because these people adapted to new situations well, worked hard and were relatively little political trouble. Thus the Chinese spread to southeast Asia and America; the Indians to south-est Asia and Africa (Fig. 4.4). Probably some 17 million Indians left India under indentured labour schemes, of whom a quarter never returned; an unknown number of Chinese, but at least several million, also 'emigrated' making these indentured migrations at least as important as the slave trade (Fig. 4.5).

> *Suggest some reasons why labourers in densely populated countries such as China and India might have become indentured in such large numbers.*

European migrants did not emigrate to tropical countries in any large numbers, for the climate did not suit many of them. Those that went became administrators. The largest expatriate community in permanent residence was in India and then it did not exceed 200 000 (Fig. 4.6). As a

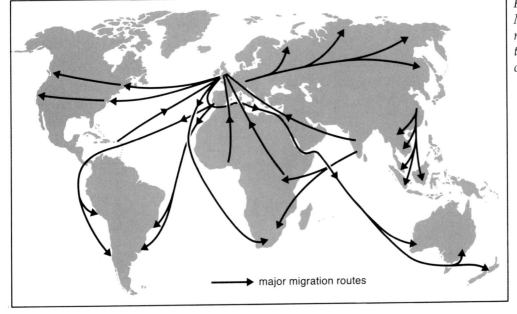

Figure 4.2 Major world migrations of the twentieth century

→ major migration routes

90%
other races

10%
black

Figure 4.3 The large percentage of people of African origin now in the US reflects the period of forced slave migration

result, colonisation did not greatly increase the European stock in most tropical countries. Many Europeans migrated to temperate lands, either in the northern or southern hemispheres. At first this migration was slow: in the first 200 years of European migration in what is now the USA, the population grew to just over 4 million, and in Australia the population was still only 200 000 by the mid-nineteenth century.

European migration is thus a phenomenon of the nineteenth and early twentieth centuries. In this time over 50 million people migrated (about a fifth of the entire population). The reasons for movement were:

(i) the rapid pressure on the resources of Europe associated with the second phase of the demographic transition (which came to a head with starvation in Ireland, for example);

(ii) the invention of the steamship made the passage more possible;

(iii) the presence of Europeans in north America and Australasia, even in small numbers, had sufficiently 'tamed' the wild lands to make them appear to be more desirable places;

(iv) migrants wrote back extolling the benefits of the new lands;

(v) products from the new lands (e.g. wheat) competed with those of Europe worsening the plight of the Europeans and making the new lands seem even more attractive; and

(vi) some religious groups were persecuted, especially the Jews in Central Europe.

Student enquiry 4A

Examining the pattern of long distance migration

Here is a chronology of the main events that took place during the main phase of colonisation of the American west.

1. From the chronology draw a graph of population movement against time.
2. A1 shows a model of migration across an ocean. Describe the stages shown by the model.
3. Using the information on the Great Platte River road, construct a parallel model to that shown in A1. You should put your model on a real base of the USA, using an atlas. A Rand McNally road atlas of the USA (obtainable in British bookshops) will be the most useful because it marks parts of the trail as national monuments.

4A1

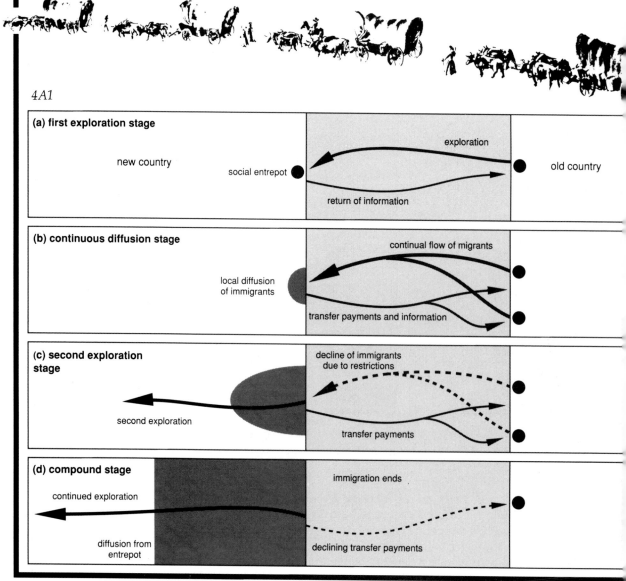

(a) first exploration stage
new country
social entrepot
exploration
return of information
old country

(b) continuous diffusion stage
local diffusion of immigrants
continual flow of migrants
transfer payments and information

(c) second exploration stage
second exploration
decline of immigrants due to restrictions
transfer payments

(d) compound stage
continued exploration
diffusion from entrepot
immigration ends
declining transfer payments

The road west: a chronology of the main events leading to the opening of the Great Platte River Road in the USA, often called the Oregon trail.

1804 Lewis and Clark explore the mouth of the Platte River.

1812 Robert Stuart and six others returning from the Pacific discover the South Pass. In the spring of 1813 they reach the Missouri, becoming the first white men to travel the trail.

1819 The US army establishes a fort on the route at Council Bluffs.

1820 Lt Long leads an exploring expedition up the Platte, making observations and sketches. Long reports 'The Great American Desert' (later called the Great Plains) uninhabitable.

1824 William Ashley leads an expedition to explore the Rocky mountains.

1830 Smith-Jackson-Sublette partnership leads a caravan from St Louis to make the first wagon train on the trail for fur trading.

1834 Fort Laramie and Fort Hall are established as forts and potential supply posts on the trail.

1835 Presbyterian missionaries join the fur traders' trail.

1838 Fur trader Andrew Drips is accompanied by John Sutter, who establishes a ranch on the Sacramento River which becomes the scene of gold discovery in California ten years later.

1840 The last American Fur Caravan to rendezvous in the Rockies is accompanied by Joel Walker, the first avowed Oregon emigrant, and father Pierre DeSmet, missionary, explorer and historian.

1841 The Bidwell-Bartleson party, the first emigrant party, leaves Kansas River for Oregon. One of the party writes a detailed diary of events. 100 migrants move.

1842 Oregon Trail from Independence is noted for fatal misinformation included in a later guidebook written by one of the party. In the same year Lt Freeman produces a narrative and map and gives the first reasonably accurate guidebook for the Great Platte River Road. 200 on the trail.

1843 The first large migration to Oregon, from Independence, Missouri contains 1000 people. This is a family affair including 130 women and 610 children.

1844 Four Oregon trains leave (perhaps 2000 people).

1845 Over 5000 people flock to Oregon. This is also the year of the first US military expedition up the Platte.

1846 California is involved in a war with Mexico. The Donner party, starting late, are nearly frozen to death by having to spend winter in the Sierra Nevadas. News of the disaster gets back East. Mormons are ousted from their bases in Central American towns (1000 people on the trail).

1847 Brigham Young and his first small party of Mormons go via Fort Laramie to the Great Salt Lake of Utah (2000 migrants).

1848 About 4000 Mormons follow the advance party. News of James Marshall's discovery of gold at Sutter's Mill electrifies the country.

1849 The mass migration to California begins. Something like 30000 people use the trails. The Gold Rush people are mostly men. Lack of preparedness exposes them to natural hazards and some do not make it.

1850 About 55000 hopefuls set off for California. Because of the dissemination of information from the 1849 experience the 1850 parties are better prepared. Nevertheless, drought sets in , the prairies are parched and oxen die by the thousands. Many people have to abandon their loads.

1851 Largely as the result of the calamities that befell the 1850 migration, the curve this year takes a nose-dive, with only about 10 000 emigrants.

1852 The California Gold Rush is revived by an influx of 50 0000 adventurers.

1853 About 20000 take their chance this year.

1854 The passage of the bill creating Nebraska Territory. Indian warfare becomes a problem. Only 10 000 migrate.

1855 Continued Indian wars keep the numbers down to 5000.

1856 Migration continues at 5000.

1857 The Union Pacific Railroad track is surveyed. 5000 migrate.

1858 The trail improves to support military activity in the Indian wars. Fortified ranches, offering accommodation and supplies, are established. The US mail service becomes established. Numbers travelling are 10000.

1859 Numbers rise to 30000.

1860 The famed pony express service is launched. Overland stages are in regular service. A silver strike occurs in Nevada. 15 000 emigrate.

1861-2 Civil War brings much migration to a halt and numbers remain at five thousand.

1863 10 000.

1864 20 000.

1865 25 000.

1866 25 000.

1867 Trail gives way to the railway, which is about to be completed. Total migrants to this date 350000.

1869 The railway is completed across the continent. Numbers soar to perhaps 100000 as travel becomes so much easier.

Figure 4.4 Indian people form large sections of the population in many continents. They are the main commercial group in Africa, and form a substantial group in many Middle Eastern countries such as Dubai, shown here

Figure 4.5 The Chinese are found as a dominant group in many south-east Asian countries. This street in a Malaysian city is dominated by Chinese shop signs

The migrations had very important effects on demography. They took the strain off the donor countries, allowing a breathing space and preventing the population exceeding the carrying capacity of the land (except in Ireland, Fig. 4.7); and they stimulated fertility in the new lands where every available hand was needed to help in development.

Migrants often reached the maximum possible levels of biological reproduction under such circumstances and families were huge. Thus between 1750 and 1930 the populations of the new lands increased 14 times, nearly six times as fast as the old world.

The results of these forced and chosen migrations were profound. By 1970 more than half of all caucasians did not live in Europe and more than a fifth of all negroes did not live in Africa.

By the Second World War the great European emigrations were over, but a new wave was just beginning: the emigration of people from the colonies of the developing world to the colonising countries in the developed world. Here, for the first time, people became aware of the possibility of moving from their impoverished states to lands of plenty. In this they were no different from the Europeans who migrated a century

earlier. Only this time the European population increase was slowing down and there were not enough people to do the work. So the increased perception by the developing world of opportunities abroad was matched by an open arms policy from Europe including payment of passages (Fig. 4.8).

There was another significant move afoot. In the aftermath of the Second World War, the mood was for every nation to claim its own sovereignty. But the world was now racially very mixed by wave after wave of migration. As nations sought to gain rapid independence there were a wide range of wars, revolutions and ideological struggles as nations sought to attain routes to development overnight. In an effort to provide separate territories, nations were carved up: the partition of India into India and Pakistan (now India, Pakistan and Bangladesh), of Korea, Vietnam, and Palestine are a few examples of a conflict which has raged up to the present day. Almost arbitrary division of land created minorities who were often forced to flee from persecution. Probably over 70 million people became refugees at some time or another between 1913 and 1968.

And so began the long trail that has led to the present world refugee problem in which 12 million people are displaced from their homes.

Fig. 4.6 *This British boy sits outside a part of Bombay built by his grandfather during the period of Indian colonialism called the Raj*

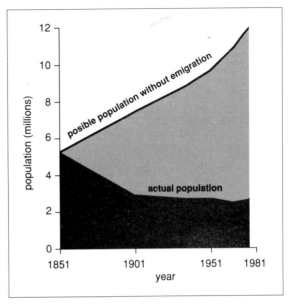

Figure 4.7 The impact of emigration on the population of Ireland since 1851 is only exceptional in that Ireland was the only European country whose population declined absolutely as a result of emigration

> *Consider the argument that, as a result of the displacement and mixing of the races, there are more racial problems in the world today than at any other time in the past.*

The principles of migration

The pattern of migration described above shows that people move long distances for two reasons:

(i) they perceive the situation in the destination location to be better than that prevailing in their home location; or

(ii) they are forcibly expelled from their home location.

However, experience shows that the majority of people move much shorter distances, moving from one home to another in the same town, or between towns as they change job, etc. This can be described as an **unconscious drift** of people.

When people migrate internationally or for long distances within their own country, their perception of the new environment is very limited and they therefore tend to migrate to large centres which they have heard of, for example, from central Scotland to London, from the UK to Los Angeles (Fig. 4.9). A large centre also offers a wider range of possibilities for adaptation and survival; people prefer to reduce the range of hurdles they must overcome; they therefore tend to move to places which share some culture or at least language. Thus special relationships between countries stimulate immigration routes: Commonwealth citizens to the UK; north-west Africans to France, etc. International migration is like a conveyor belt, with people moving to more advantageous locations. Some countries, such as the UK, have a net balance of migrants, but the UK loses people to other developed countries while it gains those from developing countries. Often such migration results in a net loss of skills.

The most prosperous countries are those with the highest net immigration if this is allowed (Fig. 4.10). Countries with a net loss of migrants are usually the losers because it is the most skilled

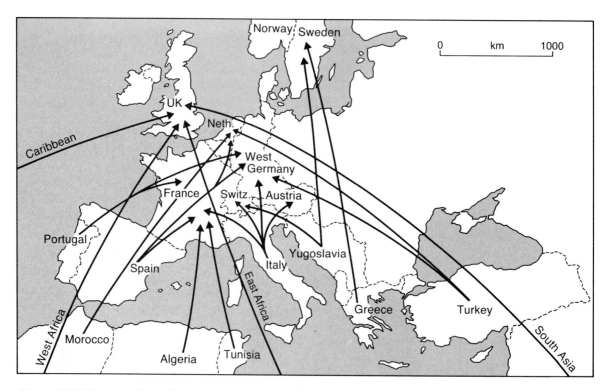

Figure 4.8 This map shows the most common routes for migration from the developing world since the Second World War

and able that migrate, while the less adventurous stay at home. Thus migration of doctors from the developing world deprives them not only of health care, but also of the ability to build up their own medical schools.

When people move short distances or internally they tend to be more acutely aware of a wider range of possibilities and thus migrate to smaller centres (i.e. inner city to suburbs; suburbs to commuter villages). Migration is thus a step by step process, requiring a springboard reason for movement at each stage of migration.

Government attitudes

Governments do not necessarily play a passive role in international migration. Their role is to try to provide the best for all of their people. Thus, if they are likely to be a recipient country and they see resources being stretched, they are likely to put up obstacles to migration. If the resource base appears large and there are too few nationals effectively to exploit the resource then immi-

grants, either temporary or permanent, will be welcomed with open arms. Of course, the resource base may change over the years, and countries may, for example, experience economic depression. Migration policy is therefore very dynamic.

Donor countries are those with less favourable resources. They tend to help migrants either because their removal from the country puts less burden on the meagre resources, or because they are likely to send **remittances** back to the country and help its balance of payments. In some developing countries such remittances form a major part of the national budget.

The governments of Bangladesh, Pakistan, the Philippines, Thailand and others have set up overseas employment companies to promote foreign employment. They realise that rural workers have little hope of finding a job abroad on their own nor will they have the finance to make the journey. These companies operate to bring overseas employer and the workers together. At the same time they try to attract remit-

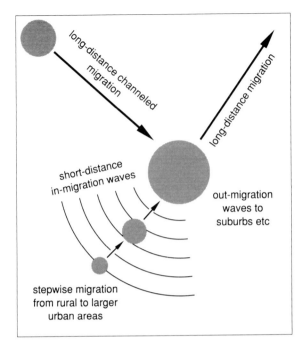

Figure 4.9 *The stepwise pattern of migration*

Figure 4.10 *Shops in Leicester cater for the substantial immigrant community and their specialised requirements*

tances back to the country through a variety of financial incentives. By contrast these countries have few schemes to assist migrants to find jobs when they return home: the country's best objectives are served if the migrant stays abroad! Consider, for example, the 3.5 million Asian workers that have gone to the Middle East since 1975 primarily as construction workers. This movement followed the expansion of job opportunities in oil-rich countries following the oil price rise in 1973. About 2 million Pakistanis, 1 million Indians and a third of a million Thais are currently abroad.

Ex-colonial countries such as Britain and France enouraged migration of whole families from their former colonies; other European countries such as Germany and Switzerland and Middle Eastern countries allowed only working adults who had already been promised jobs. Suggest what this difference might make to the countries concerned (i) over a period of decades; and (ii) during a recession.

International migration has severe social consequences for it interrupts family and community life. The scale of the migrations highlights the desperate need for money experienced by people in the developing world. Even the loss of 1 million males in a country the size of Bangladesh (population 90 million) has some impact on society. In the tiny Pacific island of Tonga a third of the population (30000 of 100000) presently lives abroad. In these circumstances disruption to the society is severe.

It can be argued that migration cannot be the panacea to development that it once was; there are no new lands to be colonised and developed, and no amount of migration will make a significant difference to the strains on the developing world. Indeed, the developed countries would have to take 80 million migrants a year to curb the growth in the developing world. This would result in a doubling of the developed world population every 11 years. Discuss this statement with respect to a policy of stopping all migration to Europe.

Laws of migration

1. Ravenstein's laws

The first formal study of migration relationships was produced by Ravenstein in the nineteenth century. He observed:

> (i) that most migrants only move short distances, and that numbers decrease as distances increase;
>
> (ii) people moving long distances are only poorly aware of the possibilities at their chosen destination: they tend first to go to large urban areas, rather than to small towns or rural areas;
>
> (iii) after arrival at a place, migrants will often then disperse, as they become more aware of their local environment;
>
> (iv) as people leave a place so others often migrate in; and
>
> (v) urban people migrate less than rural people.

Ravenstein made his observations at a time when the urbanisation of the industrial world was at its maximum. However, taking the world as a whole, the statements remain valid as huge numbers move within the developing world.

2. Zipf's inverse distance rule

The first of Ravenstein's laws was quantified by Zipf in the 1930s. He maintained that the volume of migration was inversely proportional to the distance travelled by the migrants:

$$N_{ij} \text{ is proportional to } 1/D_{ij}$$

where N_{ij} is the number of migrants between towns i and j, and D_{ij} is the distance between the towns.

3. The gravity model

Ravenstein's law (ii) can also be expressed as a relationship, called a gravity model. This makes a parallel with the laws of gravity and suggests that, if P_i and P_j are the populations of the towns, then the number of people migrating between them will be:

$$N_{ij} \text{ proportional to } (P_i . P_j)/D_{ij}$$

Note, however, that in the decision to migrate people rarely think in terms of physical distance, but more in terms of remoteness (i.e. time and difficulty of travel) and this is less easy to quantify. After a certain distance, people have little appreciation of real distances and they tend to foreshorten long distances.

The city migrant

When people move to a city they often enter an environment that is totally different from the one they are used to. The structure of the society may be different, people may speak a different language. Immigrants have two basic problems which must be solved quickly:

> (i) they must find somewhere to live; and
>
> (ii) they must find some means to support themselves.

In the developed world people usually migrate after considerable preparation. They come to a job that has previously been arranged and they move into a home that has been selected by an advance visit. People find migration very much easier if they are reasonably wealthy; those living in council accommodation must be accepted by the destination council. This may involve extensive waiting and may not be allowed at all unless there is a guaranteed job on offer. It is not in the receiving council's interests to bring more unemployed people to add to its own social service problems.

In the past migration was often by the most disadvantaged part of society. In today's highly structured society the disadvantaged are often the least mobile. Explain how this change has come about.

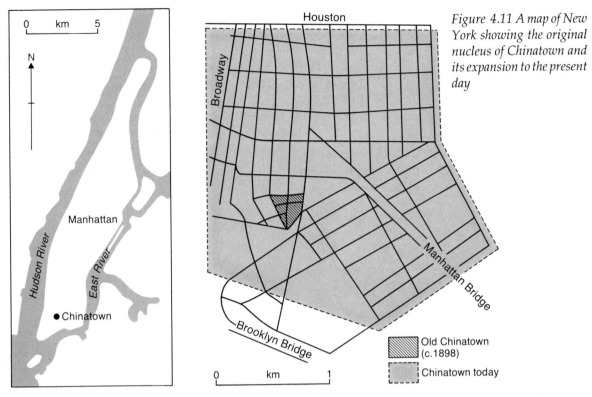

Figure 4.11 A map of New York showing the original nucleus of Chinatown and its expansion to the present day

(Map labels: Houston; Broadway; Manhattan Bridge; Brooklyn Bridge; km 0–5; N; Hudson River; East River; Manhattan; Chinatown; km 0–1)

Old Chinatown (c.1898)

Chinatown today

The privately rented accommodation sector bridges the gap between buying and council provision for those who cannot afford to buy a property (about 40 per cent of the UK households, for example) and yet still want to move quickly. Such accommodation is normally found in inner city areas where large, older houses can be subdivided as flats. In this manner the student, the single young person, and the young family usually manage to find a home while they save for the time when they can buy their own house.

The cultural barrier

In general, provided people move within their own country or from one country to another that speaks the same language and has more or less the same culture, the location of a home is only dictated by what can be afforded. But if there is a cultural and worse, a linguistic barrier to the new arrival, then it is very much in the migrant's interests to seek help from those already established within the city. In this way areas with well defined cultural contacts – **enclaves** (sometimes called **ghettos**) – develop.

A cultural enclave is a very supportive area within a city for new immigrants but it does have the penalty of being well defined. In times of social stress it is the area most likely to be identified and in which racial conflict develops. Notice that this is not just true of the least advantaged enclaves but also those which are, for example, very prosperous. The prosperous enclave is a well defined area for attack and burglary. In many cities such areas have homes patrolled by security guards and contained within barred boundaries.

Chinatown: an example of minority segregation

The Chinese first became aware of the opportunities offered in the west when European and American vessels began to trade in Chinese ports. The nineteenth century was also a time of great hardship for many of the Chinese and many of those in coastal regions wanted to try to earn money in a new land. At the same time the need to industrialise in America and many European colonies provided the demand for cheap labour

Figure 4.12 Chinatown, New York with its distinctive telephone boxes

that was prepared to work hard and not cause any trouble. The Chinese went to work at jobs as diverse as railway construction and tin mining, and to places as far apart as Malaysia and the USA. The US Central Pacific railway, for example, had a workforce which was 80 per cent Chinese.

The intention of the Chinese indentured labourers was to earn enough money to return to their homeland where they would live the rest of their lives in prosperity. As a result the early Chinese did not seek to integrate and become part of the American people. The rule that immigrants are only welcome while there is work for all applied to the Chinese in the USA at the end of the nineteenth century. When the railway was built and the mines worked out the slogan 'the Chinese must go' echoed throughout California and there were many discriminatory laws passed specifically against the Chinese, e.g. the Anti-Queue (pigtail) Law which forebade pigtails, then worn as a heritage from Chinese law. Economic com-

petition caused discrimination because the Chinese worked hard and were willing to accept low wages.

The Chinese settled first in California, but familiarity with the country and discrimination caused them to venture to other major cities. The first Chinese person to leave San Francisco for New York migrated in 1850. Early Chinatown in New York consisted of three streets: Mott, Pask and Doyer (Fig. 4.11) and from this nucleus it gradually expanded. By the 1920s there were 5000 Chinese in New York (Fig. 4.12). It was attractive because:

(i) it was a vast city with many different races, a place where small groups of newly arrived immigrants would not 'stand out';
(ii) since it was located on the East coast it was less influenced by the Californian anti-Chinese sentiment;
(iii) New York offered more economic opportunity for those who did not want to be labourers;
(iv) there was a large market for services such as hand laundry and restaurants.

Notice that the Chinese are not a nation of launderers and restaurant owners. Rather they *selected* these careers after 1884 in an effort to avoid competition with white labourers in the job market. Hand laundry was considered women's work and Chinese restaurants required ethnic skills. Chinese laundries and restaurants remain the most important businesses within New York's Chinatown.

Before 1945 there were very few women and children in Chinatown. Most were men who returned to China periodically to get married and have children. Their intention was to earn enough wealth through hard work to retire to China. Those American-born Chinese who were US citizens and could not find Chinese partners also returned to China to get married. Furthermore, US immigration laws discriminated against Chinese women until 1965. This family separation caused great stress and was one of the factors that led to the rise of prostitution in US Chinatowns.

The Communist revolution in China in 1949 led to a new wave of emigration from China, although 99 per cent of migrants were still from the

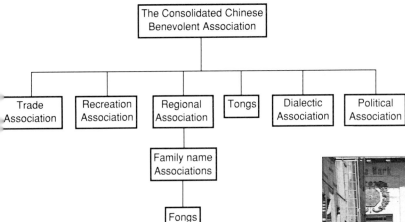

The Consolidated Chinese
Benevolent Association

- Trade Association
- Recreation Association
- Regional Association
  - Family name Associations
    - Fongs
- Tongs
- Dialectic Association
- Political Association

Figure 4.14 Chinatown's traditional associations were developed as a response to external hostility. We see parallels to this in Britain and other countries today. The attempts to establish Black Sections of the Labour Party is one such manifestation

coastal province of Kwangtung. These new political refugees were the first group of Chinese not to seek to go back to China and this began to change the whole character of Chinatown. These people had an incentive to learn English, seek a better education and integrate more widely with the rest of American society.

As a result of the 1965 relaxation of the immigration laws, by 1970 there were 69000 Chinese in New York's Chinatown, and by 1980 this had swollen to 150 000. In 1970 the sex ratios became equal for the first time in US Chinese history.

The trials that befell the Chinese after their immigration to the US led to the establishment of some special social structures (Fig. 4.13). Among the most important is the Consolidated Chinese Benevolent Association, a welfare grouping designed to help the Chinese in a hostile environment. In many ways this type of structure is inherited from the systems of traditional China. Kinship is a strong tradition in rural China and part of this has been carried over to the US with the migrants' surnames. Family name associations play a strong part in the social structure as do regional associations related to place of origin and trade associations. Many of these are supportive in providing credit to members of the community to build their businesses. Close family ties also provide the basis for the activities of the secret societies or 'Tongs', the groups who allegedly persue illegal activities much as the Mafia does.

The rapid changes that are occurring within the Chinatown societies mean that the traditional support structures are, to an increasing extent,

Figure 4.15 Traditional areas in Chinatown owe more to their tourist potential than they do to the preservation of a cultural identity

being taken over by the state run social agencies. There are also generation gaps opening up between the traditionally-minded Chinese and those with a more American outlook, derived from the knowledge that they will never go to China but must integrate into the US society (Fig. 4.14). However, they suffer a special identity crisis because they come from a culture which for centuries considered itself to be technologically and morally 'advanced'; only in the last century has China been left behind and become a developing country. It is hard to go from the top of society to the bottom when you migrate.

Student enquiry 4B

The role of the Chinese in US cities

Chinatown is naturally heterogeneous, although this may not be apparent to an outsider. Locals see their social differences as due to dialect, locality of origin, profession, prestige, time of arrival, lifestyle, degree of Americanisation, attitude toward China, income and age. In this they are just a microcosm of society at large.

1. Explain the factors that have led to the following statements:

(a) The old immigrant

'The traditional associations gave me a lot of help. I celebrated festivals and all the Chinese holidays with my Tong (brothers of the same village in China). Before my wife and children joined me here, my family name association was my family... Raising children does not do any good in this country. They leave when they are grown up. I seldom see them nowadays, with the exception of my younger son who is running the factory in Chinatown. They are too independent in this country! They are selfish, too!'

(b) The new immigrant (of five years residence)

'I am not interested in having a (association) name. I am interested in my work and in making money to support my family. I want my family to have a good life. I will retire after all my children are educated from college and have become professional people.'

(c) The second-generation Chinese-American:

'We were ridiculed by the old immigrants as "bamboo-stick" for not being able to speak Chinese and not being accepted as "white people". We are not here. We are not there. White people consider us to be inferior to the educated Chinese from China because we lack the "exotic value". That is why many of us do not want to socialise with the China-born Chinese-American. Most of us are proud of our Chinese cultural heritage, but due to the pressure to assimilate and the lack of opportunity, we don't know much about the Chinese way. We don't understand the lifestyle of the new immigrants or the older generation. When I visited Hong Kong and Taiwan last year, my friends and I were treated as foreigners. I am an accountant with a Wall Street firm. Chinatown is a ghetto. People there are ignorant of the workings of American society and they don't take advantage of its benefits, not even social security.'

(d) Chinatown planning official

'The Chinese immigrants are generally apathetic about politics because they don't know the American political system. They don't know that the American government is supposed to exist for the benefit of the individual. Many of them still hold the view of the traditional Chinese peasant that it is good to stay away from government, to live in a faraway place, to be separated from the influence of government by high mountains. The majority of the Chinese immigrants take it for granted that, because they are a minority group, they therefore have to swallow many grievances. They don't know that they have to fight for their rights in this country. This is America!'

2. What do these statements tell us about the probable distribution of urban Chinese minorities in the future?

Student enquiry 4C

Issues of ethnic minorities in Britain

On the following pages you will find some information about the nature of immigrants to Britain.

This information is only part of a wealth of literature that is available. It is suggested that you make yourself familiar with the issues involved in your own community and that you use this information to act as a springboard for local appreciation of this important topic.

1. Look at the series of maps showing the changing pattern of the Asian population in Leicester. Describe the changes shown by the maps.
2. It is sometimes said that a minority at first focuses on one part of a city for security, but as the people become more familiar with their surroundings they tend to diffuse into the rest of society. Using the map evidence consider how far the Asian population appears to fit this diffusion model. Consider carefully why areas of very high ethnic concentration remain.
3. On the map of London boroughs, draw the information of the 1981 census using a suitable cartographic scheme.
4. Draw a further map, this time using deviations from the mean for Greater London. Calculate categories for (i) within 1 standard deviation; (ii) between 1 and 2 deviations; and (iii) more than 2 standard deviations. Illustrate positive and negative values separately.
5. Describe the pattern you see, contrasting it with the impression from the first map you drew.
6. Compare and contrast the map you have drawn with the information for Asians in Leicester.
7. Plot the census figures for total immigrant populations in the cities shown on the table and obtain a regression line. Try to outline some factors that might be responsible for any large deviations from the regression line.
8. Using the map showing total coloured population, suggest how far the Laws of Migration may be reflected in the distribution of England's coloured community.
9. From the article 'Firm, but fair controls', and the answers to the previous questions, try to draw out and discuss as a group parallels and differences to the Chinese experience in the USA.
10. What are the social results that may follow from ethnic minorities (i) being concentrated, and (ii) being dispersed within a city?

MUSLIM MOSQUE ATTACKED

Imagine for a moment that you are at your place of worship, quietly praying to your God.

Suddenly, the peace of prayer is shattered by windows being smashed. You dodge to avoid being cut by the splinters of glass flying through the air.

After the initial shock, you realise that a hostile mob is outside, shouting obscenities and looking for a fight.

It slowly dawns on you that the reason the mob are there is because they don't like you or your choice of God.

Not possible, you may say. That sort of thing doesn't happen here. We're a civilised country, aren't we?

It seems that a small minority of thugs would lead us to believe otherwise.

The events I have described above actually happened on the evening of October 28th, at the Markaji Mosque in Christian Street, E1 (London).

The police say that they are doing everything possible to track down the perpetrators of the attack.

(Source: Anoushka Faroughy, *Tower Hamlets News*, Jan. 1987)

Firm but fair controls

Immigration has been one of the most difficult issues of British politics over some twenty years. Sensational and emotive statements have caused dismay and have damaged race relations. It is an issue which politicians must handle with care and sensitivity. But too often sensible discussion has been hampered by knee-jerk cries of 'racism' whenever a change in the operation of our entry controls is proposed.

A case in point is the hullabaloo over the introduction of visit visas for India, Pakistan, Bangladesh, Nigeria and Ghana last year. This came about because of the large number of dubious visitors seeking entry who had to be turned back upon arrival at the ports – almost 1500 nationals of the five countries had to be refused admission in July 1986 alone.

The Government argued that it was in the interests of bona fide travellers and of the smooth operation of the control, for eligibility to be sorted out before embarkation. The move was roundly denounced by the Opposition, their exaggeration fuelling fears in the minority communities.

In the event the visa regime is running smoothly, as I found when I was in the Indian subcontinent in September.

The Government believes that firm but even-handed control of immigration is a crucial factor in the building of better race relations.

When it was at its height there was a real danger of a public backlash against primary immigration. That is why immigration controls have been maintained by governments of both parties and why, after a brief wobble

during Neil Kinnock's visit to India last year, the Labour front bench now affirms its belief in a firm control.

This is not to belittle the very major contribution made to our national life by the minority communities – particularly in inner cities where their contribution is crucial to the drive for regeneration

There is still a fair way to go before we achieve the goal of a society which is not marred by racial discrimination, but progress is being made and that is our clear objective.

The Immigration Bill, now before Parliament, is a modest measure. It will not fundamentally alter the nature of the controls imposed by the Immigration Act 1971. However, in such a complex area, where the pressure points on the control can shift, and where there has been a good deal of judicial activism, it makes sense to repair loopholes. It will improve the working of the control and close off avenues for abuse.

The pressure to emigrate from parts of the developing world to the West grows stronger. It is not a problem peculiar to Britain. The most recent route through which an increasing number of people have sought to come to the West is as refugees.

Denmark, Canada, the United States and France have all had to counter illegal immigration based on dubious claims to refugee status over the last year; the Federal Republic of Germany received some 100 000 refugee claimants in 1986.

It is of great importance that genuine refugees should be protected from persecution; but we must not

allow this proper protection to become the object of abuse. It was with this in mind that we secured the passage of the Carriers Liability Act earlier this year.

It is not sufficiently understood that once a person gains admission to Britain, even on a temporary basis, it is often well nigh impossible to return them to their port of embarkation should their claim to admission prove false. Last year some 1500 women and children arrived here claiming to be British citizens but with no supporting evidence and it is clearly an avenue for further trouble

It is with this problem in mind that we intend, through the Immigration Bill, to remove the appeal rights in this country of such people but instead there is, of course, a full right of appeal from abroad.

The bill will also prevent the admission of more than one wife of a polygamous marriage. This does not affect more than tens of people entering this country each year.

I am anxious that the forthcoming debate on the bill should not release the old poisons. The Government believes in maintaining a firm but non-discriminatory and fair system of immigration control. We shall stand by this and keep the control in good repair – it is to this end that the Bill is directed. Public confidence in these controls is of benefit to all sections of the community in this country.

Timothy Renton is Minister in charge of Immigration.

(Source: *The Guardian*, 13 Nov. 1987)

Asians in Leicester

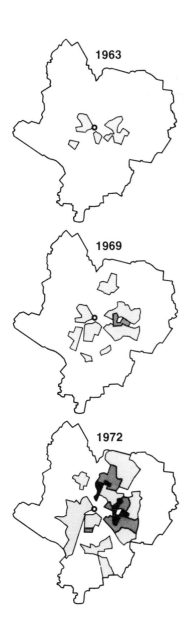

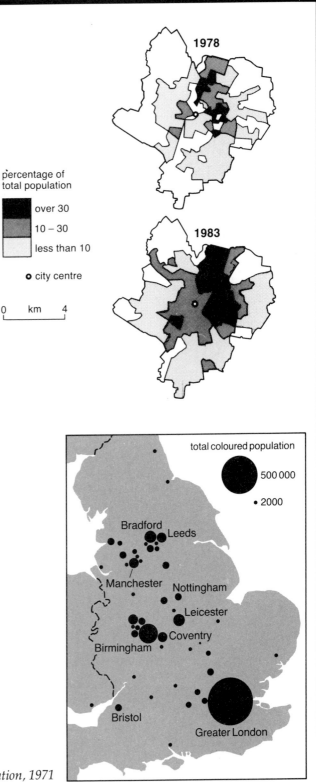

1963

1969

1972

1978

1983

percentage of
total population

over 30

10 – 30

less than 10

○ city centre

0   km   4

total coloured population

500 000

• 2000

Bradford

Leeds

Manchester

Nottingham

Leicester

Birmingham

Coventry

Bristol

Greater London

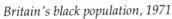

Britain's black population, 1971

Enquiry 4C concluded

Statistics from London Boroughs 1981 (Source : *Census*)

region	number on map	percentage of usually resident population in households with head of household from the New Commonwealth and Pakistan	region	number on map	percentage of usually resident population in households with head of household from the New Commonwealth and Pakistan
Barking	1	5.02	Waltham Forest	19	17.48
Barnet	2	12.83	Outer London	(pop 4.2mill)	11.81
Bexley	3	4.19	City	20	4.53
Brent	4	33.46	Camden	21	10.77
Bromley	5	3.60	Hackney	22	27.77
Croydon	6	12.04	Hammersmith	23	15.28
Ealing	7	25.41	Haringay	24	29.78
Enfield	8	14.04	Islington	25	16.90
Greenwich	9	7.97	Kensington	26	9.53
Harrow	10	15.28	Lambeth	27	23.48
Havering	11	2.38	Lewisham	28	15.12
Hillingdon	12	6.64	Newham	29	26.61
Houslow	13	17.08	Southwark	30	16.49
Kingston	14	5.39	Tower Hamlets	31	20.27
Merton	15	10.66	Wandsworth	32	18.20
Redbridge	16	11.22	Westminster	33	12.47
Richmond	17	4.53	Inner London	(pop 2.4mill)	19.37
Sutton	18	3.80	Greater London	(pop 6.7 mill)	14.50

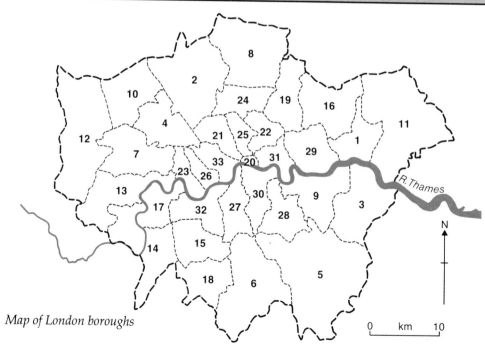

Map of London boroughs

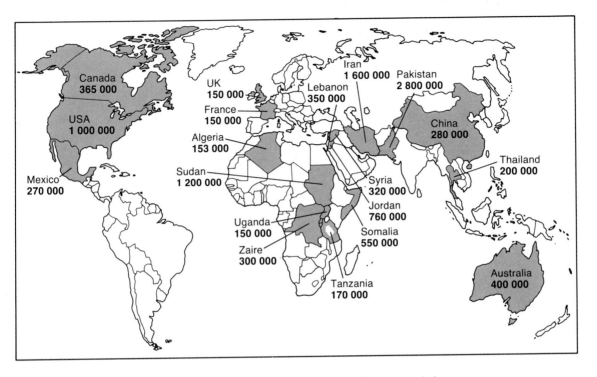

Figure 4.16 The distribution of international refugees today

Refugees today: the unwanted international migrants

Twelve million people are now refugees (Fig. 4.15). Nine million of them have sought refuge in the poorest countries of the world and as such these unwanted people now constitute a 'fourth world', with virtually no rights or ability to speak for themselves.

The UN High Commission for refugees has an inadequate budget for the job it is required to do, but even so the amount allocated reflects the increasing scale of the problem. In 1965 the budget was $5 million, by 1975 this had risen to $50 million and by 1985 it had mushroomed to $500 million.

The greatest surge of refugees occurred between 1974 and 1982 due to a combination of international conflicts and drought. Since then the rate of increase has slowed. However, today there is a new trend: that of semi-permanent concentrations of refugees in parts of the Middle East and north-east Africa.

The African crisis

The largest concentration of refugees is in Africa. Of the 4 million refugees, most are found scattered in camps in Sudan, Somalia and Djibuti. Many have fled from the wars in Ethiopia and Uganda. These people are very badly off because they have had to face the twin miseries of civil war and drought. These two causes compounded to produce a situation which was seen on the world's television screens and which culminated in the public appeals such as Live Aid and Band Aid.

In some places the large number of refugees have become a special problem. For example, it is now believed that about a quarter of the total population of Somalia are Ethiopian refugees. In this circumstance a country as small and as poor as Somalia cannot cope without assistance. The tens of millions of dollars of aid given by international governments are now central to the survival of the country's economy.

Refugees do not go to the cities, but remain in the border zones of their host countries. Nevertheless, many of the refugees have built up quite established communities in the border zone, with huts instead of tents, clinics, schools, bustling

Figure 4.17 Life tries to return to normal in one of the refugee areas just over the border of Somalia

markets and areas of crops (Fig. 4.17). When the war problem has subsided, people have returned to the time-honoured nomadic ways, simply using these new settlements as bases and sources of food. In this way 'refugee' becomes a blurred concept. The UN now gives aid equivalent to a refugee population of 700 000 but it has no way of knowing whether this is the correct guess; it is just a humanitarian gesture of the right order of magnitude.

In addition to the war refugees a further influx of people from south-east Ethiopia occurred because of the way the Ethiopian government had gone about the resettlement of people from their scattered communities – regrouping them into villages. This was done with the intention of providing better access to scarce services. However, the nature of the coercion used resulted in a further exodus of 30 000 people.

Sudan, too, has been affected by Ethiopia's troubles. But it also has to deal with the results of its own civil war, a drought at least as severe as that in Ethiopia and further influxes of refugees from Chad (where there is a civil war) and Uganda (where there was a civil war). The famine of 1984 brought 1 million more refugees to Sudan and only in 1987 did some of them begin to go back to their homes, realising that conditions were getting worse in Sudan than they were in their homelands.

While northern Africa is the focus of that continent's refugee problems, southern Africa also has severe problems, albeit on a smaller scale. The conflict in southern Africa, for example, has led to significant refugee movements. Because of its central position, Zambia has had to open its borders to waves of refugees from virtually every direction in the past decade. In 1987, for example, there were 200 000 Mozambicans fleeing from their civil war and 130 000 Angolans fleeing from a war with the Russian backed government that had lasted for 11 years. To add to these Zambia also has 'guerilla' refugees belonging to the resistance movements in Namibia and South Africa.

The only way Zambia survives this onslaught of the poor is by trying to make these people as self-sufficient as it can. Unlike Somalia and Sudan, Zambia still has spare land, and some land near its margins has been temporarily allocated to refugees in an effort to make them self-sufficient in food.

Refugee problems in Asia

In Asia there are startling numbers of refugees from the Afghan war that began with the Russian invasion of 1978. Over 3 million refugees have fled across the border to temporary refuge in Pakistan and Iran. The effect on the Pakistani border area has been devastating; the forest cover

Figure 4.18 Stages in the refugee crisis. This model describes the typical progress of a refugee movement applicable throughout the world

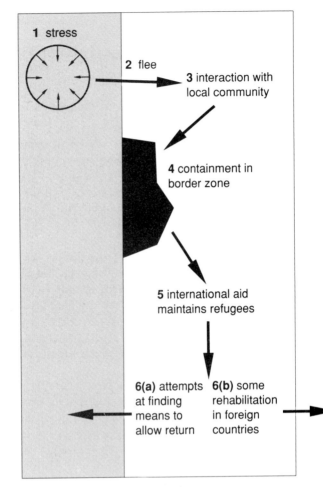

has been stripped for firewood and pasturelands have been turned into barren wastes by the flocks of goats and sheep the refugees brought with them. Thus there is intense competition between locals and refugees (Fig. 4.18). The main saving grace in this situation is the fact that the same tribal groups occur on both sides of the border and in this the Pakistanis feel a kinship with the refugee Afghans.

In Indo-China there is a further concentration of refugees. The UN High Commission for refugees, for example, spends $20 million a year in Thailand coping with people who flock over the borders from Kampuchea, Laos and Vietnam. For the most part these people are held in camps on the border, often still within the bombardment zone of the Vietnamese.

Thailand illustrates a refugee problem in a more mature phase. In the examples outlined above the refugee numbers are swelling rapidly because the situation has become critical relatively recently. In Thailand numbers hardly vary. This is because a booming birth rate in the camps balances the loss of people back to their country of origin.

The luckiest refugees in south-east Asia are those Vietnamese who are allowed to leave home under the 'orderly departure' programme operated by Vietnam and several western governments. Since it began over 120 000 have been flown out of Ho Chi Min City (Saigon) to new homes in the west. Nevertheless there are still 'boat people' who risk all to leave Vietnam in an assortment of small boats just as they have done since the mid-1970s. They are subject to attacks by pirates and if they go to Hong Kong they effectively go to prison. Hong Kong has never turned away a refugee but neither does it have the resource base or the land to house them and so it takes refugees only on the basis of a port of first asylum, assuming they will move on elsewhere. The 'prisons' are simply to contain them while they seek alternative homes. There are now more than 8000 on the closed island camps. Many of these people are not true 'political' refugees, but simply those seeking to improve their lifestyle. Britain took 20 000 Vietnamese between 1979 and 1986 but it is reluctant to take any more because they require considerable resources to help them adjust to a new culture. Most others go to the USA and Canada.

Now there is a general feeling that refugees should stay in the Third World, however reluctantly this conclusion has been arrived at. Denmark, for example, appalled by the demands of 20 000 asylum seekers from Iran, Sri-Lanka and the Middle East have, for example, been trying to change their immigration rules and close their borders. Recently the West Germans have had to act too, since the East Germans and Soviets began ferrying refugees to East Berlin to claim asylum, making use of a loophole in the immigration laws. 100 000 came this way before new visa controls were introduced.

Student enquiry 4D

The environment of refugees

The status and environment of refugees around the world change so quickly that it is important for you to supplement information presented in this enquiry with current material from newspapers.

The Middle East contains the largest number of long term refugees. Some people have been refugees for over forty years and many young people in the refugee camps know no other way of life. Most have been born and brought up in the camps that surround Israel.

The Middle East contains a complex web of interacting forces possibly unparalleled in the world. After the Second World War there was a struggle against the British Forces to establish a homeland for both Jewish and Arabic peoples. When Britain withdrew the Jews took over and declared the State of Israel. This state has never been recognised by the majority of Arab countries. Two wars have been fought over the territory that Israel annexed for itself, and the losers are to be found everywhere. Lebanon, and especially its capital Beirut, has been literally shot to pieces. Part of Jordan (the West Bank) has been annexed, together with a part of Egypt called the Gaza strip. All three areas contain Palestinian Arabs in refugee camps.

For a variety of political reasons there has been virtually no attempt to rehouse or improve the living conditions of the refugees even though they have been there for forty years.

1. Using the newspaper information comment on the environment of the refugees in the Middle East camps.
2. By reference to the Middle East refugees and those from Afghanistan, attempt to explain the common features of refugees and their environment.
3. Explain how the refugee problem and its solution might be seen from the viewpoint of
   (i) a UN delegate from a neutral country like Sweden;
   (ii) a refugee in one of the camps;
   (iii) an official in the receiving country;
   (iv) a politician in the country of origin of the refugees.
4. Some of the pressures that force people to migrate can be seen in Ethiopia. In 1985 the price of oxen fell by 500 per cent while at the same time the price of grain doubled. Farmers selling animals could not afford to buy sufficient food. OXFAM proposed to set up a scheme to purchase the oxen before the market price fell. They then proposed to keep them for four to five months in surplus fodder areas and then redistribute the oxen to farmers in time for the next planting season. Explain how this strategy could help prevent migration. Suggest other forms of help that might be appropriate to prevent farmers turning into refugees.

Caught in the crossfire of the Middle East

The Israeli reconnaissance plane drones in the distance, circling the sky above Israeli-occupied Rafah on the other side of the 40 yard wide no man's land of barbed wire and steel fencing.

The light aircraft flies towards the sea along the line of Israeli machine gun turrets which divides northern and southern Rafah, then it banks off to the right to continue its vigil over the restless Palestinians at the southern tip of the Gaza Strip.

For the 7000 Palestinian refugees of Canada camp, still stranded on the Egyptian side of the fence six years after the Israeli withdrawal from Sinai, thre is only the constant drone of the 'Intifada' (uprising) on the other side of the fence.

'Almost every day and night,' says Ziad, 'we can hear shouting, and then the shooting, and then the screaming and the crying. When they (the Israelis) throw the teargas, when it is blown across the fence and we can feel it in our eyes. And when we hear that someone has been killed, we know we shall soon discover him to be a neighbour or friend, an uncle or cousin.'

Caught at one of the main demarcation lines of the Arab-Israeli conflict, Rafah is a divided city; a dusty little Berlin at the south-east corner of the Mediterranean. The bleak barbed wire and steel fence, which marks the limit of Israel's 1984 withdrawal from the Sinai under the terms of its peace treaty with Egypt, has cut off the Palestinians of Canada camp from friends and families – and in some cases spouses – in the main part of Rafah.

For six years the camp's UN-supported refugees have been waiting to leave the unsanitary collection of low houses and return to their friends and relatives on the other side of the fence. The 'Intifada', as the refugees universally refer to the growing wave of unrest in the territories, has deepened their longing to return.

'It has given us hope,' said Mohammed, a 24-year old university graduate. 'The only hope is for the return to the homeland,' he added sadly.

Before the unrest in Gaza, the young men's only contact with friends and relatives on the other side of the fence was during the 'shouting hours' when the Egyptian and Israeli guards allowed the divided people of Rafah to shout greetings and messages at one another across the 40 yards of tangled wire. Now even that privilege has been denied.

The Israelis allow women, children, and old men to visit the other side once every six months, but the permit to do so costs £40. 'For all of us that is too much,' said Mohammed.' But even if you do get the permit, the Israelis sometimes make a point of tearing it up in front of you at the border, and sending you back to the camp. . . . For young men like me it is forbidden to visit the other side altogether.'

Ziad, also in his 20s and therefore ineligible for a permit to visit Gaza, showed me his papers — a blue travel document issued by the Egyptian Government and renewable every six months — his certificate of statelessness, as he explained. Despite a costly education at an Egyptian university, he is out of work.

The uprising in the occupied territories may have given the youths of Canada camp some new hope. But it has done little to dispel their acute frustration. In recent days, whenever the rioting starts on the other side, the teenage boys of the camp have begun to express their solidarity by shouting and burning tyres provided by the sympathetic Egyptian authorities. But this does not compensate for the camp's isolation from the events on the 'other side'.

'We feel so helpless,' said Ziad. 'We would like to be with them on the other side more than ever now that the *thawra* (revolution) has come.'

(Source: Tom Porteous, *The Guardian*, 15 Jan. 1988)

Student enquiry 4D continued

Plight of the nomads

Ahangeran camp is one of the few permanent refugee camps in Iran. It is a camp for Afghan nomads. Lying in a valley at the foot of high mountains some 60 kilometres from the Afghan border, it contains 1200 tents and close to 120 000 people belonging to eight different tribes.

At first sight these nomads continue to live in their traditional manner, in big black tents where the women weave carpets. In fact, they have been reduced to misery. They came to Iran three or four years ago with huge herds of 200 000 sheep and camels. Now they are left with only 100 000 – the rest were sold or eaten or died in the war or in the drought which has struck the area during the last three years.

Wholly dependent on the Iranian government which gives them food and medicine and tries to provide them with some schooling, these nomads wait impatiently for the coveted permit to work in a city.

Shir Ahmar comes from Hadraskan. He fled the war with 300 nomad families. By the time they reached Iran, all his animals had been killed. In Iran he works as an apprentice at a brick factory, making about 150 toman a day: $20 at the official rate. When he has some money he goes back to Afghanistan where he is a member of Jamuat Islami.

Clinging to tradition

Fierce fighters in their own country, the Afghan nomads are sometimes difficult for the Iranians to manage. CAR officials often give up any hope of bringing them to accept 'progress'. For the nomads school is the place from which their children were taken by the Russians and sent to Moscow. They are reluctant to send their children to Iranian schools even though boys and girls are taught separately.

Medical treatment is an even bigger problem. Dr. Nasrulan Hamraz, an Afghan doctor working for the CAR in Ahangeran, describes how he was forbidden by one nomad to put a stethoscope to his wife's chest – and was told to put it to the man's chest instead. When he needs to give a woman an injection, he has to cut a small hole in her dress with scissors.

There are other problems. Like all immigrants the Afghans are accused – sometimes justly – of a wide range of crimes including drug trafficking, the kidnapping of women or children and so on. Faced with the growing number of refugees, some CAR officials wonder if the Iranian government is not creating a time-bomb by accepting them all. 'We already have so many problems with them, now that we control them. What will it be like when we no longer control them?' asks one CAR official.

(Source: *Middle East*, Aug. 1986)

Chapter 5
Moving to a developing world city

" ... AND PEOPLE IN THE WEST THINK THEY HAVE A ROUGH TIME WITH INCREASING HOUSE PRICES . "

Introduction

Most people in the developing world still live in the countryside, and grow their own food. But because the land can provide a living for only a limited number of people, an increasing proportion of the world family cannot be directly supported by the land The redistribution of people between the countryside and the city – called **rural to urban migration** – has been occurring for centuries, but there are many factors that have recently hastened the transfer, causing many social problems. In this chapter we shall focus on this relatively local migration within a country and see some of its effects. To gain some insight as to the long term consequences of the drift to the city, however, we shall first describe the pattern of city migration that has affected Britain.

The most important factors influencing country to city migration are:

(i) **how easy it is to migrate** (have people enough money, is there a good transport system?);
(ii) **how easy is it to survive** (do the migrants have a job, do they have savings to tide them over a difficult first period, can they afford to rent or buy a house?);

(iii) **how easy it is to become part of the city community** (are migrants welcomed, can they easily integrate, are there enough jobs to absorb migrants without causing stress to the inhabitants already in the city?); and
(iv) **how quickly people migrate** (are the numbers so great as to upset the city lifestyle, can the services and infrastructure cope?)

During the nineteenth century most of the developed countries saw the majority of their populations move from the country to the towns and cities causing rapid **urbanisation**. In the last few decades the developing world has experienced the same phenomenon, but at a pace that now threatens to disrupt many societies.

Because major cities are such a conspicuous element of the human landscape, there is a tendency to see the exchange of people between country and city only in terms of stress to the city. In this chapter there is much evidence to show that the impact on the country is equally profound within the developing world. In this chapter we shall discuss how in the developing world the countryside is deprived of its best workers and often becomes more impoverished.

The developed world experience

The developed world has experienced country to city migration throughout the period of industrialisation – in many countries for over a hundred and fifty years. Because Britain was the first country in the world to industrialise, it was the first to experience many of the changes that eventually affected society world wide. It is therefore extremely valuable to look at the history of the British country to city migration to find out the pattern that evolved.

The British rural to urban migration has so far progressed through five stages (Fig. 5.1):

Stage 1

Most people produce only enough to feed themselves and there is very little surplus to trade. As a result there is limited surplus food to support an urban population and towns and cities contain less than 10 per cent of the national total.

Stage 2

An agrarian revolution begins. New techniques, seeds, better breeding of animals and mechanisation yield both a surplus of produce and a surplus of people. At the same time the means of transporting produce improves and this allows better contact between city and country. Poor prospects on the land for many labourers also encourage a move from the country (i.e. a push factor occurs).

Stage 3

The urban population is easily supported by the agricultural surpluses while the country helps to provide a demand for goods and services from the towns and cities. Towns and cities now develop based on manufacturing and can provide employment to more and more people.

Stage 4

Mobility improves and allows people to travel to the city from ever wider catchment areas. Some people perceive the city environment as too crowded, congested and polluted and look for homes in the countryside surrounding the cities. Changes in the nature of work also allow more businesses to be situated in rural rather than urban environments. The outward drift is called **counter-urbanisation**.

Figure 5.1 The relationship between cities and migration pressure (a) Developed world city

Stage 1 : The subsistence cycle in rural Britain

Stage 2: Early labour-intensive factory production

Stage 3: The growth of high density towns with low quality housing

Stage 4: Counter-urbanisation

Stage 5: Urban redevelopment

Stage 5

In an attempt to arrest the progress of counter-urbanisation, governments seek to rehabilitate the inner cities by improving the environment. The more affluent, who could choose to live outside the city, are attracted to refurbished central sites.

*Notice that one of the most important factors in the migration decision is the poor living conditions in the countryside. This can be called a **push** factor. Using Figs 4.1 and 5.1 try to produce a list of factors that could be called push factors and those that could be called **pull** factors. When do you think each factor might be the most important?*

When industrialisation began, few products were made and little money was available to buy them. As a result the transition from a nation of country people to one of city dwellers took place slowly. Nevertheless, there were both winners and losers.

The first people who suffered from the industrial revolution were the craftsmen and those who worked part-time at cottage industries in the back rooms of their dwellings. However, manufacturing in specially designed buildings – factories – was still heavily labour intensive and it quickly began to absorb as many people as the agricultural revolution displaced. And although most factory work was arduous and people were paid very poorly, many saw it to be a better way of life than the near starvation levels that existed in many rural areas.

Notice that in the British transition there was industrial work to be had for the displaced and, in general, some form of housing was also provided. At the same time urban growth was relatively slow, held in check by the rate at which increased farm output and transport systems could supply the urban needs and also by the gradual build up of an industrial society. Lack of transport placed further severe restrictions on the size and form of these early cities. When people entered the city they had to live very close to the factories. In part this was because transport systems were poor, but also because wages were too low to allow any of it to be spent on fares. Thus the early phase of rural to urban migration of poor people caused cities to become typically high density, with houses built in the most compact form and of the simplest style possible. Indeed, in these early years, the rapid growth of the population was only made possible by the building of large quantities of this low quality housing.

For many generations families shared rented houses of low quality. In the early years public assistance was simply not possible. However, low quality housing did not stem the tide of migration in nineteenth century Britain, any more than it stems migration in the developing world today.

Gradually workers' wages improved and many could afford to rent better quality housing, and some could even afford fares. Thus the form of migration changed from a once in a lifetime move to a pattern of daily migration called **commuting**, based initially on horse drawn trams or the railway and subsequently on motor cars.

Figure 5.1 continued **(b) Developing world city**

Stage 1: Subsistence cycle

Stage 2: Most production uses labour intensive methods

Stage 3: Rapid pressure on the city leads to high density, low quality shelter

Stage 4: . . . . ?

Urbanisation in the developing world

1. Pre-independence

In most of the developing world rapid and large scale migration began at a time when there had been no drive to industrialise in a comprehensive way. This was because the majority of countries, as colonies, had been organised to supply primary materials to the colonising country rather than to make their own goods. There were exceptions of course, and India, for example, stands aside from this pattern as we shall see later. Nevertheless, many urban areas of the developing world served a primarily administrative role in which there was relatively little opportunity for the untrained rural worker (Fig. 5.2).

Only in places where there were minerals to be won, such as gold and diamonds in South Africa, copper in Northern Rhodesia (now Zambia) or tin in Malaya (now Malaysia) was extensive help sought and urban communities developed. And even then, for many skilled projects it was common not to use the indigenous labour, but rather to use imported labourers. Many colonial policies only allowed non-Europeans to stay in the urban areas by permit, thus keeping the number of immigrants from the countryside relatively small. This policy also prevented permanent migration of people from the country and built up a great reserve of people who would flood to the cities after independence.

Figure 5.2 The imposing skyline of Nairobi, Kenya, owes much to the colonial emphasis on one centre for development. It acts like a beacon to those moving from the country

2. After independence

By the time the developing world's urbanisation began, technology had advanced to a point where there was less and less need for unskilled people in manufacturing. Thus the traditional way of helping rural people to fit into the urban environment had been closed – at least in the 'modern' sector of manufacturing.

Some, notably the Far East countries, were able to achieve very high productivity with their labour force and did become important manufacturers. The effect of their success was, however, to soak up the world demand for unskilled manufacturing labour and make the plight of the city dweller elsewhere all the more difficult.

Another factor important in influencing urbanisation was the pattern of colonial development. Each European colonising power operated from seaports (Singapore, Rangoon, Jakarta, etc.), developing rail links to the country interiors in order to transport the agricultural and mineral products. Thus development was confined to small urban areas and the countryside left undeveloped. This process continued past independence as politicians saw their priority as the need to protect and develop their manufacturing industry rather than agriculture. Thus, although the majority of the people might still live in the countryside and work on the land, attention was focused on the urban, manufacturing minority. This had a profound impact on the subsequent pattern of migration because it resulted in:

(i) an economic core, usually a single major metropolis containing both a capitalist or modern sector and a traditional or bazaar sector; and

(ii) an economic periphery dominated by the traditional rural peasant sector.

The imbalance in urban centres is striking and quite different to the situation found in most of the developed world. Towns in the rural centres are of no use to country people desperate for a job,

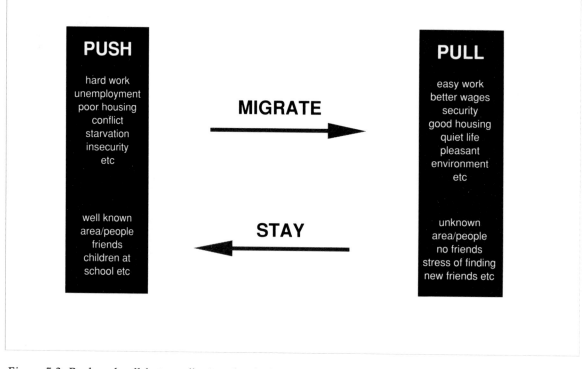

PUSH

hard work
unemployment
poor housing
conflict
starvation
insecurity
etc

well known
area/people
friends
children at
school etc

MIGRATE

STAY

PULL

easy work
better wages
security
good housing
quiet life
pleasant
environment
etc

unknown
area/people
no friends
stress of finding
new friends etc

Figure 5.3 Push and pull factors affecting the decision to migrate to the primate city

because their range of activities is so limited. As a result people have bypassed them and concentrated on the few major cities.

Usually only a single centre stands out as a centre of growth and wealth in many developing countries, and it is to this that the vast majority of the migrants flock. Its image, if not its reality, is almost like a guiding star of hope. Because it is so much bigger than other urban centres, and its political and economic importance so dominant, it is known as the **primate city** (Fig. 5.4).

Reasons for the rush to the city

People in the post-independence developing world have found themselves in countries with little wealth and therefore little in the way of social welfare programmes. But more than this, factors governing production have not required an expanding workforce. Rather, the manufacturing workforce is steadily decreasing in the face of automation and changing materials. The only way to survive is by reducing the quality of the

working conditions and paying very low wages. Thus the developing world city migrant probably has to look for a back street manufacturer and has to expect very low wages. (Back street industry of this kind makes up the so-called informal sector of developing world economies.)

In a thriving developed world society the wealth created in the manufacturing sector pays for people to be employed in services. People entering services where the manufacturing wealth is small can only look forward to a situation of shared poverty.

With such apparently limited opportunities in the cities, it at first seems unlikely that anyone would want to migrate at all. Nevertheless, with landlessness in the countryside ever more common and the opportunities for education, health and any other small degree of welfare service almost non-existent, many people feel their chances of survival in the city are better. And the bigger the city, the more niches there may be to fill and the greater chance people have of at least eking out a living.

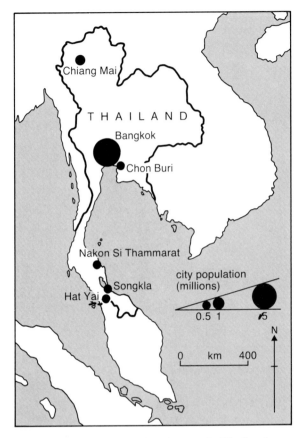

Figure 5.4 The pattern of settlement in Thailand, showing the dominance of the primate city

The scale of migration to cities

For reasons of pressure as well as attraction, therefore, people have flocked to the developing world cities in their hundreds of millions. The rate of rural to urban migration has been very rapid. At the same time, the people already in the city have benefited from better health care and nutrition, their children helping to swell yet further the numbers in the cities. Whereas in Britain in the nineteenth century the annual rate of population increase never exceeded 7 per 1000, in Africa today 20 and even 30 per 1000 is common. This has made the rural to urban migration a much more difficult problem to deal with than it was in the past (Fig. 5.5). Furthermore, the pressure on cities in nineteenth century Europe was greatly relieved by massive migrations to the New World and existing colonies. Such opportunities do not exist today.

Figure 5.5 Pulling a handcart is the kind of low paid service job that people from the countryside can take on. This killing work pays very little. The handcart is rented

The scale of the rapid urbanisation is staggering. In 1950 an estimated 38 per cent of the total urbanised population of the world lived in developing world cities. By 1985 this had grown to 50 per cent and by the year 2000 it is expected that 66 per cent of all people in cities will live in the developing world. In many cases annual growths of urban population now exceed 5 per cent with no indications that they are slowing down.

At present only about a quarter of the developing world populations live in cities, while the developed world has stabilised at about 70 per cent. If this proves to be the level of stabilisation for the developing world then the scale of migration will be virtually impossible to cope with. There are already over 3 billion people in the developing world; if half of these are involved in migration, the number of people seeking new jobs and new places to live will be 1.5 billion; and the population is growing all the time (Fig. 5.6).

On average, it appears that the population increases of those already settled, and the arrival of new migrants assume roughly equal proportions in the growth of cities, which have now reached a point where it is almost impossible to cope with the results of intrinsic growth alone. Adding rural to urban migration under these circumstances simply makes the problem unmanageable. Indeed, it is the scale of city growth that forces most people to rely on their own resources for housing

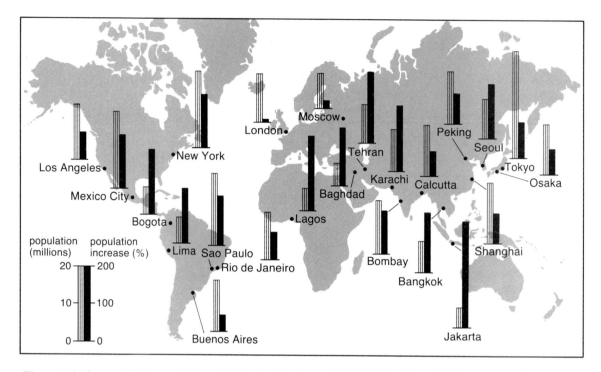

Figure 5.6 The population projections for the developing world cities. By the end of the century the world's largest cities will also be the poorest

and gives rise to that most characteristic feature of nearly all developing world cities – the **slums** (places of low quality official housing) and the **shanty towns** (buildings on illegally occupied land).

The impact on the countryside

Although they may be strangers to a city, those who migrate represent the most adventurous sector of the rural community. As a result their chances of success in finding a job are greater than average. Indeed, because of the energetic nature of the migrants to a city they often fare better in getting employment than the indigenous population.

Their chances grow rapidly if they find other people from the same home area and can thus spread their net of contacts. They are not limited to marginal forms of employment and their unemployment rate is often lower than for indigenous city dwellers. Thus, although they may start their employment in low paid jobs within the informal sector, migrants frequently advance into the better paid jobs of the formal sector. But there are several factors that may alter this situation. For example, as the number of city dwellers rises, urban costs will rise and the environment may deteriorate under the pressure of pollution. If, at the same time, jobs become more scarce than people and shared poverty becomes more of a problem, people will find themselves in an environment where their costs are rising and their incomes decreasing.

One major disadvantage of migration to the city is the loss of the relative security of the extended family. When people move to a city they enter a world which is inherently insecure and unstable. The perceived advantages have to be very great to make such a sacrifice worth while.

One example of the perceived, and real advantages of the city can be seen in food prices. Although you may think that the cheapest way of getting food is to grow it for yourself in the country, this is rarely the case because many countries operate a subsidy on food prices in the city. The objective of this policy is to prevent political discontent in the city and the possibility of the government being overthrown.

Impoverishment of the countryside comes about because it is the more energetic part of the population that moves to the city, very often depriving the countryside of its most able-bodied people. This in turn may lead to a reduction in productivity. Thus a reduction in the rural labour force may not necessarily take away the real 'surplus' labour, and allow those who remain to increase productivity and become more wealthy. Instead, it may leave only the more elderly and less dynamic on the farms. Further-more, those who stay are usually the poorest sector of the community who have accrued debts to money lenders and who must remain in the countryside to work off such debts. They may, at best, only be able move to the city on a temporary basis. Such people also tend to be illiterate and this is a handicap in the urban market.

Rural-urban migration harms the countryside not only in removing able-bodied people and those who would most likely be leaders, but also the countryside does not benefit from the skills such people acquire. Thus the structure of the countryside becomes more unequal, with the landowners and the employers remaining to-gether with the poorest of the landless. As the contrast grows so the poorest lose their bargain-ing strength and their incomes may decline even further.

Only the flow of capital from the migrant back to the family in the countryside helps alleviate the real poverty of the countryside. However, it is worth noting that it is the *less* poor who obtain the better paid jobs in the city. Thus their remittances act to make the better off wealthier and increase further the differentials in the villages.

To illustrate the complexity of the migration process, we will study examples from some con-trasting environments. Notice that in each case the particular historical and political events and the resource base of the country are extremely strong factors in influencing the migration proc-ess and its effect on the country.

The case of Zambia

In some countries the dispossession of land forces entire families to move to the city. In other coun-tries people are able to retain their land and use

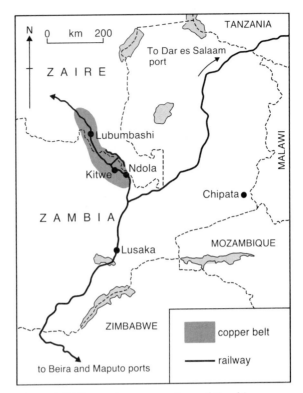

Figure 5.7 The main resource base of Zambia

the city as a source of additional income. This produces a very different population composi-tion in the city and puts strong demands on services in the city and the country. In Africa, in particular, the concept of 'land is mother' is so powerful that complete family movement from country to city is limited. The effects of this pat-tern, where people do have some degree of choice in where they will live, are seen in countries like Zambia.

Zambia, formerly Northern Rhodesia, was a British colony in south-east Africa. It contains a great variety of land, some of which is poor, but much of which can support good crops of corn, tobacco and livestock. Zambia has extensive mineral resources in the west in an area known as the Copper Belt (Fig. 5.7).

The Chipata province illustrates the effects of historical events on a fertile region. Large scale migration developed in 1901 after the imposition of a poll tax on the population. The tax could be paid either in cash or by work in the European sector of the economy. Furthermore, the land in the country was allocated either for European or

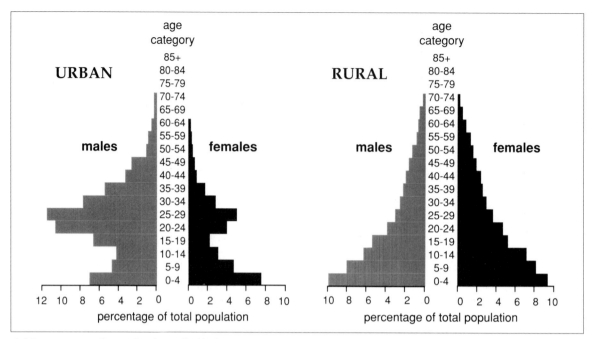

African use, so that only about half of the country was left in African hands in the form of 'reserves'. Gradually, the increasing pressure of people on too little land added a push to migration with the pull of a wage. This was accentuated by the growth of the copper belt and its need for manual labour. For much of this century there has been no shortage of jobs in the cities.

In 1951 about 60 per cent of all taxable males had left their homes for wage employment, although this did not remove the desire of all men to own land and acquire livestock; they simply saw the wages earned as a means of gathering sufficient wealth to own land and animals sooner.

After independence in 1964 the rate of migration to the cities has been 1.2 per cent per year, roughly half the natural population increase. Urban populations have soared so that now the population is more or less evenly divided between country and city.

Comment on how the population pyramids for Zambia have been distorted by rural-urban migration.

What does the small age range show about the nature of migration?

Suggest why the pyramids may become less distorted with time.

Figure 5.8 The contrasts between the urban and rural populations in Zambia are clearly shown in population pyramids

Men still dominate the migration, leaving population compositions in the countryside of about 85 men per 100 women (Fig. 5.8). Today it is difficult to find an adult male in the countryside who has not worked in the urban areas for several years.

The official guess at the unemployment rate in the Zambian capital, Lusaka, is about 25 per cent. Nevertheless, the estimated ratio between the annual income of farmers in Chipata and the average urban wage was about 1 to 7. With such differentials there has been a virtual scramble for urban jobs, the object being to provide the funds needed to supplement, not replace, the farm income and provide money for a dowry.

Explain why the official unemployment rate may be far below the real rate (information about Ahmed in 5A may be helpful).

Is the unemployment rate the best measure of city jobs?

Many costs arise out of the move to the city. Chipata trades agricultural produce with other

Figure 5.9 Rural to urban migration of the head of household and other able-bodied people puts an enormous workload on the women. These women have even had to take responsibility for improving their own mobility by digging an access road to their village

districts of Zambia. But as people leave and fewer people are left to tend the land the composition of crops changes to match the available labour. Cash crops (those that can be sold off the farm for money) require, in general, more labour per hectare than traditional subsistence crops (995 person-hours per hectare for hybrid corn; 1645 for cotton; 4300 for tobacco against 610 for local corn; 875 for beans and 2425 for groundnuts). While the money is still not available for the machine inputs and fertilisers demanded by the green revolution hybrid crop varieties, out migration also works against employing a technologically advanced system of farming and this too works against increasing the farm profit.

The trouble with this change is that the supply of subsistence crops begins to exceed their demand, since they are only traded locally. This depresses the prices and leads to a reduction in rural incomes. Thus as a result of migration the welfare of the non-migrants as a whole has fallen. In Chipata the remittances from the urban workers are quite small, so the loss in rural income is not balanced by the gain of urban wages from the migrants. Single parent families where the woman was the head of the household (i.e. the husband as opposed to the sons migrated to the city) suffered particularly because women were unable to do the heavy work of breaking new ground as well as a man. In particular this meant the households headed by women produced small cash crops and thus their income fell sharply (Fig. 5.9).

The households which have been most severely affected by out migration will want to minimise their risks: they need to ensure there is food and will not be as prepared to take the risk of commodity price fluctuations that occur with cash crops. Thus, corn can be eaten if there is no market for it, whereas cotton cannot.

The result of these technical and risk factors is that the 'strongest' rural households (those with male members between 20 and 40 years) that engage in growing cash crops get the highest return, whereas the weaker, low risk strategies make families even poorer. This leads to increasing inequalities in the rural areas.

Out migration leads to a serious scarcity of labour in peak times such as ground breaking and harvesting. If the male members cannot come back to the farms at these times the amount of land that can be brought into cultivation remains small. Animal power would speed up this process considerably (ploughing a hectare of land by hand takes 240 person-hours; ox ploughing takes only 60 person-hours) but those in most need of

Figure 5.10 Basket weaving is one way of supplementing a rural income when the male members are away in the city. The pay for this skilled activity is low

such help are the very people whose incomes are too low to be able to afford to buy animals or ploughs. Renting oxen is also an expensive business, with those hiring them out charging in real terms up to about a third of the final value of the crop. Also, because oxen are all needed at the same times, there is a restriction on the amount of renting that can be done. For all these reasons, in Chipata only 8 per cent of households used ox power.

One way to help supplement incomes is to engage in some form of indoor work at night when work in the field is impossible. Few alternatives are available, brewing being the favourite if households have enough money to buy in sugar and other inputs. Alternatively some form of textile making is the only other practical activity. Basket weaving, using local sisal plants and local vegetable based dyes, is usually the only way people can earn enough to provide the money to buy salt, sugar, clothes and perhaps pay for school books (Fig. 5.10). Again there are penalties, because working late hours at textiles or brewing makes people tired for the next day's farming. Furthermore such piecework is never highly paid and can do relatively little to supplement incomes. In Chipata 70 per cent of households had no form of supplementary income.

So what happens to the money saved by those who went away to the cities to earn the nest egg that could buy more animals or otherwise improve the land? Many who return have been away a long time, and their perceptions of what to do with their money have changed. They no longer see the farm as the best place to invest. Rather they tend to prefer to invest in shops, some form of minibus service or other non-agricultural enterprise. In practice, then, the land system loses out all the way along the line.

Student enquiry 5A

Reasons for migration to the cities

The decision to migrate, as seen from the point of view of the prospective migrants, is a complex one.

1. Study the migration stories of Joseph, Timbau and Ahmed and comment on the problems that each migrant faces.
2. What is the long term goal of each migrant? How likely are people in their position to fulfil this ambition?
3. Using the tables provided, choose some examples from various continents to support the view that migration from country to city provides an improvement in the quality of life. Using these figures, outline the main improvements that a migrant can expect to achieve.
4. Study the article 'The pavement people of Bombay'. Comment on the contention that rural–urban migration is always a success.

Joseph, a farmer's son

Joseph is a 20 year old whose home is still in the countryside about 80 kilometres north-east of Nairobi in Kenya.

'My brother has migrated to Nairobi. He trained hard and is now a policeman. Of course the money is good and the job is secure, but he still comes back on the bus whenever he can. The trouble is that the bus journey takes most of a day and so he can't do this often.

I am training to be a teacher. During the teacher training terms I also have to live in Nairobi, in a student hostel. I suppose we are fortunate; both of us did well at school and we have enough land to support the family while we are away. Everyone helps to pay for my education. It's different for some of the families who are not so well off or well educated. Some of them become labourers in the city; one of my friends mends shoes on the streets of Nairobi. The trouble is he can't get a permit to work in the city centre, so he has to work the side streets where there are fewer people who pay well. Still, he says that even in this position, and having to live in a room in the Kibaragwi slum, and with the bus fare to pay from the slum to the city every day, he is still better off in the city. There was just no more land left to support him and he was becoming a burden to his family.

We don't have too many really poor people here; this is a favoured part of the country; but elsewhere there is difficulty and many people are on the verge of starvation. Being in more remote areas they are less well educated and their chances in the city are more limited.'

Joseph is a quite well educated person from a productive rural area. He is a Kikuyu and part of the group who form the more upwardly mobile sector of the community. He was already familiar with the urban environment before he left the farm. Rural–urban migration may end up being permanent for him, but he will not face much of a cultural adjustment problem. Below, you will read the story of Timbau, a Masai man who has a low level of education and who had no connection with any city before he moved to Nairobi. He was brought to Nairobi by a middleman who tries to find people for specific jobs. His move to the city would have been a decision of the tribal elders, rather than his own. He did not have to make his own way to the city.

Student enquiry 5A continued

Timbau, a Masai pastoralist

The Masai are semi-nomadic pastoralists, long revered as fierce warriors and defenders of their cattle and grazing territory, renowned for their stately posture, and as drinkers of cattle blood. Timbau, like all Masai, is proud of his heritage; it has been a struggle for him to change. He abhors the thought of a settled life and a change to cultivation. He rejects the western style of dress, and prefers his red cloak, called a shuka. But times have changed. All around land has been fenced off for ranching or taken into cultivation as shambas. Traditional grazing grounds have been made into a National Park. The Masai are now short of land and recent droughts have made them short of cattle. To supplement their diet they must now eat maize meal and because they are not cultivators this must be bought in the market place. And there are other pressures to have money: education must be paid for and there are advantages to having a small portable radio. All these changes mean that Timbau and his family must earn money and so he has been sent to Nairobi to work as an askari(night watchman and guard) for one of the middle class families.

Timbau has no formal education but he is bright – when he arrived he could speak only Masai, but within a week he has learned enough Swahili to buy things in the local Nairobi market. As he finishes his meal and prepares to walk the several kilometres from his shanty district home to his work, he thinks back on his first night of duty. Some Europeans arrived by car and as he rushed to open the garden gate his shuka sailed majestically out behind him. He was confused by the looks of surprise. It was not his spear or knobkerrie club that surprised them but his frontal nakedness. Other Africans have also treated him as a primitive because of the way he dressed and because he has cavernous holes in his ear lobes. He makes a mental note that he must buy some western clothes and a proper charcoal stove with his first wages. After that he will be able to send spare money home. he earns enough in a few years he may be able to go back to his beloved cattle.

The pavement dwellers of Bombay

Homelessness has been a continuous problem in India for decades. The proportion of wage earners to the total pavement population was 43 per cent in 1985. Seventy four per cent of the pavement people earned less than $1.80 a day, well below Bombay's minimum wage. Overall, 67.6 per cent of the working men fell into this category, along with an overwhelming 90.9 per cent of the women wage earners. Only one quarter earned more than 19 rupees a day.

In all, over 90 different occupations were listed during a 1985 sample census. The largest group – 33.4 per cent – were unskilled workers toiling away at strenuous jobs as manual labourers on construction sites, as dockworkers and as headloaders (porters who carry heavy goods on their heads). The second largest group (21.5 per cent) consisted of people working as agents for traders or vendors of edible goods and other items, usually hawked from door to door in the middle-class neighbourhoods of the city. Self-employed people accounted for only 14 per cent, due to the large amount of capital needed to set up in business. Domestic servants comprised 12 per cent, followed by less than 12 per cent engaged in skilled labour such as metal-working, machinery, tailoring, and plumbing.

Almost 60 per cent of all the pavement people surveyed had migrated to Bombay over a decade ago; only 20 per cent had arrived within the last six years. This discovery dispels the widespread notion that pavement people are rootless transients and terminal derelicts. Living in the street has become a way of life for most of them. For the remainder, a short period of pavement dwelling has been followed by a move to a shanty or slum dwelling. Only the least successful are therefore left as permanent pavement dwellers.

When asked why they migrated to Bombay, 67 per cent cited abject poverty, landlessness and lack of employment opportunities in their native provinces. The majority of pavement dwellers (52.4 per cent) claimed to own no assets whatsoever before coming to Bombay.

This entire segment of the population – at the bottom of the economic ladder – has been almost totally neglected by city administrators and planners. This group of displaced people performs important and vital tasks for the economy of the city, such as collecting garbage and recycling discarded metals, plastic and glass.

If city planners in India and other Third World countries are to begin to tackle the immense human problems posed by slums and squatter settlements, they must also recognise the plight of the pavement dwellers.
(Source: *World Resources*, 1987)

Datafile 5A concluded

Ahmed, a rural migrant in Egypt

This has been the momentous day on which Ahmed has made the trek from his small village near Zagazig in the Nile delta to the metropolis of Cairo. Life was so hard in the village, and the land he owned with his brothers was too small for all of them to get a good life. The village had bought a communal TV and he had seen people in western clothes living at ease in tall buildings. And these selective images had touched his imagination.

'Surely if life is so good and easy in Cairo for those people, there must be work and good wages for me, he said to himself. 'Don't go to the city,' friends had counselled. 'You know nobody there; it is harsh and friendless.'

Filled with his dreams Ahmed had finally made up his mind. Early in the morning he had taken the train to the city. Gazing in almost stupefied disbelief, he stood on the steps of the city railway station, gulping in the sounds, the scale, the bustle of everything. Then, where

to stay? He withdrew a small scrap of paper on which a friend in the village had written the name of a contact. Eventually he found the place, a dark, small dwelling house in a narrow back street. People thronged everywhere. Keeping a firm grip on the bag with his spare Galabieh (cloak) and his

precious small quantity of savings he knocked on the door and asked for a place to stay. He was shown to a room where three other people were talking. This was to be his new home. The others came from many different villages so he would have to make new friends or city life would be very lonely.

Clearly a job must be top priority. But how to get one? Ahmed consulted his new friends. It was then he discovered they were sitting there because they had no full-time job. 'We get work sometimes,' they told him, 'but only on a casual basis.' They had heard you could get some goods from a wholesaler and then try to sell them on the street. He could try that, although the money was poor and if the police caught him in the city centre without a trading licence he would be 'for it'. Or perhaps he could find a job in a small metal repair shop — but what skills could a farmer offer a mechanic?

Still, all these worries could be put off till tomorrow. And if only small jobs arise Ahmed is sure he can save enough for a deposit on an airline ticket to Saudi Arabia. And everyone knows that as a construction worker in Saudi Arabia you can earn in one year what would take 20 years to earn as a farmer . . . .

Details of sample countries of the developing world (per cent)

Houses with electricity

country	urban	rural
Bolivia	76	6
Cameroon	19	1
Egypt	77	19
Indonesia	47	6
Panama	91	33
Peru	18	4
Thailand	92	12

*Mortality rates for those under five
(per thousand births)*

country	urban	rural
Senegal	167	332
Indonesia	143	188
Kenya	145	165
Panama	46	76
Peru	76	222
Thailand	57	122

Houses with toilets

country	urban	rural
Bolivia	48	4
Cameroon	93	64
Panama	96	75
Thailand	95	42

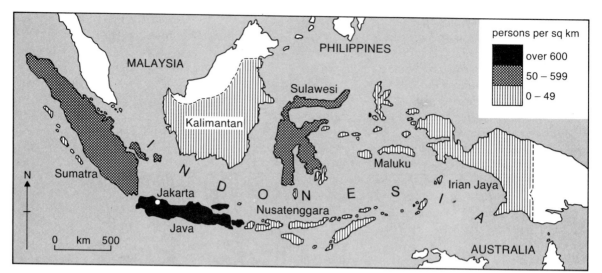

Figure 5.12 The distribution of people in Indonesia

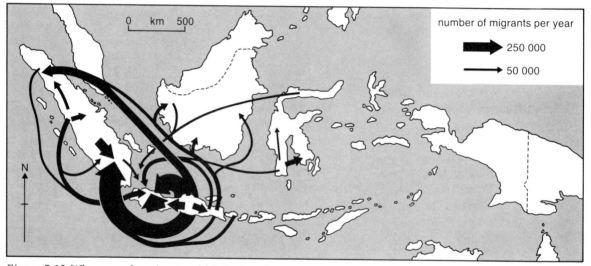

Figure 5.13 Where people migrate within Indonesia

Transmigration in Indonesia

In 1971 just over 7 million of the 165 million people in Indonesia were classed as migrants. Most Indonesians could be regarded as immobile peasants who were born, lived and died in the same house, scarcely travelling beyond the confines of their village. But if people are anxious to move to the economic core of Indonesia they must migrate to the area of 'inner' Indonesia (Java/Madura/Bali) . This is the area of the big cities and rural areas where population densities are over 500 persons per sq km (Fig. 5.12).

Over the past 40 years people have come from farther and farther away to seek work in the capital, Jakarta (Fig. 5.13). This has happened because of:

(i) an increasing awareness of the advantages of Jakarta due to the spread of radio and TV; and

(ii) the increasing efficiency and lower cost of transportation which makes it easier to get to the capital.

The government has tried to decentralise its ministries, but the shift is small in comparison to the large influx of rural people, and most decentralisation of government has been from Jakarta to other large urban areas. The other people leaving the city are migrants returning to their place of origin, often on retirement.

In 1970 the governor of Jakarta said 'Urbanisation has come to such a hopelessly bad situation that it can endanger the safety and order in the capital.' Legislation was introduced to make Jakarta a 'closed city' to try to stem the influx of people. However, the laws largely failed as people found ways to register themselves as 'temporary' residents or did not register at all. Political control of migrants does not seem possible and the only way to alter the growth of Jakarta is to try to divert migrants to other places where employment prospects are perceived to be as high.

Transmigration: a solution?

Indonesia's transmigration began as early as 1905 under colonial rule. It is a process of relocating people from the densely populated areas of Java, Bali and Lombok to new agricultural areas opened up by the government in other areas of Indonesia. Unfortunately the sheer scale of the population increase and the technical difficulties of opening up the area for agriculture mean that the impact on the country has so far been minor.

The theory behind the present transmigration policy is stated in legislation:

> ' . . . to raise the level of security, prosperity, and general welfare of the entire people and strengthen the feeling of unity of the Indonesian nation by means of
> (a) exploitation of natural resources and opening of land in a regulated manner;
> (b) reduction of population pressure in regions of dense population and populating empty or sparsely inhabited regions;
> (c) populating and developing regions which play a vital role in achieving a higher level of national endurance in all fields of life;
> (d) the formation of a just and prosperous Indonesian socialist society . . . . '

The difficulties faced by the transmigration programme in meeting its targets can be divided into:

> (i) administrative problems;
> (ii) lack of a data base such as a soil survey or land capability survey; and
> (iii) sociocultural problems as migrants are given new land and financial help but the poor indigenous farmers in the receiving areas are not.

The dramatic differences between the population densities of the inner and outer islands gives the comforting impression that the outer areas are well below their carrying capacities and that there is much more resource base for the nation to exploit. However, the special carrying capacities of Java, with its basic volcanic soils and a long dry season which favours the ripening of rice, are not repeated elsewhere. In many areas the volcanic rocks yield acid soils and there is no dry season: in fact the land is typical lowland equatorial rainforest. It is rather like looking at the moorlands of Scotland and assuming, just because they are inhabited by relatively few people, that they can be made as productive and support as many people as the lowlands of England. The problems associated with exploiting the rainforest are described in *The Challenge of the Natural Environment*, Chapter 12. As one prominent academic has said, 'few spheres of economic development have a history of, or reputation for, failure to match that of government-sponsored colonisation in humid tropical zones'. The Indonesians were fortunate to be able to colonise Lampung, but the resource base elsewhere is much more limited. They will increasingly have to look to birth control as a more effective way of keeping down pressure on scant resources.

Student enquiry 5B

Can transmigration work?

In this study you will be asked to consider the issues raised by Indonesia's transmigration policy. The material to help with this task is given in the chapter and also in this enquiry.

1. What is the reason for the high population pressure in many parts of the developing world?
2. How did the population of Indonesia become concentrated in a few of the many islands?
3. What are the objectives of transmigration? Have they remained the same or are they changing?
4. What are the cultural and ecological effects of transmigration?
5. Can the policy offer any real relief to the problem of population pressure or should it be abandoned because of the harm it causes elsewhere?
6. What are the alternatives to transmigration?
7. How far has the transmigration policy met its objectives, and has the cost been worth the effort?

Jakarta: no wish to add to the slums

Millions on the move as crowd eases its burden

Wild elephants have trampled surrounding fields, rats are eating much of his rice crop and he has no spare cash to improve the rude wooden house he inhabits with a horde of children and grandchildren.

But sitting on his porch surveying his plots of land in the south Sumatran settlement of Air Sugian, Kusman, a 55 year old farmer from the neighbouring island of Java, is pleased with life. Whatever else may be wrong, he owns land.

Kusman is one of millions, perhaps eventually tens of millions, whom the Indonesian government is resettling under a voluntary migration programme bigger than anything attempted anywhere else. Smaller neighbours such as Australia and Papua New Guinea are nervous about possible regional destabilisation resulting from this human tidal wave, and the programme has proved controversial with groups concerned about the cultural dislocation for different ethnic groups in the areas of resettlement.

The Government knows the problems but is accelerating the process – and for obvious reasons. Indonesia has serious population headaches. Its present 160 million people will rise, if current growth rates are maintained, to 216 million by the end of the century, and to make matters worse, their distribution is acutely uneven.

Miles of neat rice terraces climbing precariously to every cultivable inch of steep hillside are one sign of overcrowding in Java, which holds 90 million people or 60 per cent of the population in what is just 7 per cent of the land area.

On average there are now 690 people to every square kilometre of Java and the figure rises in irrigated areas to 2000. By contrast, neighbouring Sumatra holds 59 people per square kilometre, Kalimantan 12 and the even bigger territory of Irian Jaya, only 3.

While the larger outlying islands lack the manpower to develop, Java's overcrowding translates into widespread rural poverty and migration to cities where poverty is accompanied by outright unemployment. To make matters worse, much of the urban unemployment is concentrated among the young, particularly those with education.

Hopes that transmigration would check the rise in Java's population provided the initial impetus for the programme, but these have proved an idle dream. The government moved some 531 000 families – about 2.6 million people – in the five year plan ending in March 1984, but the population of the island grew by 10 million in the same period.

Transmigration can still ease the burdens of communities from which migrants are drawn, but the focus of the programme has shifted from redistribution of Javanese. Officials are more interested in the impetus it can give to development by opening up and exploiting the untapped natural wealth of the outlying regions.

Indonesia

By building roads and other infrastructure and moving people, the Government hopes not only to develop agricultural potential but eventually to attract industries as well. Beyond that there is also the strategic objective of what officials call 'nation-building'. In part, that seems to mean simply increasing the exposure of outlying areas to the influence of the Java-based Government. More specifically, as one official explained, 'We have to secure our country, we want to settle people along its borders.'

Accordingly, the Government tempts officially-sponsored migrants with free transport to their new settlements, free land, housing and assistance ranging from free food to free fertilisers and pesticides for the first year to 18 months after they move.

To the extent that transmigration attracts more migrants than it can accept, and has also given momentum to 'spontaneous migration' by people who move at their own expense, the programme works. In other respects, however, it is proving controversial.

Indonesia's neighbours and social groups have expressed concern about the impact on small ethnic communities facing a flood of Javanese migrants.

'Our state philosophy doesn't allow us to destroy local cultures and habits,' one senior transmigration official said. 'If we provide facilities it is not only for the people who have migrated, but for all the people there. We bring local leaders to Java and Bali to inform them.'

That's the theory, according to the critics, but they believe it is one that has little to do with reality. Scant allowance has been made in the past for ethnic groups that do not want to be integrated with migrants in resettlement areas, they claim, or for protection of traditional land rights and cultures. The Government is now beginning to weigh the possibilities for parallel development, independent observers say.

The dangers are most pronounced for the small Melanesian population of Irian Jaya and its primitive communities of hunter-gatherers who are used to roaming across large tracts of land now targeted for the biggest resettlement effort. The Government wants to move a million or more people into this area in the current five year plan.

Transmigration efforts to date have already roused local fears, prompting some drifting across the border into Papua-New Guinea and drawing rumblings of Irianese separatism. Plans are being formulated for a World Bank-funded study of the difficulties, largely in response to the criticism the resettlement plans have attracted.

With a programme of this magnitude, the Government has other headaches. With the growing emphasis on transmigration within the context of overall development, the programme has swung from being an often totally haphazard and unplanned process to a vast exercise in bureaucracy. Installation of a transmigration site with all the social and economic back-up can now involve up to 53 different government departments, experts say.

The government is budgeting the cost of establishing sites for transmigrants at $6000 per family and on that basis would be spending some $4.5 billion, not including the cost of the roads or other infrastructure development associated with any one project. But as more accessible areas start to fill up and movement of transmigrants shifts to more outlying areas, the costs are rising.

There also appears to be a need for more back-up for some of the communities that are already established. Settlers are supposed to achieve self-sufficiency after the first year or 18 months, but may have proved unequal to this.

Attention to the needs of migrants has generally improved since 1982 when angry settlers in Sulawesi expressed their frustration by beating a transmigration officer to death. But the Government maintains a critical list of communities that need extra back-up, particularly those that have suffered natural disasters ranging from volcanic eruptions to floods. It also has proposals for the World Bank on a study to rehabilitate other sites that need extra infusions of capital to succeed.

Even at sites reckoned self-sufficient, levels of productivity are often low. At Air Sugian, rated one of the more successful sites, farmers such as Kusman had far more land than they were able to cultivate.

When free fertilisers and pesticides had stopped, he simply coped without, being unable to afford them. But unable to raise production, or deal with such problems as marauding rats, he saw little prospect of generating sufficient income to clear, let alone cultivate, the other half of his land. The hardships are worse for transmigrants in more isolated sites facing a frequently more inhospitable environment.

Just how successful transmigration has proved in raising income levels of settlers is unknown and will eventually be the subject of yet another study. In the meantime the scope of the Government's ambitions is being checked by another problem: the increasing difficulty of identifying suitable sites, given the competition for land, particularly from forests that have suffered terribly in recent years and are now a target for conservation.

One response may be to broaden the scope of the transmigration programme to include, in addition to arable farming, other types of activity such as tree crops or fisheries. But as one expert remarked, 'we're not slowing down the realisation of sites now, but I can't see transmigration continuing at this rate.'

(Source: Nicholas Cumming-Bruce, *The Times*)

Student enquiry 5B concluded

Transmigration to catastrophe

On June 18th and 19th, Ministers from 17 industrial nations will meet in The Hague to decide funding allocations for one of the most controversial projects carried out in any developing country: Indonesia's Massive Transmigration Programme.

Aid from these countries, and from multilateral agencies like the World Bank, has helped fund a programme which has resulted in the loss of millions of hectares of irreplaceable rain forests throughout Indonesia's outer islands, and in the systematic abuse of the rights of the indigenous people living there.

This meeting is the target of a campaign organised by Friends of the Earth International, Survival International and other human rights and environmental organisations throughout the world. The object is to stop the aid and to lobby for it to be used more appropriately.

Environmental Disaster

The transmigration programme involves moving millions of desperately poor people from the over-crowded inner islands of Java, Bali and Madura to the unspoilt outer islands, like Sumatra, Kalimantan and Irian Jaya. Having already moved over 3.5 million people, the Government has grandiose plans to shift a further 65 million people over the next two decades. To date, aid from the development agencies has provided nearly 25 per cent (several hundred million dollars) of the total costs.

Indonesia's remarkable rain forests are vitally important, both as a global and as a national resource. They are second only to Brazil's in extent, and are biologically unique. Of Indonesia's 500 mammals, 100 are found nowhere else; and the country harbours 1480 (16 per cent) of all bird species.

The Indonesian Government has calculated that 49 million hectares of tropical rain forest have been destroyed or seriously degraded over the past 30 years. Agricultural expansion, mostly promoted by the Ministry for Transmigration, and non-sustainable commercial logging operations have been the main causes of destruction.

Because the soil of the rain forest is so poor, clearance for agricultural settlements often fails. Sulawesi and Sumatra, which have borne the brunt of settlements to date, have many millions of acres of land reduced to a 'critical' condition, i.e. land that is so degraded that it is generally unable to sustain even subsistence agriculture. 43 million hectares of degraded land is already in need of rehabilitation.

The Minister for Transmigration has recently admitted that at least 10 per cent of all settlements have failed which is generally held to be a very conservative estimate. The only opinion open to people, once their settlements begin to fail, is to clear larger and larger areas of rain forest, simply to survive.

Further damage can be clearly seen in Irian Jaya (West Papua) where future settlements are to take place. The World Wildlife Fund has identified many supposedly protected Nature Reserves and National Parks at risk from settlements. 24 transmigration sites have already alienated 700 000 hectares of traditionally owned land from tribal peoples. These indigenous people who live off the forest without destroying it by practising sustainable agriculture, suffer the loss of their land, the depletion of natural food sources, and the deliberate dismantling of their religious and cultural ways by the Government. 10 000 tribes people have already fled over the border into Papua- New Guinea to escape persecution.

Development agencies like the World Bank and the Inter-Governmental Group on Indonesia have very strict environmental and cultural guidelines which were supposed to ensure that aid money is not used in projects which cause environmental or cultural havoc. Transmigration, coupled with its strategic military position in South East Asia, have ensured that aid has continued to flow into the Programme.

This will only stop when the disastrous consequences are publicly broadcast within donor countries, and effective lobbying of donor governments takes place. This is why the forthcoming meetings in June and October are so important.

(Source: *New Internationalist*)

Theme:
The dynamic city

Chapter 6
Settlement pattern

Introduction

Chapter 5 outlined some of the reasons why many people move from the countryside to urban areas. The challenge of planning for the growth, or even coping with the decline of urban areas requires a good grasp of the way the urban pattern works. For example, knowing what factors affect settlement patterns will help governments, at both local and national levels, decide where to set up new centres or to understand why some existing centres appear to be in economic difficulties.

The reasons for urbanisation

The change from a rural society, where people live scattered across the landscape, to an urban society, where people become concentrated into certain thickly populated nodes, takes place for several reasons:

  (i) there may be a localised resource to be exploited (e.g. coal or gold, a tourist beach, a deep water harbour);
  (ii) there is a benefit to be gained by sharing ideas and expertise, by specialising in production, or by an increase in scale of production or sales;
  (iii) it is easier to live near work, the shops, or centres for leisure and entertainment; and
  (iv) it only requires a small proportion of the workforce to produce all the food that is required.

Urban areas are very difficult to define. Britain's 'cities', for example, were designated many centuries ago by the historical quirk of possessing a cathedral (Fig. 6.1). At this time they represented the most important places in the country. However, it is a definition that has not stood the test of time and cannot be used today in any satisfactory way to compare places throughout the world. An alternative means of systematically describing urban areas is therefore needed.

" FROM UP HERE YOU CAN SEE THAT IT FITS THE MODEL PERFECTLY "

From a geographical viewpoint an urban area can be defined by a combination of :
  (i) population;
  (ii) area of built land and/or proportion of built to rural land; and
  (iii) number, size and nature of the service or manufacturing functions.

Figure 6.1 Chichester is historically a 'city' because it has a cathedral. In terms of function it is only a medium sized town

Thus an **urban area** is *a thickly populated place where the amount of built land exceeds that used for agricultural purposes and where a wide variety of services and manufactures occur.*

Using this definition, the smallest urban area in most of the developed world would be called a **market town**. However, there is no clear cut off value that separates one size of urban area from another. At some size and complexity (largely determined by common consent rather than a specific formula) a large urban area becomes a '**city**'. A closely linked group of nearly continuous urban areas (towns or cities) that often spread into one another and contain a population of more than a million people is called a **conurbation**.

The pattern of urban settlements

To understand the present urban landscape we have to discover why towns and cities have grown up in their present pattern. In some cases a town or city may have been founded and grown because of specific local advantages of site. There may, for example, have been a good fording or bridging point of a river, a gap in some hills which provided an easy routeway, or the presence of a resource such as coal. However, when we look at a landscape it frequently shows patterns that could not be explained by these local factors alone. For example, it is easy to find consistent even spacing of similarly sized villages and towns (Fig. 6.2). A common pattern such as this must be due to more fundamental forces produced by the way we live.

> *Place a sheet of tracing paper over the Cambridge regional map (Fig. 6.2) and classify settlements according to the area they cover. Divide them into villages or smaller, small towns (market towns) and medium sized towns. Measure a sample of distances and perform a nearest neighbour analysis on the result. What does it show?*

The central place model

There are many reasons for the growth of urban centres. Firstly they are convenient central places for many everyday as well as specialised activities. For instance, it is much easier to have all the shops together so that all the goods that are needed can be got on one shopping trip. While shopping it might also be useful to visit the bank, buy petrol and perhaps have a cup of coffee.

From a retailing viewpoint an urban centre provides a focus for people from the surrounding districts – a **trade area**. Other types of business also find many good reasons to locate in an urban area. It has more people, and so the chances of finding the right workforce are better. It has road and perhaps rail links with other areas, making it easy to get raw materials to a factory or to send finished products elsewhere.

Thus the network of towns and cities grow primarily as **central places** for goods and serv-

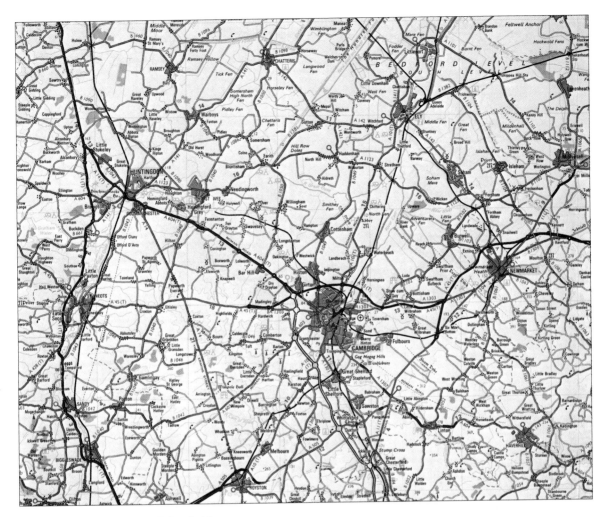

Figure 6.2 The area around Cambridge

ices. Each new service or function increases the convenience of the centre and therefore makes it a more powerful attraction for customers and businesses of all kinds.

When a network of these convenience centres has developed, it becomes increasingly unlikely that a new centre will be required or that it could survive, because the existing centres already cater for all possible needs. Because of this, some people have found the dynamics of settlements rather similar to the way an ecosystem develops. They see the following stages:

(i) a stage of pioneer settlements (villages or even individual farms), all about the same size and with the same functions;

(ii) a first stage of succession in which some

of the pioneer centres are taken over by opportunists to offer special services. If successful, these centres grow to dominate the remaining pioneers;

(iii) a second stage of succession in which some of the growing centres are chosen by entrepreneurs as the most likely places to succeed. These centres then become bigger still, offering all the facilities of the pioneers, all the facilities of the first successors, and the bonus of special facilities; and

(iv) subsequent successions occur until all the requirements of the area are satisfied (equivalent to the climax stage of vegetational succession) and the urban pattern becomes stable.

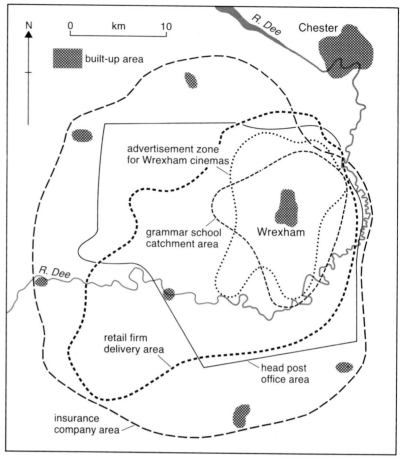

Figure 6.3 The trade areas around Wrexham

In an area where the population have much the same mobility, needs and purchasing power and where all goods and services are available uniformly, people will probably go to their nearest centre. Of course, to be commercially viable each good or service has to have a minimum number of customers – a **threshold population**, and thus a minimum size of trade area in which enough customers can be found (Fig. 6.3).

People need some goods and services more often than others, while the profit margin on some goods is better than others. A margin of 12 – 13 per cent on food items would be considered good, whereas a profit margin of 50 – 100 per cent on plastics would be normal. Thus trade areas need to be in varying sizes. For example, centres dealing with day to day requirements could expect to capture a large proportion of the

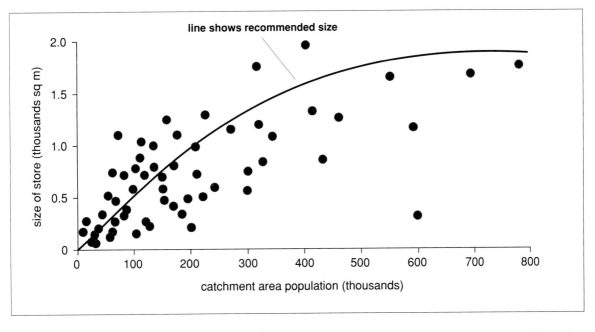

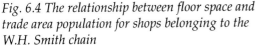

Fig. 6.4 The relationship between floor space and trade area population for shops belonging to the W.H. Smith chain

purchasing power of the local people. By contrast a specialist shop, such as one selling furniture, whose products might be bought by a family only once a decade, will have to draw its custom from a much wider area because its share of the purchasing power of each family is much smaller.

In a region of uniformly distributed wealth each level of specialisation will therefore have to seek its own relevant number of customers and this would result in an even spread of service locations. However, because each type of service has a unique size of trade area, not every function would be present in every settlement. Some centres would be home to only one function, others (but fewer)would conveniently be a base for two, yet others (and fewer still) a convenient base for three functions and so on.

One way to think about the resulting pattern is to build up from the smallest service centre (called a **first order settlement**) to the largest (a conurbation). This would produce a regular distribution of centres, formed into a dependent **hierarchy**. This was the method chosen by Christaller, a German geographer who began to develop a **central place theory** in the 1930s.

Christaller found that this simple model can be produced by approximating the trade areas to hexagons. These geometrical forms make up a precisely fitting 'honeycomb' of 'service areas' with the smallest urban area (market town) receiving its trade from the neighbouring villages. A network of market towns would similarly look towards the more specialist services of the next larger town (Fig. 6.5).

It is possible to isolate a number of economic pulls that might have especially important influences on the pattern. For example, if there is no constraint on travel and it is uniformly easy to get to all centres, pattern (a) would be produced. Here, each second order centre would need a trade area which captures the whole of its own 'first order' customers, together with approximately a third of all surrounding areas, i.e. three times the area of the first order centre. (This is called a K= 3 pattern.)

Realistically all parts of a region are not equally accessible, and many settlements are located on or near to main roads. This becomes increasingly important for those towns offering specialist functions for which people may have to travel long distances. The trade pattern that builds up when settlements are on roads (represented by the edges of the hexagons) gives pattern (b). Here communications are the deciding factor, the cap-

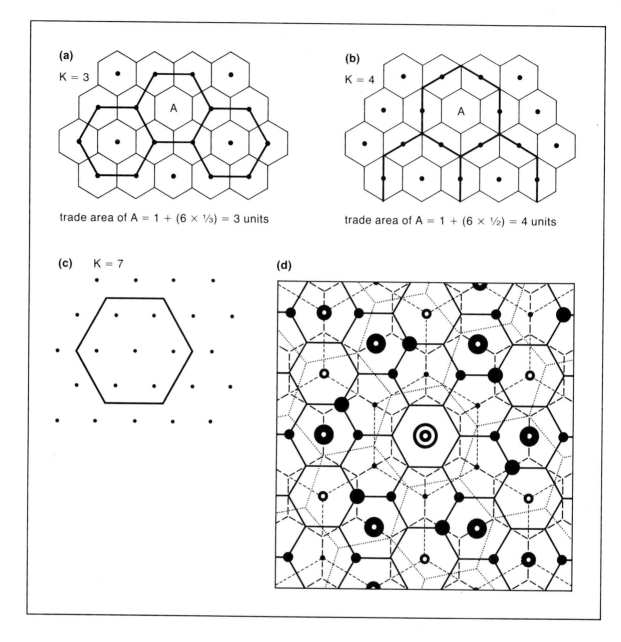

(a) K = 3

A

trade area of A = 1 + (6 × ⅓) = 3 units

(b) K = 4

A

trade area of A = 1 + (6 × ½) = 4 units

(c)   K = 7

(d)

tured trade area in each step is four times the area in the order below and the pattern is described as K = 4.

Administration has different requirements again, having the objective of gathering a number of settlements. Communication to them is not as vital as in the previous examples. The smallest hexagon which encompasses settlements is one that accumulates settlements in multiples of seven, i.e. a K = 7 pattern, (c).

Figure 6.5 Christaller's central place pattern: (a) The simple form of trade areas where each higher order catchment is nested to take three times the trade of the order below; (b) a similar pattern based on trade areas conforming to major routeways; (c) a configuration related to administration; and (d) the complex pattern that results from trying to maximise the number of functions as each of the patterns (a), (b) and (c) are superimposed. This shows how simple principles can lie behind a complex reality

Several studies in the developed world have shown that Christaller's ideas can be used as a basis for understanding the pattern of settlements. Table 6.1 gives, for example, the rank size classification of US central places in the agricultural State of Iowa in the 1960s.

When Professor Berry made an analysis of the state of Iowa in the 1960s he was able to identify the increasing numbers of functions and correlate them both with sphere of influence (trade area) and with population thresholds. Thus he found that (in the special cultural context of rural US) a hamlet might contain a general store, farm elevator, gas station, roadside restaurant or bulk fuel depot. Villages contain 20–25 types of retail and service businesses from 40 stores whose sphere of influence extended over 180 sq km, towns perform 50 different functions from 100 stores, reaching a market area of 500 sq km. In addition to the activities performed by villages they provided more specialist functions such as a hardware shop, chemist and funeral parlour.

Central place and planning

Central place theory is important because it provides a model with which to view the real world. To create the model many simplifying assumptions have to be made. Any real pattern is therefore unlikely to be a close fit with the model even though the underlying economic pulls may be the same. Regions are also dynamic, and a set of pulls that may have created a certain pattern can rapidly change and make a simple pattern very complex.

Consider, for example, the rapid change in communications and personal incomes that has taken place within the last half century in the developed world. Even in mid-century most people were relatively immobile, a large proportion of people lived and worked in the countryside and small central places thrived within very short distances of one another, each with its own more or less captive market.

Since this time there have been dramatic changes:

(i) the technological revolution in agriculture replaced people with machines and the rural population has dwindled;

(ii) personal mobility has increased dramatically – it is now convenient to travel longer distances to buy even day to day items;

(iii) disposable incomes have increased, and the cost of transport is no longer a prohibitively expensive item in the household budget;

(iv) supermarkets offering goods in bulk packs at discounted prices help offset any additional transport costs;

(v) specialisation and competition between types of service have developed very strongly.

Table 6.1 Central places in Iowa

Place	Approx. pop. size	Functions (retail and service businesses)
Hamlet	100	less than 8
Village	500	20-25
Town	1500	50
Small city	6000	100
Regional city	60 000	includes speciality goods centre
Regional metropolis	250 000	includes wholesale centre
National metropolis	1 million +	includes primary wholesale centre

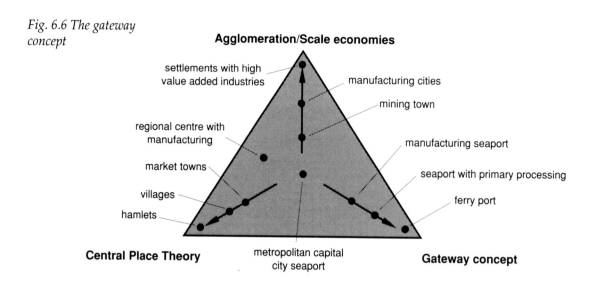

Fig. 6.6 The gateway concept

Agglomeration/Scale economies

settlements with high value added industries

manufacturing cities

mining town

regional centre with manufacturing

manufacturing seaport

market towns

seaport with primary processing

villages

ferry port

hamlets

Central Place Theory

metropolitan capital city seaport

Gateway concept

These five factors have caused a virtual revolution in the functions and size of rural central places within the developed world (see also urbanisation of the countryside in Chapter 12). As soon as people were freed from dependence on their local shop, they began to buy a wider range of goods and services. Thus simple, unsophisticated services that had been the mainstay of low order central places for centuries declined rapidly, while quite specialised services (such as garden centres) sprang up in new rural locations often not directly connected with any single settlement but in nodal communication positions.

The revolution that affected rural areas was no less deeply felt within large urban areas such as the major conurbations. This is because suburban areas can be considered in many ways as a collection of villages and towns, each with its own central services, but lacking the separation of fields. The corner shop began to be displaced by the hypermarket and the greengrocer by the boutique.

Thus dynamic change has occurred at all scales within the landscape. Today there are fewer levels of central place than was true fifty years ago, the larger growing at the expense of the smaller.

Central place theory is useful because it provides the structure for analysis, whether in the developed or developing world. Some patterns of settlement give great problems to their countries. This can often be explained by the history of

their development when the normal free market economy has been suppressed. The model also points the way to one system of planning for a more stable distribution of people.

Influences on settlement patterns

1. Resources and manufacturing

Christaller developed a model that considered settlements primarily in their role of servicing a local or regional hinterland. That is, it assumed that urban centres were mostly outward looking. However, today the outward looking city is becoming increasingly rare. As soon as urban centres develop a substantial manufacturing base, they become less dependent on their immediate trade area for their wealth. As a result large manufacturing centres can cluster and still survive.

Settlements founded to exploit a localised resource also fall outside the central place model. In this case their primary function was never related to servicing a surrounding hinterland.

The classic examples of the resource-oriented settlement are the port and the coalfield town. Ports transfer cargoes from overseas to a number of inland centres. Their functions are as **gateways** (Fig. 6.6). Site factors such as a sheltered harbour, deep approach channels and space for docks and warehouses are of central importance. Many major cities are gateways.

A localised resource such as a coalfield can only be exploited if the people are close at hand. Many of Europe's coalfields developed as miners were drawn to selected areas to dig for coal.

It is important to see that growth based on a single resource is inherently unstable because the continued success of settlements can only come during the lifetime of the resource. During the time of prosperity, other forms of employment need to be found. To this end a settlement is best placed if it is a good service and distribution centre (i.e. fits into the Christaller pattern).

2. Scale

Christaller first developed his model around a relatively small area, part of south-west Germany. At this scale it is possible to imagine that people are able to move to the largest centre for their specialist requirements. However, as countries become larger such an argument becomes increasingly less tenable. For example, people in the west of the USA cannot be thought to relate to the functions of east coast New York, despite the high mobility of Americans. Thus in large countries there cannot be one single large centre at the apex of the urban pyramid, but a number of large equal centres set in meaningfully sized regions. In countries where mobility is low, such as China or India, such an argument is particularly important. India, for example, has centres such as Calcutta, Delhi, Bombay and Madras so remote from one another as to control their own regions.

3. Culture, wealth and development

If the classic Christaller pattern is found only in agriculturally oriented regions of the developed world, perhaps it should be found more readily in the developing world where the number of manufacturing centres is more limited. However, in practice it is impossible to find any equivalence between, say, Indian small towns and those of rural USA, either in population, trade area or functions. This is because culture, wealth and stage of development play an important part in forming the hierarchy. Thus in both India and Iowa the number of small towns has decreased and the number of larger settlements has increased. However, in the case of Iowa the change was associated with increasing levels of mobility

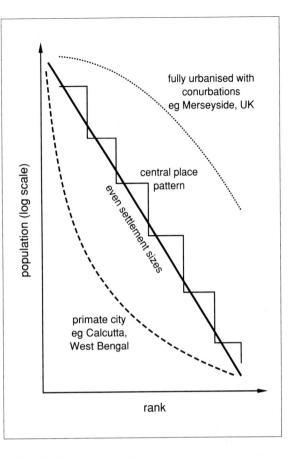

Fig. 6.7 Settlement patterns

and the reduced need for small centres; in the case of India it is due to rural – urban migration, while no new small centres are being founded.

In a country where the population is not very mobile the larger centres cannot rely on people from their 'trade area' coming to them. On the contrary, the markets have to travel round the established centres, bring goods within reach of the people. Thus the **periodic** (weekly, monthly, etc.) **markets** act as links between the towns and their regions. This helps to explain why all the small towns of Bengal, for example, belong functionally to just the lowest two orders of the hierarchy despite some having populations in the order of 20 000 (Fig. 6.7).

Further links are provided by the even more specialist '**fairs**' that visit the centres only a few times a year. In this case they attract buyers from a wider area because their products are so specialised.

Student enquiry 6A

The advantages of a central place

Information about the former steel town of Corby and the mining towns of South Wales is given below. In both cases the resource which sustained the settlements for so long has now been abandoned and the base of the town's employment withdrawn.

Corby Works Advert

1. Study the information and consider how far Central Place concepts are behind the degree of recovery of the towns.
2. To what extent do these areas act as central places in affecting the variety and character of new industries that have been established?

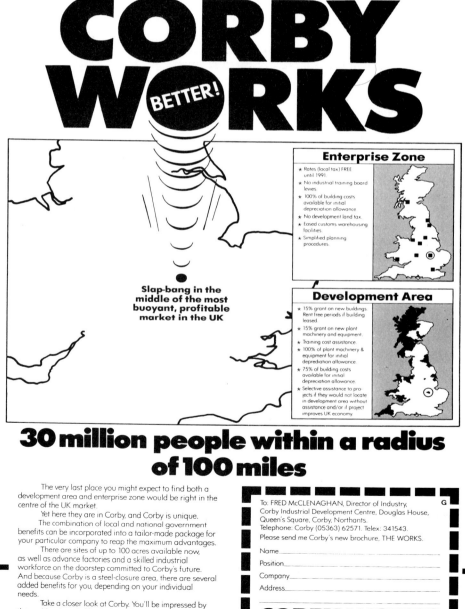

CORBY WORKS BETTER!

Slap-bang in the middle of the most buoyant, profitable market in the UK

Enterprise Zone

★ Rates (local tax) FREE until 1991.
★ No industrial training board levies.
★ 100% of building costs available for initial depreciation allowance.
★ No development land tax.
★ Eased customs warehousing facilities.
★ Simplified planning procedures.

Development Area

★ 15% grant on new buildings. Rent free periods if building leased.
★ 15% grant on new plant machinery and equipment.
★ Training cost assistance.
★ 100% of plant machinery & equipment for initial depreciation allowance.
★ 75% of building costs available for initial depreciation allowance.
★ Selective assistance to projects if they would not locate in development area without assistance and/or if project improves UK economy.

30 million people within a radius of 100 miles

The very last place you might expect to find both a development area and enterprise zone would be right in the centre of the UK market.

Yet here they are in Corby, and Corby is unique.

The combination of local and national government benefits can be incorporated into a tailor-made package for your particular company to reap the maximum advantages.

There are sites of up to 100 acres available now, as well as advance factories and a skilled industrial workforce on the doorstep committed to Corby's future. And because Corby is a steel-closure area, there are several added benefits for you, depending on your individual needs.

Take a closer look at Corby. You'll be impressed by the position, tempted by the incentives and understand the relevance of the slogan, Corby Works.

To: FRED McCLENAGHAN, Director of Industry,
Corby Industrial Development Centre, Douglas House,
Queen's Square, Corby, Northants.
Telephone: Corby (05363) 62571. Telex: 341543.
Please send me Corby's new brochure, THE WORKS.

Name
Position
Company
Address

CORBY WORKS

New life struggles to bloom as the valleys fight for jobs

England has its inner cities, Wales its valleys. Unemployment built upon dereliction is common to both; in South Wales, the problem is merely elongated.

Communities, abandoned by their traditional industries, remain locked in the deep, tightly crowded valleys that run between the South Wales coast and the hills of Glamorgan. Their legacy has been a mountain range of colliery slag, furnace waste and acres of poisoned earth that has failed to perish the strong sense of identity or a communal determination for improvement.

But at Blaenau, Gwent, where one in five is out of work, there are fears that the town could become victim of its own success at creating jobs. Companies keen to settle there are being turned away because there are not enough new factories into which they can move.

Mr Tom Gravenor, chairman of the Industrial Development Land Committee of Blaenau Borough Council, said 'We went out into the world and fought hard for more than 3,500 new jobs from America, West Germany, France, Sweden, and Belgium.

'It was bitterly disappointing to have to turn away people able to offer maybe 300 jobs because we could not give them a factory.'

Long before England's inner cities were perceived as a problem, the pits and steel plants that were the industrial heart of South Wales had shed 425 000 jobs.

When the earth movers and the landscape designers arrived, the industrial face of South Wales was lifted beyond recognition. The most striking transformation has been in the Lower Swansea Valley where 2000 acres have been reclaimed from what the city claims was the largest single area of industrial dereliction in Britain.

Mr Gwn Griffiths, head of the Welsh Development Agency (WDA) land reclamation department, pointed out that since 1966, 5000 ha of derelict land has been reclaimed.

Admiring the view across Swansea Bay from the sea wall bordering the Maritime Park, he said: 'Not many years ago where we are sitting would have been 50 feet in the air, above a huge lake of black slurry. Five million pounds later, we have this.'

The Park is a wide quadrangle of terraced brick houses overlooking the pool of the old dock, which is occupied by pontoon berths and a scribble of yacht masts.

Further up the valley, where the River Tawe was once no more than a sluice for toxic waste, and where new trees have struggled to put down roots, Britain's first Enterprise Zone has grown beside an artificial lake. The zone is a centre for more than 200 firms and 4000 jobs, a scratch on the surface of what has been lost, but a sound foundation for hope.

The 'master plan' for the Lower Swansea Valley includes five parks for industry or leisure. To the north, in the mining valleys, the change has been no less dramatic as Ebbw Vale begins to transform the derelict site of the old Victoria slag tip for the 1992 Garden Festival.

It takes quite a lot of confidence for a private industrialist to come here, but they have found a willing and adaptable workforce and a countryside that has been utterly changed.

The cost had been huge, relieved by the multiplicity of Government and EEC grants and loans. At the same time, the WDA factory building budget, set at £80 million a year at the height of the steel closures, had since been halved.

The Government giveth, the Government taketh away.

(Source: Ronald Faux, *The Times*, 9 May 1988)

Regions without a stable hierarchy

The colonial development policies that operated in many developing world cities caused the capital port cities to develop, while the remaining settlements were given only limited encouragement. Furthermore, settlements were not connected by an adequate route system, resulting in poor mobility. These twin features are contrary to the natural development of a stable central place network, and the legacy is the **primate city** whose size is grossly disproportionate to the other settlements in the country (Fig 6.7). Lagos in Nigeria, Mexico City in Mexico and Jakarta in Indonesia are just some of many examples. In large countries even several gateway centres could not achieve a good settlement hierarchy. Whereas London, the capital of the UK, has a population just over three times that of the second city Glasgow, Calcutta, for example, is over fourteen times the size of the second city of West Bengal, Patna (Fig. 6.7). The supremacy of primate cities which do not fit within a stable hierarchy has caused many problems. For example, the rural migrants do not have a selection of places to choose from. Instead they must all go to the primate city if they want to find a job. This simply makes the primacy of the capital even greater and adds further to the problems of coping with the large numbers.

Calcutta, for example, is the result of very slow growth in agricultural productivity in the surrounding regions coupled with a rapidly increasing population. The lack of growth in small urban centres makes them unable to absorb much of the surplus rural population. Thus in the absence of any real economic breakthrough in the countryside, any new investment in Calcutta draws in more people (at the rate of about 200 000 a year) and accentuates the urban problem. Indian planners clearly recognise the need to try to stimulate economic activity in the smaller centres. However, at present their aims are frustrated by a lack of mobility within the country which leaves many potential growth points still isolated and at an economic disadvantage.

Alternative patterns

History shows that the single resource urban area is not a long term survivor. Villages and towns disappeared from the map centuries ago when the demand for agricultural labour declined. Coalfield towns, lead and tin mining towns and ports have similarly lost their employment base and many people have been forced away.

However there has not always been a decline. Some towns and cities that began as single resource centres have grown big and diverse enough to be secure from the threat of decline of a single resource.

One of the largest agglomerations is London. The city docks declined to such an extent that the dockland area became derelict in the 1960s and 70s. However, this local 'black spot' in unemployment did not ripple through the whole city because the dock trade was only one facet of the city's employment. Since it first developed as a gateway, London had become a diverse centre of activity, taking on the functions of port, manufacturing centre and centre of political and financial power.

London is now a metropolitan capital city seaport. This is the most stable form of settlement because of the diversity of its functions. It can form a nodal service centre; it has manufactures, and it can use the gateway resource. This unique combination ensures a degree of stability that cannot be attained by any other form of settlement.

Urban pattern and planning

This chapter has discussed some of the reasons behind the distribution of settlements of all sizes. It has shown that a pattern established for one set of circumstances may have enough inertia to be used time after time through the centuries. The places with the greatest degree of stability are typically those with good nodal positions. These have been able to build a diversity of industry and services which buffer them against the decline of any one sector of the economy or the nature of the hinterland.

Central place theory is a useful basis for considering the sites of New Towns and expanded towns. Many of these are small to medium sized settlements, whose success depends on accurate judgements by planners.

Student enquiry 6B

India's changing settlements

The tables below show the changing populations of settlements in India. Study them carefully and make sure you understand what they are showing.

1. Complete Table 2 by calculating the percentage distributions.
2. Display the data in graphical form to show the nature of the settlement hierarchy and the changes that have taken place this century.
3. Work in pairs or small groups to produce several statements describing settlement hierarchy in India. Suggest ways in which this might differ from the nature of the hierarchy in developed countries. How important is the fact that many people in India are involved in subsistence agriculture and therefore have low incomes? (Think about their purchasing power and need for specialist goods and services.)

Table 1 Percentage population of urban settlements in India (1901-1981)

Settlement size	1901	1951	1961	1971	1981
over 100 000	22	38	45	49	60
50 000-99 999	11	12	12	13	11
20 000-49 999	17	18	20	18	15
10 000-19 999	23	15	14	13	10
less than 9 999	27	17	9	7	4
Total (%)	100	100	100	100	100

Table 2 Population of rural settlements in India (1971)

Population	number of settlements	population (millions)	percentage distribution settlements	population
less than 200	150	15		
200-499	169	57		
500-999	133	94		
1000-1999	82	113		
2000-4999	36	104		
5000-9999	5	36		
Total	575	415	100%	100%

Student enquiry 6C

A new town for Cambridge

Cambridgeshire has experienced one of the most rapid growths of any British county and there is continuing pressure from both industrial users (especially high technology and office functions) and commuters who are trying to find a pleasant location within a reasonable distance of London and yet where the house prices are not too exorbitant.

In this enquiry you are asked to suggest, and give reasons for, the selection of sites for one small new town to accommodate the brunt of the planned population expansion. While you are doing this you should bear in mind the general principles (and limitations) of central place theory.

1. Study all the information carefully before you begin. The bulk of the information is derived from the Cambridgeshire Structure Plan.
2. The map D1 shows six possible sites for a new town. For each of the sites A to F, write a few sentences, or make up a matrix, showing its advantages and disadvantages.
3. Decide upon the best site for the new settlement. Imagine that you have been asked by the Council to write a report which will become the appendix to the structure plan. Your report should include an annotated sketch map and a statement which clearly outlines the reasons for your choice.

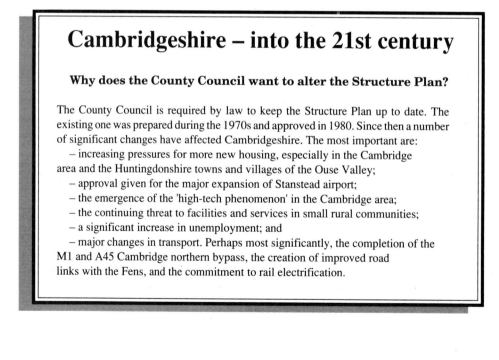

Cambridgeshire – into the 21st century

Why does the County Council want to alter the Structure Plan?

The County Council is required by law to keep the Structure Plan up to date. The existing one was prepared during the 1970s and approved in 1980. Since then a number of significant changes have affected Cambridgeshire. The most important are:
  – increasing pressures for more new housing, especially in the Cambridge area and the Huntingdonshire towns and villages of the Ouse Valley;
  – approval given for the major expansion of Stanstead airport;
  – the emergence of the 'high-tech phenomenon' in the Cambridge area;
  – the continuing threat to facilities and services in small rural communities;
  – a significant increase in unemployment; and
  – major changes in transport. Perhaps most significantly, the completion of the M1 and A45 Cambridge northern bypass, the creation of improved road links with the Fens, and the commitment to rail electrification.

Planning changes which affect you!

The County Council is considering a series of changes to the County Structure Plan. This leaflet outlines the main proposals. The Council is not yet committed to any of the changes and wants to take your views into account.

WHAT THE EXISTING STRUCTURE PLAN SAYS

The present Structure Plan, approved in 1980, was committed to slowing down the previous high rate of growth and identified four main areas of concern.

- **Jobs and services:**
  – emphasis on the needs of people already living in the County with improvements being made to the relatively disadvantaged north and east while restraining growth in the south and west to reduce demands for increased services.

- **Settlement pattern:**
  – concentrating development in towns and a small number of large villages so that more people can live close to facilities and services.

- **Transport:**
  – emphasis on improving communications to the north and east as a means of stimulating economic development; organising public transport to give as good a service as possible within available resources.

- **The environment:**
  – protection of good quality farming land, areas of best landscape and the historic heritage of our towns and villages.

WHAT IS PROPOSED?

In reviewing the Structure Plan, the County Council had to ask itself two fundamental questions:

- **by how much should the number of people living in Cambridgeshire be allowed to increase?**
- **where should any growth and change takes place?**

The County Council has recognised that there are considerable pressures for development and that people are continuing to move into the County. A level of growth is suggested which is realistic about these pressures but which still seeks to slow down the rate of development.

The proposed policies would allow the population of the County to grow by about 100 000 people between now and the end of the century.

To accommodate this level of growth some 65 000 new houses would have to be built. Just over half this increase will be needed by households arising from the existing population of the County.

THE PROPOSED CHANGES

The main changes to the Structure Plan being considered by the County Council are:

1. **Rate of growth.** Planning for future growth at a lower rate than has occurred in the past, but recognising that the current Structure Plan does not make enough provision for development up to 1991. Restraints on growth in the south and west would be slightly relaxed.

2. **Distribution of growth.** Selectively locating future growth taking into account:
   – the capacity of towns and villages with good services and facilities, but mindful of environmental limits;
   – the potential of particular locations on the A1 to A604 corridor, from Cambridge to Peterborough;
   – the need to protect the environment of Cambridge itself and villages to the south
   – the need to stimulate growth in the north and east of the county.

3. **Jobs.** Including more positive policies for economic development, including high technology, to provide suitable jobs for local people. Continuing priority for the north and east of the county.

4. **Houses.** Continuing to concentrate new house building in the main towns and villages but allowing the flexibility for more development in a wider range of villages. Some villages would be considered suitable for rural growth (housing estates). Others would be suitable for more limited growth (small estates of less than 30 dwellings). The remaining villages would be restricted to small groups of houses or infill plots.

5. **New Settlements.** Providing for the establishment of two new settlements near Cambridge to provide attractive locations for homes, jobs and shops, without swamping existing towns and villages with new development.

6. **Shopping.** Some relaxation of existing policies to allow new forms of retailing in appropriate locations.

7. **Roads.** Seeking road improvements to deal with new problems of congestion, and proposing solutions to the problems caused by heavy lorries.

8. **Environment.** Strengthening conservation policies both in the countryside and in towns and villages.

9. **Tourism.** Promoting tourism where it can bring local benefits.

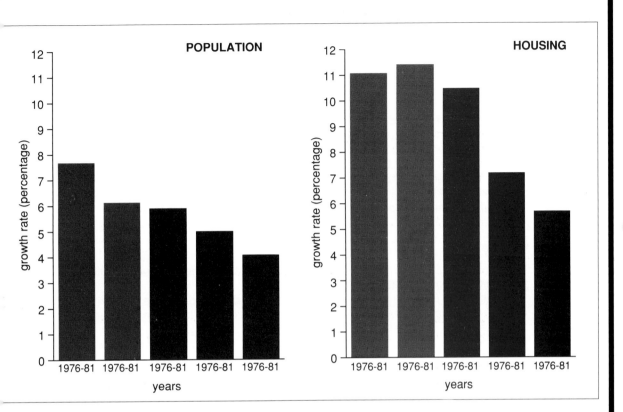

EXTRACTS FROM THE STRUCTURE PLAN CONCERNING:
(numbers at left refer to the paragraph numbers of the original document)

Environment/infrastructure/land quality

20 The County Council has conducted a series of major investigations into these aspects of future growth through:
   a) Formal and informal consultations with District Councils and service providers including Anglian Water; and
   b) Assessments of the capacity of major settlements to accommodate future growth.

21 Bearing in mind that it is not the function of the Structure Plan to determine development sites, the examination of environmental and infrastructural constraints was taken as far as necessary for strategic planning purposes. Possible broad areas for developments have been considered and evaluated. Site potential in villages and towns have been discussed informally with District Councils or their officers.

23 Broadly the following conclusions were reached:
   (i) There are few remaining opportunities for significant growth in Cambridgeshire which do not have significant adverse implications for the environment bearing in mind:
     – the extremely high quality and versatility of agricultural land in the County (70 per cent grades 1 or 2);
     – the location of the most attractive landscape and important wildlife habitats is in the south and west of the County where development pressures are most pronounced;
   (ii) There is little spare capacity in existing services and infrastructure, particularly in those areas

continued overleaf

Student enquiry 6C continued

of the County most under pressure for growth. A number of services are under significant strain, e.g.:
- there are significant congestion points and overloading of roads;
- many schools are using temporary classrooms;
- hospitals have long waiting lists for operations; and
- a recent survey by Anglian Water showed a deterioration in the quality of some water services.

(iii) In Cambridgeshire there is much low lying land, and flooding and flood control are significant factors restricting suitable areas for development.

Green belt

171 . . . those strategic considerations which are relevant to the determination of Green Belt boundaries:

(i) containing urban growth. The boundary is clearly intended to be close enough to the existing urban edge to act as an effective limitation on development during the plan period;

(ii) preserving the unique character of Cambridge. The boundary of the Green Belt should protect those areas on the periphery of Cambridge which contribute to the special character of the City; and

(iii) maintaining the present setting of Cambridge. As Cambridge is still a small city in a rural setting, the boundaries of the Green Belt should be drawn to maintain the essential relationship between town and countryside.

Size and broad location of a new settlement

106 Early in the preparation of a strategy for the Cambridgeshire area the County Council became aware that it might be necessary to plan for the creation of a new settlement. The capacity of existing settlements in the Cambridge Sub-Area to accommodate new development is limited by the following factors:

(i) Cambridge Green Belt;

(ii) Capacity limits in the larger villages in terms of infrastructure, environment and physical barriers;

(iii) Rural character and minimal service base in most of the smaller villages making them unsuitable for expansion;

(iv) Anglian Water has indicated that in many cases 'modest' expansion in villages would tend to be too small to bear the costs of infrastructure improvements yet too large to be 'absorbed;' without serious adverse consequences for river quality and land drainage; and

(iv) Restraint south of Cambridge where new development is particularly susceptible to long distance out-of-County commuting.

107 In identifying a broad location(s) for a new settlement the County Council has had regard to the following major strategic factors (in no special order):
   (i) Positive contribution to growth prospects of areas to the north east;
   (ii) Good relationship to areas of housing demand/need;
   (iii) Locations on a major transport route;
   (iv) Avoiding areas to the south of Cambridge where development would most favour long distance commuters rather than local requirements; and
   (v) Avoiding the Cambridge Green Belt.

112 The County Council has also concluded that one new settlement only is required because:
   (a) 2000 – 3000 dwellings is the minimum viable size for a new settlement for the following reasons:
      – smaller new settlements may not attract services and facilities to support the local community life;
      – smaller new settlements are unlikely to be attractive to private developers. None of the many proposals for a new settlement in Cambridgeshire has been less than 2200 dwellings and most have been for 3000 or more.
   (b) the commencement of more than one new settlement at the same time may affect the viability of one or both.

136 The concentration of high technology development in and around Cambridge can be seen in the distribution of high technology permissions by sub-area:

gross floorspace permitted 1980-7		
Fens		1
Peterborough		3
East Cambs		3
Ouse Valley		8
Cambridge	city	36
	science park	21
	rest of sub area	28

137 In the submitted Plan there are no strategic constraints on the expansion of high technology industry in the County outside Cambridge. An adequate quantity of land is to be made available and of the right quality for the type of employment activities needing sites and accommodation.

138 Within the Cambridge sub-area, research and development activity is to be encouraged. However, significant new manufacturing capacity will be restrained to avoid the unnecessary build up of population and other growth pressures in the City, in accordance with the overall strategy for the sub-area.

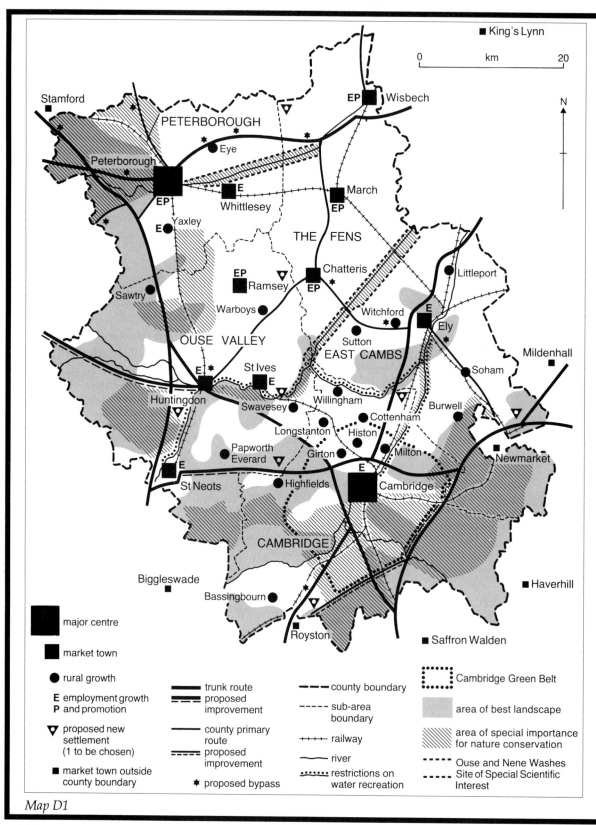

King's Lynn

0　　km　　20

N

Stamford

PETERBOROUGH

EP Wisbech

Eye

Peterborough
EP

E
Whittlesey

March
EP

E Yaxley

THE FENS

Sawtry

EP Ramsey

Chatteris
EP

Littleport

Warboys

Witchford

E Ely

OUSE VALLEY

Sutton

EAST CAMBS

Mildenhall

E
Huntingdon

St Ives
E

Willingham

Soham

Burwell

Swavesey

Cottenham

Longstanton

Histon

Papworth
Everard

Girton

Milton

Newmarket

E
St Neots

Highfields

E Cambridge

CAMBRIDGE

Biggleswade

Bassingbourn

Haverhill

Royston

Saffron Walden

◼ major centre

◼ market town

● rural growth

E employment growth
P and promotion

▽ proposed new
settlement
(1 to be chosen)

◼ market town outside
county boundary

━━ trunk route

━━ proposed
improvement

━━ county primary
route

━━ proposed
improvement

✶ proposed bypass

━ ━ county boundary

- - - sub-area
boundary

+++ railway

──── river

•••• restrictions on
water recreation

⁝⁝⁝ Cambridge Green Belt

area of best landscape

area of special importance
for nature conservation

- - - Ouse and Nene Washes

━ ━ Site of Special Scientific
Interest

Map D1

Chapter 7
The form of cities

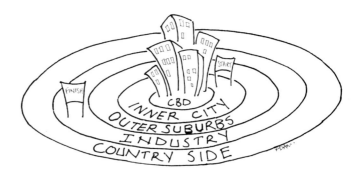

" TRY TO GET FROM THE INNER CITY TO INDUSTRY EACH
DAY FOR WORK IN TWO BUS JOURNEYS, DO NOT
PASS THROUGH THE CBD, DO NOT COLLECT A
PRIVATE HOUSE."

Introduction

Cities are the most tangible and profound expression of people's ability to forge their own environment. In the previous chapter some attempt was made to define categories of urban development. For those settlements of greater than market town size there is no ready definition, so here the word city is used as a shorthand for any large urban area containing a mixture of housing, service and manufacturing functions.

To many people cities look a mess, consisting of a tangle of roads, houses, offices, factories and randomly dotted open space – places where people do their best to get by. So have the struggles of people to plan cities as good places to live been to no avail? In this chapter we try to examine the purposes of the developed world or 'western' city and see how these have resulted in recognisable patterns and problems. Developing world cities are considered in Chapter 10.

Investigating city pattern

The city is so complex that it is best to begin with an example on which to focus ideas. Figure 7.1 shows the pattern of south-east Birmingham as seen when following the approach road A34 from Stratford-on-Avon. Here we find several elements. The first is described in some detail, the others are only briefly described because they form part of student enquiry 7A.

Over 13 km from the city centre, and adjacent to farmland is a new housing estate (Monkspath) for owner occupiers built on a new (green field) site. The photographs show the economic status of the occupiers to be upper-middle income. Most have at least one car, and although there is a bus service people obviously have considerable personal mobility. Adjacent to the housing estate is an industrial estate (Cranmore), made up of medium sized manufacturing factory units built in the 1950s and 1960s. Beside this is a business park (Monkspath) designed in the 1980s to provide facilities for high tech industries. Housing and industry are flanked by open space and the residents of the housing area have good access to the countryside for recreation. All of these developments are still in Warwickshire and not officially part of Birmingham, but they are obviously very firmly associated with the conurbation.

11 km from the centre lies the 'town' (really suburb) of Shirley, also in Warwickshire. The photographs show older (mainly 1930s and 1950s) housing in tree lined avenues. The shopping centre is spread around the axis of the main road. Notice the type of shopping facilities.

At 9 km from the centre is Acock's Green.

Figure 7.1 Birmingham - map continued overle[af]

showing elements of earlier building (turn of the century) especially along the main road in a form of elongated (ribbon) sprawl from the centre. There is a railway station which may have been the original focus of the suburb.

At 5 km from the centre there is a radical change of settlement and functions in the areas called Sparkhill and Sparkford. The photographs show many clues as to the character of this area and the status of the shopping.

At about 2 km from the centre lies Bordersley which includes the first evidence of the blocks of flats built in the 1960s phase of inner city housing renewal.

The centre is focused on the Bull Ring shopping centre.

Hall Green housing

rural village

0   km   1

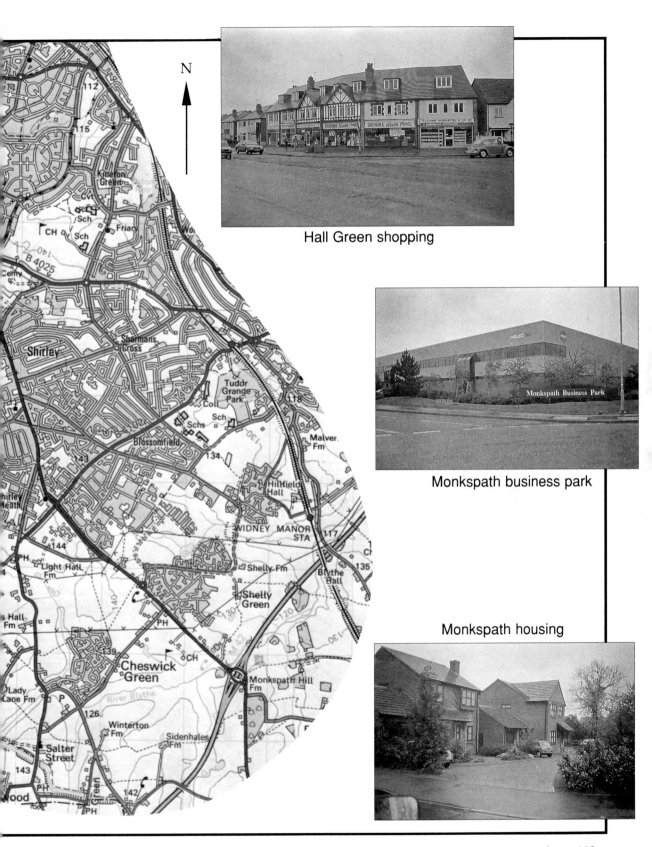

Hall Green shopping

Monkspath business park

Monkspath housing

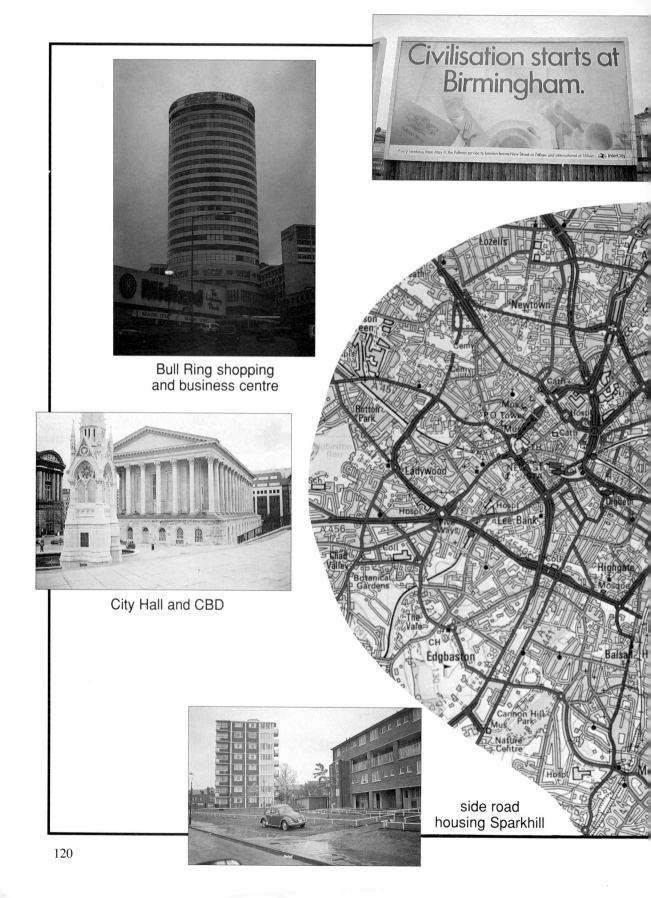

Bull Ring shopping
and business centre

Civilisation starts at
Birmingham.

City Hall and CBD

side road
housing Sparkhill

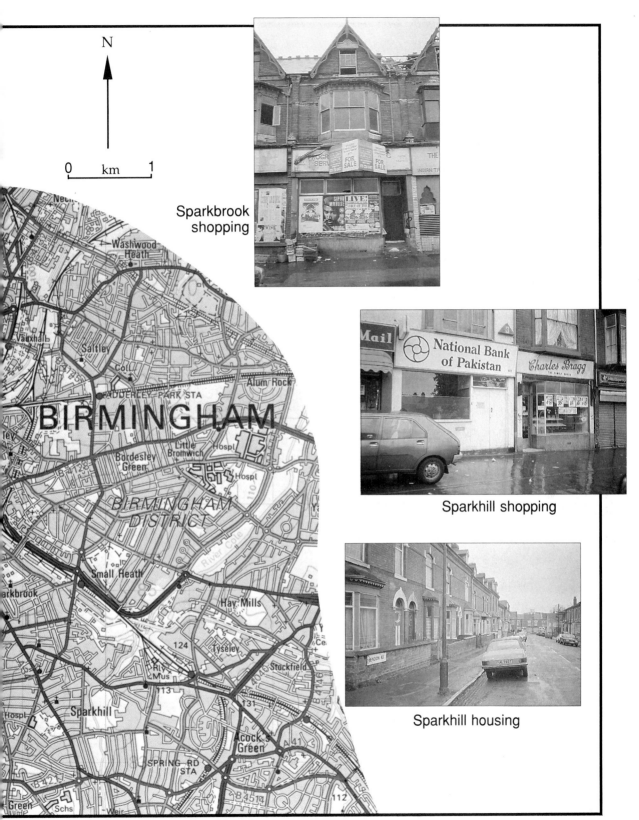

Sparkbrook shopping

Sparkhill shopping

Sparkhill housing

Figure 7.1 Birmingham - map continued from last page

Student enquiry 7A

Study the four page spread of south-east Birmingham (Fig. 7.1) and the land use map of the whole of Birmingham (A1) and selected population details (A2, A3).

1. Plot column graphs to show the characteristics of the population in Sparkbrook, Sparkhill and Hall Green.
2. Describe the pattern at each of the locations using both the photographs and the OS base map. Use the following headings:
   (i) housing age, density and character;
   (ii) shopping facilities;
   (iii) signs of industry;
   (iv) pattern of roads; and
   (v) characteristics of population.
3. Try to explain some of the reasons for the pattern you see. At this stage you should not try to look up theoretical answers but simply express your own ideas. These can then be set against the theoretical models later in the chapter.
4. By referring to A1, comment on how far the photograph transect gives an accurate representation of the distribution of city activities. How would you make a more statistical survey of the city using an alternative survey system to a transect? Compare and contrast the transect system with the one you have suggested.

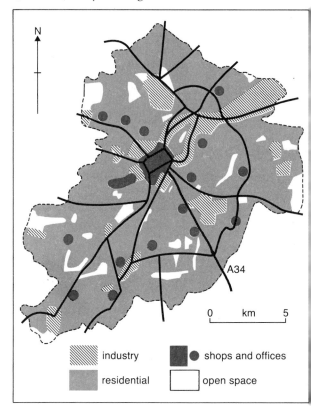

A1 Land uses of Birmingham

industry   shops and offices

residential   open space

A3 Table: Details of wards, 1981

(Figures are percentages unless otherwise stated)	0-4	5-15	16-64	65+	births	deaths natural increase (per 1000 population)		accommodation owner occupied	rented local authority	other	households without cars	unemploy
HALL GREEN	4.9	14.9	58.4	21.8	10.7		-1.4	80.0	12.1	8.2	35.6	8.1
SPARKHILL	9.5	17.8	61.6	11.1	23.3		15.9	55.6	7.2	37.2	56.2	21.6
SPARKBROOK	10.6	21.7	57.3	10.4	23.9		15.2	26.4	56.2	17.4	72.7	30.5
BIRMINGHAM (AVERAGE)	6.4	16.7	59.5	17.4	15.5		3.8	52.6	34.7	12.7	49.5	15.2

Source: *Census 1981*

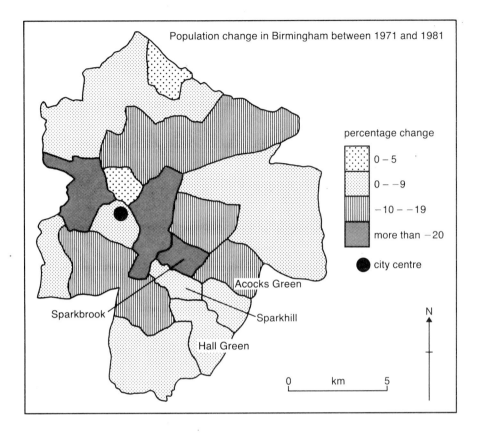

Population change in Birmingham between 1971 and 1981

percentage change

- 0 – 5
- 0 – -9
- -10 – -19
- more than -20
- ● city centre

Acocks Green
Sparkbrook
Sparkhill
Hall Green

N

0   km   5

	socio-economic groups							residents headed by person born			
	professional	employers	skilled		semi-skilled	unskilled	other	UK	Eire	New Commonwealth	Other
			manual	non man							
HALL GREEN	3.8	12.5	21.9	36.5	14.2	3.7	7.4	84.6	8.7	4.5	2.2
SPARKHILL	2.1	5.8	23.2	24.9	25.4	8.6	10.0	37.5	11.5	47.8	3.2
SPARKBROOK	0.7	3.1	20.2	13.5	30.0	10.4	22.1	35.7	11.1	50.4	2.8
BIRMINGHAM (AVERAGE)	2.6	7.9	23.5	25.6	22.1	6.7	11.6	76.3	6.8	15.1	1.8

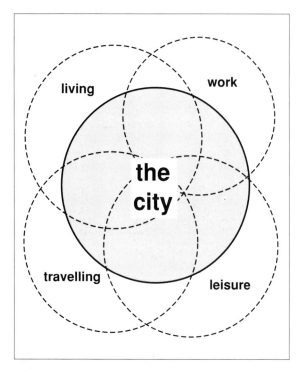

Figure 7.2 Garnier's functional concept of a city

The purpose of the city

If we are to disentangle the complexity of cities we must understand how they try to fulfil a well defined set of human needs. As Garnier explained at the turn of the century, a city is intended to perform certain basic functions (Fig. 7.2):

> (i) it is a place for living in;
>
> (ii) it is a place for working in;
>
> (iii) it is a place where people seek recreation and leisure; and to achieve all these aims
>
> (iv) it has to be a place where people can move about and to which people can easily come from the surrounding towns and countryside if they wish to share in the range of services.

However, Garnier was concentrating primarily on just one aspect of a city. The shape and fabric of a city are best understood by realising that people demand two quite different things from their environment:

> (i) it should be a place that caters for people's physical needs. This means it must have houses, shops, roads, utilities, etc. just as Garnier said; but

(ii) it must also cater for people's emotional needs. Thus the urban space must feel comfortable to be in, it must be pleasing to the eye, etc. This is sometimes achieved if buildings have a human scale (such as in an ancient market town) or they can be successful with an awe inspiring scale (such as Manhattan's skyscrapers): what is important is that the juxtaposition of buildings and the pattern of spaces pleases the eye (Fig. 7.3).

The basic functions such as shelter and employment, security and welfare must be provided in a convenient and effective manner. However, these requirements can compete for space. In practice it is very difficult to arrange for people to do all the things they want easily. City planners have the difficult task of seeking the best compromise.

Paying for city space

Society revolves around work and earning a living. In the city this is reflected in the large numbers of businesses that are present. A business has to select its position very carefully (see also *Challenge of the Economic Environment*, Chapter 10). Whether it be a shop, a factory or an office, it has the potential to be most successful if its position in the urban structure gives the greatest advantage. If the position is good, the business will thrive; conversely a bad location can spell ruin.

Because success or failure depend so closely on location, businesses are prepared to pay heavily to secure an advantageous location. That is, they are prepared to pay more than any other section of society for city space.

Companies large and small jostle with one another in the city fabric in an attempt to secure their most advantageous location. In a free market economy those who end up in the best positions are those with the ability to pay most. This is expressed in the term '**bid rent**'.

Bid rent model and city pattern

In modern cities most of the industrial and commercial land is owned by property companies (Fig. 7.4). This land, and the buildings built on it,

Figure 7.3 Two contrasting forms of city pattern that are commonly regarded as pleasing to the eye: (a) the old buildings of Tudor Chester with their ornate style; and (b) the towering skyscrapers of Manhattan. They both match the surrounding environment

are leased or rented to potential clients.

Some companies own the sites they occupy, especially if they have been trading for a long time and they bought the land when it was of low value. However, few companies buy their premises today because:

(i) the purchase of property locks up large amounts of capital that could be more usefully employed in the running of the business; and

(ii) the lack of a property makes them more 'footloose' and able to relocate at short notice should trading conditions so require.

The expression of competition for a particular location is seen in the pattern of rent cost. In the centre of London, office rents can be over £150 per square metre per year , whereas in the centre of Reading, a provincial town 60 km west of the capital, the rents are £50 per square metre. Away from the centre space is valued at £30 per square metre in both Reading and some parts of London. In Didcot (less accessible to London and 100 km from the capital) the rents are £18 per square metre. Similar patterns are found surrounding all cities.

The general pattern of industrial and commercial users is clearly determined by their profitability per square metre. In a shop the profitability depends on the value of goods that can be sold for each square metre of shelf space. It is a factor that, for example, accounts for the high density and height of supermarket shelves! But whereas it might be possible for a major supermarket or department store to support a high rent, a builders' merchant, for example, who deals in high bulk, low value commodities, will only be able to survive in a much lower rental environment.

Figure 7.4 The signboards in this street advertise many commercial properties for lease; few are for sale.

Most businesses can identify their prime location; the place where they will make the most money. In the case of a shop it will be the place where most people visit. This could be a corner site, a regional shopping centre, the centre of the city, or increasingly a peripheral site near a motorway or bypass. At this location they would be able to maximise their profits. Away from this site the profits drop and the amount of rent that can be afforded is therefore less. The profit made at various sites can be plotted to obtain a curve showing where it is best to be located (Fig. 7.5). This is called a **bid rent curve.**

Each business has its own bid rent curve. Clearly the business that can generate the highest profit from a site will be able to pay the most rent. In this way the pattern of bid rent curves can determine the actual pattern of businesses in the city. You can see that very few businesses will be able to get their ideal location; most will be a compromise based on rental competition.

The bid rent system will result in a pattern of essentially concentric zones each spreading away from prime sites. In a small centre the prime site may well be the centre, where all the roads converge. In a larger centre there may be several equally suitable prime sites.

Most buildings can house a number of different businesses. The top floors of a central site will be of no use to a retailer, but they may very well suit a solicitor. Without rent competition from the retailer the rents for the upper floors in buildings will be less. Many buildings therefore show a 'vertical bid rent' pattern (Fig. 7.6).

The same system of bid rents will apply to the private housing market. Although the majority of people own their homes, the price they pay for the freehold still contains a strong element of bid rent. Advertisements sometimes indicate the bid rent directly in statements such as 'near to shops', 'St Francis school catchment area', or 'near university' and 'near golf course'. None of these

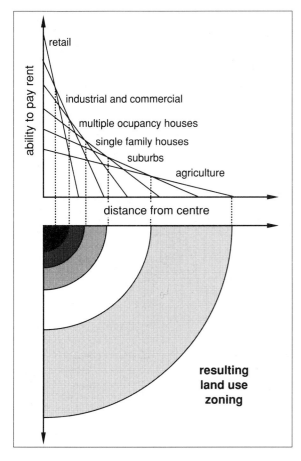

Figure 7.5 Bid rent curves for various functions

Figure 7.6 Vertical bid rent is shown here by the solicitors' and accountants' offices above the shop

elements is related to the size of the property or its character, simply to its bid rent value. Some houses can increase their bid rent only by being sub-divided. This is the reason it is quite common to find large older properties divided into several flats.

Community space

Bid rent theory is only one factor in producing patterns within a city. Nevertheless, in most circumstances it is of overriding importance. But the community does have a say in the use of urban space through the local government representatives that they elect. Most countries also have legislation that gives the local authorities power to decide on land use. In Britain the most important piece of legislation is called the **Town and Country Planning Act**.

Using legislative powers the community has a say in the pattern of the city, for example, on the zoning of land for particular purposes. It may be decided that the land in a particular district should not contain any commercial development, or that it should only be used for industry. Further, the community can decide where to place its public buildings such as the town hall, public parks, swimming pool and library. All these can be outside the bid-rent framework and add to the complexity of the urban pattern (Fig. 7.7).

The influence of the past

As we have seen, the city pattern at any one instant is the result of a number of compromises in trying to achieve certain defined aims. But most

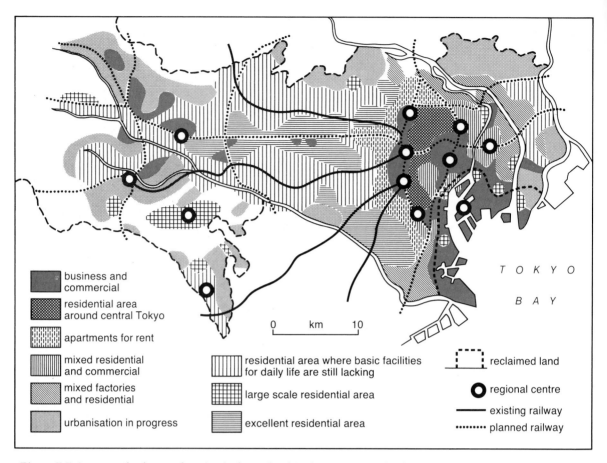

Figure 7.7 An example of town planning is shown by this planning map of Tokyo. Notice the plan separates various land uses and also provides for recreation, transport and so on. (Source: Government of Japan)

cities have also existed for many centuries and therefore they bear the imprint of compromises of the past. It is the combination of past and present that gives yet another twist to the pattern. Also, bear in mind that buildings often outlast the uses for which they were designed. Some city space is inevitably going to consist of buildings that nobody wants, or that have yet to find an alternative use. This would have been true of the Albert Dock in Liverpool for decades, although it is now a much treasured tourist centre, or the Central Station in Manchester, now the centrepiece of the GMEX exhibition area (Fig. 7.8).

The quality of a city

In the introduction we mentioned that cities are both functional and emotional. Ebenezer Howard, one of the first British planners, ex-

pressed the idea of an emotionally satisfying city at the end of the nineteenth century when he was considering what provisions ought to be made for people in the future. In his book *The Garden City*, he showed the forces that attracted people in the form of three magnets (Fig. 7.9).

Howard thought that people enjoyed the dynamism of the city and yet wanted the feel of space and tranquillity that can be found in the countryside. He concluded the most powerful form of magnet (i.e. most attractive situation) would be a garden city where the positive attractions of each type of environment could most readily be satisfied.

Howard's desire for 'pattern' and order come through very clearly in his plans for garden cities. He was formulating a design for people's lives on a piece of paper. It is a problem that has haunted planners ever since.

Greater Manchester Exhibition and Event Centre

Howard's garden city idea produced Letchworth, just north of London. This was the first planned 'new town', but his scheme has not been as widely adopted as might be expected for reasons we shall see later.

Howard's perception is important because it allows us to understand yet further forces that underly the nature of our cities. We have already seen that cities develop to satisfy physical and emotional needs of the people who live or visit there, but we can now see that there are two other factors:

> (i) the sociological factors that affect people in power, particularly in local government; and
>
> (ii) the desire of architects not only to create a functional structure, but also one which fulfils their ambitions.

The most famous and important architect who had great influence on the way the cities of the western world were built after the Second World War was the Frenchman, Le Corbusier. He made his attitude to city pattern very clear when he declared that 'A house is a machine for living in' (Fig. 7.10a). Shadows of some of his concepts can be seen in many of the urban renewal programmes of the 1960s (Fig. 7.10b).

This section has focused on the role of the architect, but it is important to understand that much power resides in the hands of politicians and it is they who mould the city structure through planning controls, compulsory purchase orders and the awarding of public building contracts. They are also responsible for the overall quality of the environment, where they exert an ever more powerful and shaping influence (Fig. 7.11).

Figure 7.8 (a) The centre of Manchester is now dominated by GMEX, (b) the pattern of building in central London is still controlled by the shape of the old street pattern

The urban pattern as a model

Because there are so many different forces at work in a city, it will inevitably be difficult to isolate a single driving force and create a very simple model. Nevertheless, models have their place because they help people to look systematically at a complex world; they are the skeleton around which the detail appropriate to each individual example hangs.

Several models have been formulated to try to provide a descriptive and analytic framework for city patterns. These have mostly been for the developed free market economies ('the west'), where a wide spectrum of wealth occurs and where people have a large measure of control over their location.

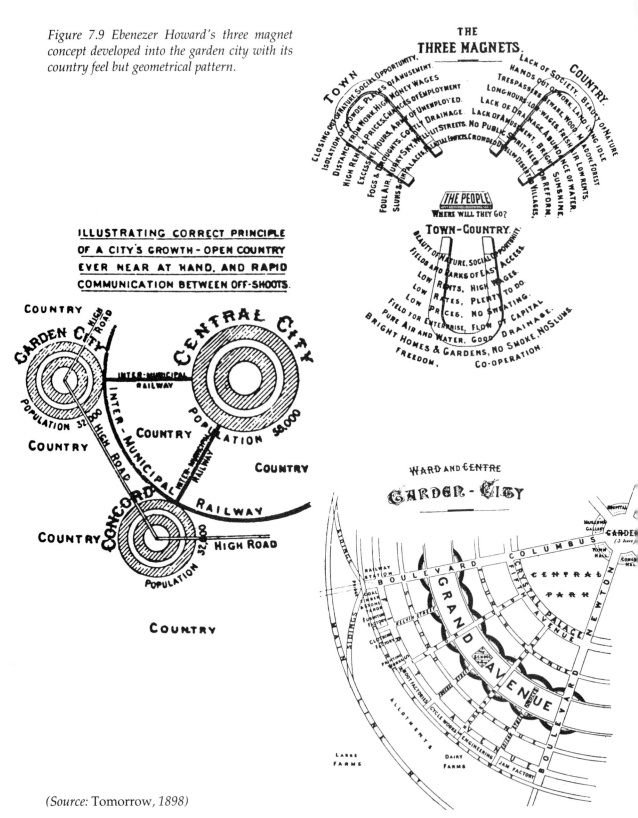

Figure 7.9 Ebenezer Howard's three magnet concept developed into the garden city with its country feel but geometrical pattern.

(*Source:* Tomorrow, 1898)

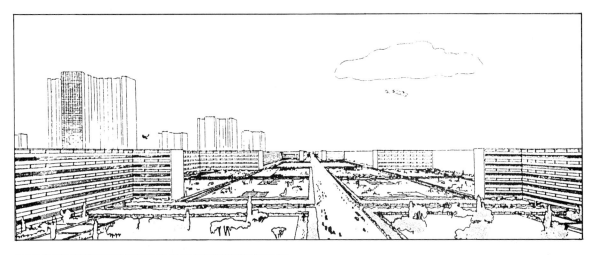

Figure 7.10(a) The city pattern as suggested by Le Corbusier, (b) how it partly came to reality in some inner city renewal schemes

Given the complex interacting factors mentioned above, it may seem a fruitless task trying to extricate the framework of city space. However, there have been several attempts to provide a guide to pattern. Three of these are given below.

Burgess and the concentric ring model

In the 1920s, the American economist Burgess recognised a basic pattern of concentric zones of development and land use. His model was based on city dynamism, noting that the only way in which a city can normally grow is by marginal accretion. Because there is no more room left in the centre, people are forced to build their new homes and workplaces in green field sites on the periphery. The result is a pattern of concentric zones (Fig. 7.12).

Those with the greatest wealth could select their locations: in general these would either be in the centre of the city near to all the facilities of entertainment and communications and business, or on the periphery where new houses could be built on green field sites. As people moved to the green field sites so they sold their houses to the less wealthy and automatically changed the character of the zone. Thus, for example, large

Figure 7.11 This shopping centre's character is the result of sympathetic planning decisions excercising guidance over the commercial developer

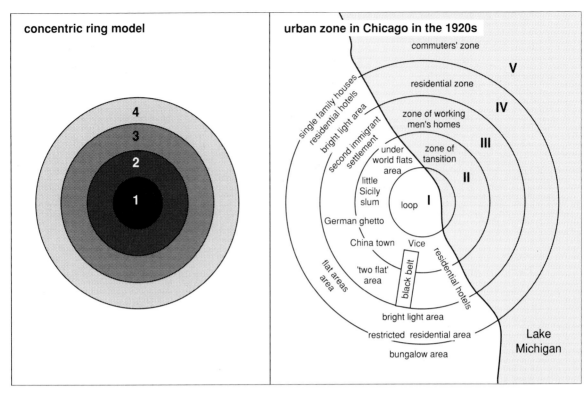

Figure 7.12 The concentric pattern of functions suggested by Burgess to describe Chicago has been widened to form a general model

merchants' houses built at the turn of the century to suit big families with servants were sold when the wealthy families became smaller, lifestyles changed and large houses were not required. Such houses were subdivided and converted for those with lower incomes.

Only when the landscape makes concentric development impossible to achieve, or when accessibility is not uniformly available to the city centre, should there be significant variations to this fundamental model. For example, Chicago's lakeside location caused it to grow in a pattern of semicircular zones.

Hoyt and the sector model

Hoyt recognised that the need to seek continual expansion for living space is not the only force determining city pattern. People with similar lifestyles or similar businesses also tend to cluster and this causes wedges or sectors to develop (Fig. 7.13). Again those with the greatest purchasing

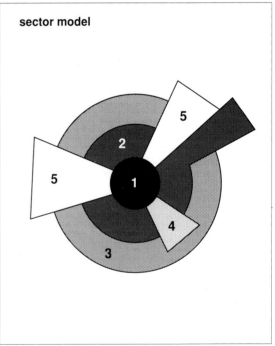

Figure 7.13 The sector model developed by Hoyt to account for the clustering of people within a city

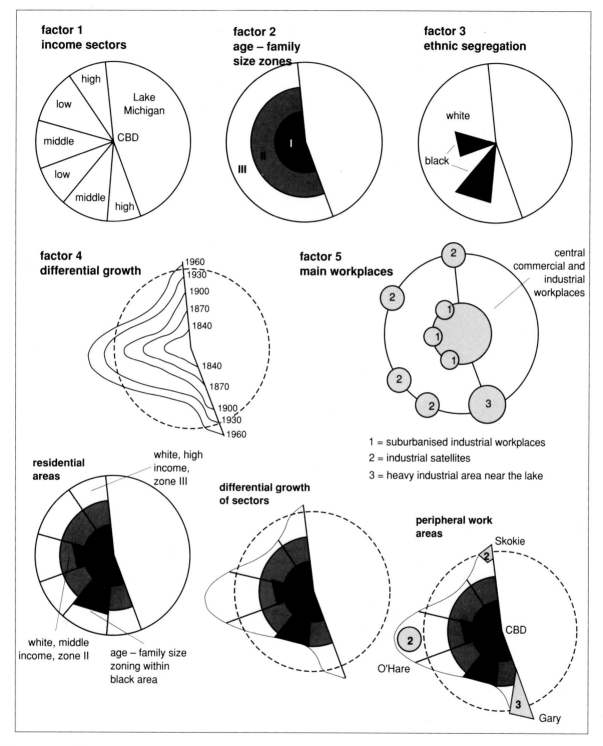

factor 1
income sectors

high
low
middle
low
middle
high
Lake Michigan
CBD

factor 2
age – family size zones

I
II
III

factor 3
ethnic segregation

white
black

factor 4
differential growth

1960
1930
1900
1870
1840
1840
1870
1900
1930
1960

factor 5
main workplaces

2
2
1
1
1
2
2
3
central commercial and industrial workplaces

1 = suburbanised industrial workplaces
2 = industrial satellites
3 = heavy industrial area near the lake

residential areas

white, high income, zone III
white, middle income, zone II
age – family size zoning within black area

differential growth of sectors

peripheral work areas

Skokie
2
O'Hare
2
CBD
3
Gary

Figure 7.14 Chicago's present character can be defined by a combination of concentric ring and sector models. In this version Professor Haggett accounts for the pattern by mapping five factors: income, age/family size, ethnic segregation, differential growth, and main workplaces

power set the pattern. They are able to secure the most desirable locations and in this way control the location of many other people within the city. Different sectors in a city include the wealthy housing sector, the industrial sector and the commercial sector, all embedded within the general sea of dwellings that make the main body of the city. It is also possible to recognise a poor sector and an immigrant sector (ghetto) because these are the areas left over after the more wealthy have made their locational decisions.

Many attempts have been made to combine elements of both patterns. Figure 7.14 shows one such combination applied to Chicago.

Harris and Ulman's multiple nuclei model

Harris and Ulman looked at the largest cities and saw that a single centre of attraction did not really exist. They concluded that the largest cities and conurbations are best regarded as having multiple nuclei or being multi-centred (Fig. 7.15). Thus the commercial centre, administrative centre, cultural centre, jewellery centre and many other specialised clusters develop more like *islands* near the *centre of gravity* of the city, simply because there is not room for them all at the core. They are supplemented by regional and neighbourhood centres each designed to offer a range of more local services.

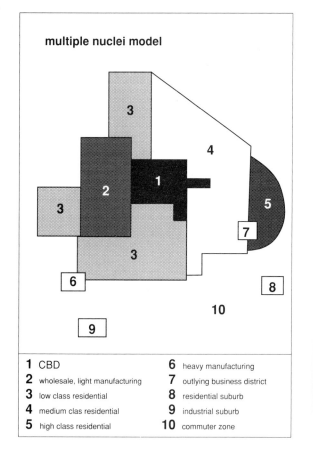

1 CBD
2 wholesale, light manufacturing
3 low class residential
4 medium clas residential
5 high class residential
6 heavy manufacturing
7 outlying business district
8 residential suburb
9 industrial suburb
10 commuter zone

Figure 7.15 The multiple nuclei model used by Harris and Ulman to describe the patterns seen in very large urban centres

Chapter 8
Infrastructure

Introduction

Infrastructure is the basic network of public facilities upon which nearly all economic activity depends. It is one of the most important features of the geography of an area.

The infrastructure facilities come in a wide range of shapes and sizes: they may be the road or rail network, the pattern of water, gas and other utility lines, the waste disposal systems, or street lighting. In a wider context infrastructure might apply to the provision of all public facilities, such as schools, police stations, fire services, hospitals, welfare and public housing (Fig. 8.1).

The people who operate these networks form part of the service industry (doctors, police, teachers, local government officials) or the construction industry (road makers, public building construction workers, etc.). In most developed societies they form one of the largest groups of workers and consume nearly all the publicly gathered rates and other taxes. Many people regard the degree of sophistication of the public infrastructure as an indicator of the stage of development a country has reached.

Responsibility for infrastructure

Infrastructure involves community services. Most important are communications and provision of facilities for health, education and security.

The most basic parts of the infrastructure are so fundamental to society that they are provided as a statutory right to everybody. For example, everyone in Britain has the right to use all public roads, to attend school free, to be housed, to be able to see a doctor, to go to hospital without charge, to be protected by the police, and so on.

Not all infrastructure facilities need be provided by the community from public funds. Toll roads, private hospitals, and many other infrastructure operations are paid for as they are used, rather than paid for under a general rate. In most countries there is a combination of public and private services.

There is no single formula for the provision of services, and no one pattern most suitable. But at the same time there are acceptable levels of provision which act as guidelines. Everyone can expect to be provided with 'adequate' public services and with an 'adequate' route network. What is

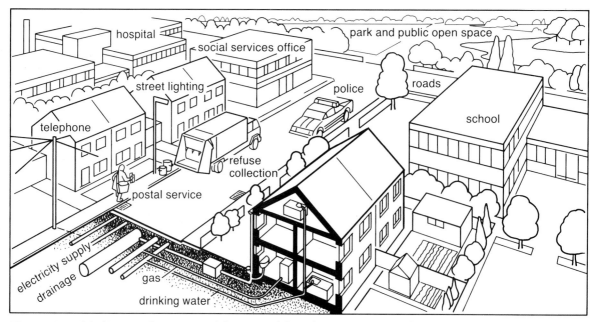

Figure 8.1 This diagram shows some of the parts of the urban environment that are provided as basic facilities in the developed world. Together all the community services make up the infrastructure

'adequate' is a matter of political judgement and varies from time to time according to the proportion of taxes made available and the philosophy of the party in government.

Norms for infrastructure provision

Comprehensive planning norms have existed in Britain for more than a hundred years. For example the Victorian town planners tried to ensure that there would be a primary school in each square mile of urban area, a church and some form of public open space (Fig. 8.2). Today the provision depends on:

> (i) the perceived level of service that government and the community think should be provided;
> (ii) the ability of individuals to pay for their communal services; and
> (iii) the mobility of the population.

Thus if everyone in a community still had to walk everywhere there would be a need for a larger number of small scale facilities such as cottage hospitals and parish schools. A more mobile population can choose to retain the small scale pattern or to consolidate small units into larger, more widely spaced facilities.

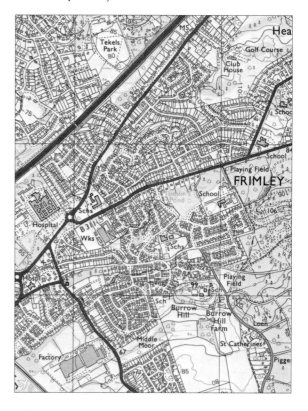

Figure 8.2 A map example of an urban area with basic communal infrastructure planned in

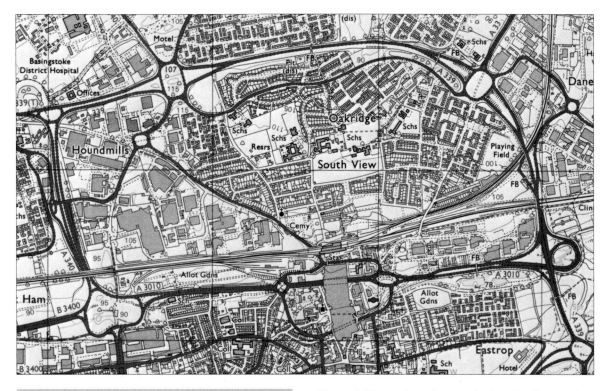

Figure 8.3 Part of a road network, showing the complexity of the planning required

Road networks

An adequate network of roads provides the most flexible means of getting about – we may use them to walk on, to pull carts along or to drive lorries and cars on. They provide arteries of public land through otherwise private property, allowing people to communicate effectively (Fig. 8.3).

It is much easier to plan for and then provide an infrastructure for a new town than to modify one that has grown over centuries. Roads and railways, for example, take up large amounts of space, and they have to be laid in reasonably straight lines. If a new road is needed in a built up area, then much private land will have to be bought and if necessary compulsory purchase orders issued. Thus a major scheme may take 15 years from planning to completion.

Because of the time involved, many schemes get overtaken by events. Therefore, the provision of road networks is always a matter of compromise – a feature that can lead to much frustration on the part of the users who see only one aspect of the problem.

The kind of road network that needs to be provided depends on its function and the funds available. Figure 8.4 shows the networks of roads that will achieve different levels of direct contact (called **connectivity**). Overprovision of road services will use up land and resources that could be spent on other parts of the infrastructure. At the same time underprovision leads to bottlenecks and delays. The increased time and distance to make a journey can be a major economic handicap to businesses and can put an area and its workforce at a competitive disadvantage.

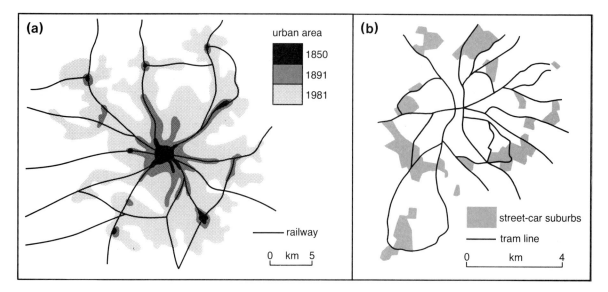

Figure 8.4(a) The early growth of Manchester owes much to the pattern of railway development ; (b) Leeds grew outwards to the limits of the tram routes. It is a more compact city than many other urban areas that sprawled with the train networks

Transport infrastructure and the city

Cities in Britain largely grew around the economics of nineteenth century transport systems. As a result the emphasis was first on canals and then railways. Canals and railways are good for moving goods cheaply over long distances, but the inflexible networks keep people relatively immobile within the city.

The early **mass transit systems** defined the sphere of influence of the city as is shown by the railway system of Manchester (Fig 84a). In an attempt to increase flexibility trams were introduced. The growth of Leeds shows how a much more dense network of development was possible with this road-based transport network (Fig. 8.4b).

Public transport keeps people tied closely to the lines of the service. The rapid expansion of cities that occurred in the twentieth century, and particularly since the Second World War, has been the result of increasing personal mobility. People began to own cars, or to be able to use more flexible transport means such as buses. This allowed the major areas between railway and tram lines to be **backfilled**.

The result of these developments has created some very distinctive shapes: cities like London, Manchester and Frankfurt stretch out long tentacles of ribbon development into the surrounding countryside, giving them a shape and character like an octopus. By contrast, cities such as Los Angeles and major New Towns such as Milton Keynes, which have developed more recently, are enmeshed by a great web of major roads.

The influence of personal mobility

Shopping trips represent one of the major journey patterns within a city. Increasing personal mobility has allowed people the choice of using a car to reach the shops and conveniently to carry their purchases. However, it has also led to conflict within the city centre and a great strain on many infrastructure systems.

Traditionally public transport systems were built to converge on the city centre, making it the most accessible place. This allowed people to change services and get to any point in the city easily. Because shops need to maximise their custom the centre was also the sensible location for major shopping areas to develop. The continued focus on the city centre has often caused intolerable central congestion. Many cities have introduced pedestrian only zones and inner distribution roads (effectively, ring motorways).

Communications networks

Communications **networks** (patterns of routes or **links**) connecting particular locations (**nodes**) play an extremely important role in our lives (Fig. 8.5). Each pattern, whether it be roads, railways, gas pipelines or telephone lines, evolves or is designed to suit its particular requirements.

A telephone network, for example, needs to connect together every household or commercial and public building. This person to person network is fundamental to the system. Nevertheless it would be impractical and uneconomic to connect all buildings together directly. Thus a branching system is used, with single feeder lines connecting to more major shared lines. Road patterns follow similar principles, the roads designed to serve small communities connecting to major roads and then to motorways.

(a)

(b)

(c)

(d)

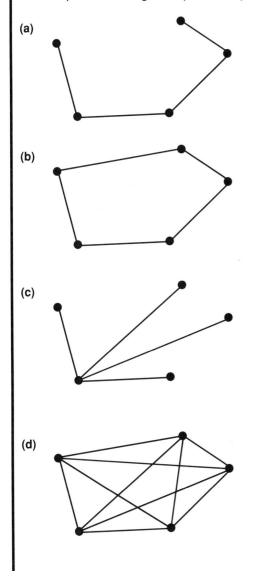

(e)

(f)

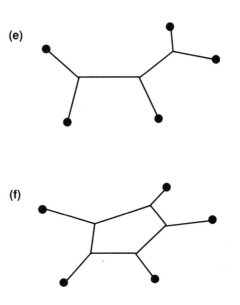

Figure 8.5 Networks are designed to achieve a variety of degrees of connectivity: (a) the minimum distance network for visiting all points (such as a bus route); (b) the minimum distance to perform a circular tour (such as a newspaper round); (c) a radial pattern to connect one point to all the others (such as the arterial roads from London); (d) connecting every point to every other (such as a local road pattern); (e) the shortest route pattern that would connect all places (cheapest building cost); and (f) a ring road with spurs as a compromise between (d) and (e) as adopted in some New Towns

Student enquiry 8A

Should there be development at the M25 junctions around London?

Ring roads have often been forged through existing built up areas. This has involved a considerable amount of demolition. The roads are a major help in improving mobility for the majority of the people of the city, but they have seriously affected the quality of life of many who live close to them.

Although London's planners envisaged a system of three concentric ring roads for the conurbation, when the inner one was begun, so great was the disruption involved and so strong the opposition, that the complete scheme became politically unacceptable.

The inner sections thus do only part of the job for which they were designed.

The outer ring road (designated Ringway 3 on the early planning maps) was to be built almost entirely in London's protected ring of countryside (the Green Belt, see Chapter 13). Its intention was to link all the motorways as they approached London, allowing through traffic to bypass the city.

The information in this enquiry shows that, despite being a three lane motorway, the M25 has quickly reached saturation levels.

£30m scheme to start on fourth lanes for M25

Work to construct a fourth lane on both carriageways of the London orbital motorway, between Chertsey and Staines in Surrey, is expected to start early next month.

It is thought that the Department of Transport will announce next week that the contract, worth more than £30 million, is to be awarded to Balfour Beatty.

Plans to install a fourth lane on both carriageways, between junctions 11 and 13, which are among the busiest sections of the road, were announced more than a year ago.

Even then traffic densities were far exceeding the 80 000 vehicles a day for which the existing road was designed

The latest figures, for last September, show that those sections were carrying about 130 000 vehicles a day. Apart from the building of the fourth lanes between Chertsey and Staines, improvements will be made to the junctions between Wisley and Staines.

It is understood that in the event of the contract overrunning, the contractor will be liable to pay penalties of nearly £13 000 a day.

The Department of Transport is also commissioning a consultant's report into the possibility of putting fourth lanes in a further section of the M25, between the M4 and the M40, north-west of Heathrow.

In addition it will carry out a comprehensive review of the whole of the M25 because in almost all sections the volume of traffic is exceeding predicted levels.

A week ago the Costain construction group floated some radical ideas for easing traffic problems in London and the south-east. These involved constructing a second tier above the entire 120 mile length of the M25.

That scheme, which would be financed by private capital with tolls to be levied on users, would cost about £3 billion.

Other schemes put forward by Costain included sinking a tunnel under the River Thames from Chiswick to Blackwall, which would accommodate a motorway and rail links.

The company also proposed the construction of new fast rail links which would run around London, direct to the Channel tunnel, which is planned to come into use in 1993. Those schemes taken together are estimated to cost about £7 billion.

(Source: *The Times*, 9 Jan. 1988)

1. Outline some of advantages and disadvantages of Birmingham's ringway as far as can be deduced from the photograph 8A1.
2. Suggest reasons for building a motorway through London's Green Belt.
3. The average urban speed is 11 miles per hour, and the motorway speed 55 miles per hour. Assume the M25 is roughly circular and of length 210 miles. Calculate how long it would take to cross the conurbation of London compared with the time to travel by motorway.

How does this calculation influence the planning of motorways?
4. Read the article 'M25: a fast way to lose jobs', and explain the pressures that have built up for development at the motorway intersections. Put forward a case for and against development.
5. Suggest, and give some specific examples of how the M25 may change the accessibility of places other than London and thus cause problems elsewhere.

M25: a fast way to lose jobs

London's new orbital M25 motorway will be a mixed blessing for the capital when it is fully open to traffic in 1986.

This is the verdict of a major economic planning study of the motorway's implications by County Hall.

It warns that unemployment in inner London could get worse as firms are attracted out to key sites alongside the 120 mile motorway.

On the credit side, the planners forecast that journey times in London will be speeded up by around 10 per cent as traffic switches to the M25 circuit.

It is calculated that this will save motorists and hauliers more than £100 million a year.

But it is the loss of even more jobs in the service industries and manufacturing that worries County Hall planners. As the Labour leader of the GLC, Mr Ken Livingstone, told colleagues: 'The motorway will be a major blow to employment in London.'

'Already we are seeing a massive increase in land prices on sites adjoining the motorway.'

Mr Livingstone said firms would be faced with tremendous economic pressures to move out to a motorway site, preferably one near an interchange with links to other parts of the country.

DANGER

In transport costs alone firms would find it cheaper to get out of the Capital. He forecast that few of their workers would be prepared to make a long and difficult journey to the fringe of Greater London.

'Although there are advantages to the M25, there are major economic dangers,' said Mr Livingstone. This was one of the main reasons why the GLC had pressed the case for cheaper bus and Tube fares.

The aim of the policy had been to sway the economic and transport arguments in favour of firms staying in London.

GLC planners reckon that in addition to the outward shift, East London will suffer with West London benefiting proportionately.

The report says: 'Outer London may gain some service jobs but it is likely on balance to lose manufacturing jobs.

'Inner London may also lose further manufacturing jobs and face a major new threat to its service employment.'

The report points out that much of the motorway is in the Green Belt where development is restricted.

Hypermarkets and superstores have so far been contained near town centres. But the report warns: 'Applications for development on green field sites close to the M25 are expected to increase.'

At present 46 miles of the M25 are open to traffic. More than 34 miles are under construction while the remaining 41 miles are at various planning stages.

(Source: Michael King, *The Standard*, 4 Jan. 1983)

Student enquiry 8A concluded

Going nowhere fast on the South

There are 33 pedestrian crossings and 47 signal controlled crossings along the South Circular. We seemed to stop at every one.

Not to mention the hold ups when we let traffic filter in from the 320 streets with direct access to the A206, or the delays when buses blocked the only lane by stopping at some of the 144 bus-stops on the route.

Edged

We joined the South Circular at the Kew end and stopped and started and edged our way over Kew Bridge and down Kew Road. The traffic flowed more freely down Mortlake Road until we hit the first of Andrew Warren's 'black spots' – East Sheen.

He said: "The big problem here is one that is repeated along the South Circular – vans and trucks have to unload in front of the shops. Queues also build up through people waiting to use the two car parks behind Waitrose"

It was not far to the next Warren black spot, Putney. We queued up to the approach of the traffic lights where the Upper Richmond Road (i.e. the South Circular) crosses Putney High Street.

Mr Warren said: 'Government statistics prove that a High Street is ten times more dangerous than something like a motorway which has limited access.'

We press on through the mass of lanes and signs that make up the Wandsworth one-way system. 'Even the signs are confusing for the stranger', says Mr Warren. 'If you are heading for Woolwich, how do you know here which way to go?'

He was looking at two signs, one above the other. The top one said: 'South Circular Rd, The City, Brighton, Folkstone'. The bottom one said: 'South Circular Road, The North, The West , Oxford'.

On to Clapham Common, down The Avenue and across the A24 at Balham Hill. As we approached the main Brighton Road, the A23, at Streatham Hill, Mr Warren said:'This is the first bit of dual carriage so far.'

That's what is so bad with the South Circular. So much of it is single-lane traffic, sometimes it goes to two lanes each way, but compared to the North Circular there is very little dual carriage way, let alone three-lane traffic in each direction.

The South Circular is just a series of high streets and residential roads linked by signposts. To suggest it acts as a viable inner by-pass for London, as is officially claimed, is a very sick joke.

Hampered

Across the A23 the three lanes almost immediately became a single. From there the South Circular winds across Dulwich Common and along to Forest Hill – another black spot. Vans unloading in London Road hampered progress and bus stops and traffic lights meant more queues.

Through Catford, the shops give way to houses and in Brownhill Road the front doors are just a car's length from the road.

Mr Warren said, 'Think how miserable that must be for the people living there – and how dangerous. A dog or a child could dash right out of the door and straight into the traffic.'

Past Hither Green the road widens to a dual carriageway and we reach the legal speed limit of 40mph. 'This is the best part of the South Circular', said Mr Warren, 'but it also has its dangers.'

Circular

'After all the frustrations of the past miles you're tempted to put your foot down and take silly chances.'

We negotiate the Well Hall roundabout – another notorious rush-hour trouble spot – without hold-ups and the rest of the journey to Woolwich was problem free.

Journey's end and Mr Warren summed up: 'The GLC is talking about doing something about odd junctions but that's just tinkering.'

(Source: *The Standard*, 1986)

Figure 8.6 The National Exhibition Centre near Birmingham is at the most accessible point in the Midlands. This is not the centre of Birmingham, but at the junction of the motorway M42 and the A45 on the eastern outskirts of the conurbation

Changing the road infrastructure in this radical way has drastically altered urban accessibility. The intersections of radial roads with the city ring road are often far more accessible points than the centre. This has led to pressure for the growth of shopping and other facilities at these communication nodes. In turn this has produced conflict in the countryside, as developers attempt to seek planning permission on green field sites at the city periphery for hypermarkets, shopping malls or even an exhibition centre (Fig. 8.6).

The infrastructure of a new town

You can most easily see the variety of infrastructure facilities needed by following the planning of a new town such as Runcorn New Town in North Cheshire.

Runcorn was planned as a community of about 90 000. It provided an exciting opportunity for those concerned with urban design to implement the theoretical concepts and to try to correct problems that occur in established urban areas.

When the planners of Runcorn set about the task of creating a new town, and were given target populations to accommodate, their first task had to be to plan the pattern and nature of the infrastructure. In the case of Runcorn they were developing a small site. They therefore had to opt

for a design that featured high density housing. They were also taking a large part of their population from the areas of Liverpool where people had traditionally earned low incomes and therefore were less likely to be able to own private transport. Nevertheless, Runcorn was envisaged as a focus of new industry and it would be expected that the level of earnings would rise. In time, it could be expected that the level of private car ownership would increase. Furthermore, the more successful the new town, the more freight transport would be attracted to the centre, adding additional traffic movements. With the twin concepts of (i) preventing traffic congestion; and (ii) making provision for those without private transport, the 'figure of eight' busway became the central focus around which the whole town structure developed.

Features of Runcorn's plan

Perhaps more than any other feature of the urban scene, infrastructure determines the quality of the environment. Getting an acceptable level of environmental quality was a paramount consideration for the planners. Some idea of the importance of infrastructure can be gained from the following selections from the Runcorn New Town master plan (Fig. 8.7).

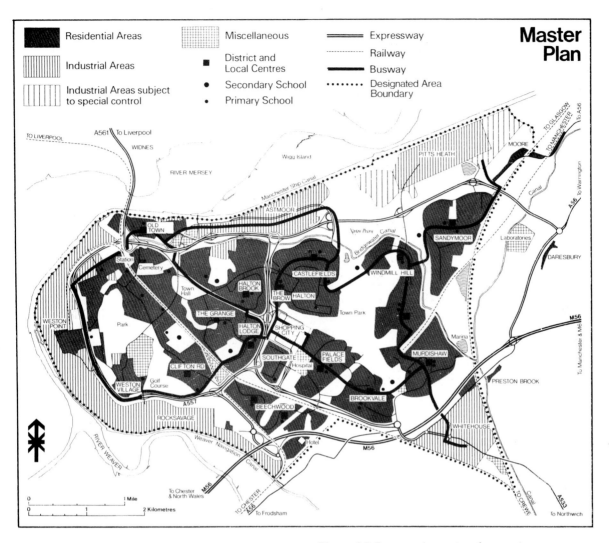

Figure 8.7 Runcorn's master plan
(Source: Runcorn Development Corporation)

What they said about . . .

Roads and public transport routes

' . . . good accessibility to all parts of the town . . . could be achieved in three ways: firstly, by a planned balance between the use of the private car and public transport; secondly by planning for a high degree of use of the private car; or thirdly, by designing a compact town where it would be possible for everyone to walk to the town centre and places of work. The third possibility of designing the town on a "walking" basis was rejected as impracticable . . . the need to increase (the population) to at least 90000 would make walking distances far too great.

'To design the town dominantly for the motor car would require the maximum expenditure on highways to cater for peak-period traffic and a more extensive provision of car parking spaces at the Town Centre and in the industrial centres. In addition, public transport operating on all purpose roads would be little used and therefore it would be uneconomic to operate a frequent bus service. This would cause a sense of social isolation for those without the use of a car, such as children and old people, and also members of the family to whom the car is not available at a particular time.

'A linear arrangement of the new residential communities, on either side of a spinal public transport route, has been evolved so that the majority of people will be within five minutes walking distance, or 500 yards, of a route which is especially reserved for buses. This distance is considered to be the maximum which car owners are prepared to walk to a public transport system. A linear form of development has the advantage of a minimum length of public transport route serving a constant density of population on either side. The requirement of five minutes' maximum walking time to the public transport system coincides with similar desirable maximum distances to the local shopping and community facilities. Local centres have therefore been planned along the public transport route at approximately half mile intervals to serve a series of communities each having a population of 8000 (Fig 8.8). Complementary to this public transport system, a road network is proposed for private motor cars and other vehicles, consisting of an expressway road outside the residential communities, with distributor roads to the residential areas.

Figure 8.8 The bus terminal at Runcorn's Shopping City. It is directly linked to the shopping area by an escalator

Consider the argument that a five minute walk should be the basis for the town plan.

'The application of the linear principle to the topography of the [New Town] leads naturally to the "figure of eight" plan shown (Fig. 8.9). The town centre is at the intersection of the "figure of eight", the residential areas are on either side of the public transport route and the industrial areas are on the edges of the town.

'The solution adopted provides the buses with a separate track so that they are not subject to the delays of traffic congestion and at the same time provides other vehicles with a road system which is free of the delays occasioned by buses which stop and start at frequent intervals. With such a system it is possible to plan on the assumption that there is no discouragement to the use of public transport on the grounds of delay and inefficient service.'

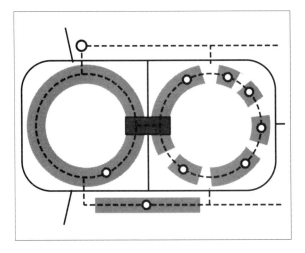

Figure 8.9 The figure of eight plan used as the basis of the infrastructure networks

Parking and garaging

'With garages and roads to each dwelling the maximum convenience is provided for private cars and service vehicles, but the environment is largely dictated by the road layout. With grouped garaging and parking this distortion can be avoided and a safer and more private pedestrian environment provided around the dwellings which need only single access. Cars are parked or garaged on the edge of each residential area from which residents walk a maximum of 150 yards to their dwellings.'

Suggest some objections to the plans for garaging based on (a) security, and (b) on desired life-style.

Parks and recreation

'An integrated open space for the town as a whole is proposed. The central town park . . . links the town centre with the local centres . . . . Within this park, buildings for recreational and cultural activities will be located. A landscaped parkway around part of the town contains the expressway and separates the residential areas from industry.'

Housing and industry were to be segregated by the use of parks. Suggest other patterns of land use that use parks differently. Would segregation be a top priority for today's planners?

One of the most striking features about Runcorn New Town is the ease with which you can travel around. There are no great hang-ups in traffic jams – nor are there likely to be in the future when the town is fully occupied and the roads a lot busier.

There are two major road systems in the town: the busway and the expressway in figure of eight pattern, closing the existing town in one half of the loop and the new residential areas in the other. Complementary to the expressway is a special road for buses only, which links all residential areas and which, when completed in the late 1970s, will be about 12 miles long.

When the visitor to the town approaches the new shopping centre he is confronted by an elevated roadway catering only for buses. This graceful structure is the brainchild of Professor Arthur Ling, then of the Department of Architecture and Civic Planning, Nottingham University, who was appointed by Runcorn Development Corporation to prepare a master plan for the new town.

It was while working on the overall plan that the Professor considered the private car in relation to the town. And it was while sketching on the back of an envelope that he conceived the figure-of-eight roadway system with a 22 ft wide track reserved for public transport.

The expressway is a far different proposition and has been designed to deal with the expected growth of traffic without detriment to the town's amenities. It has inward access to the residential and industrial areas and outward access to the regional and national road systems.

To a great extent the busway owes its birth to mistakes made in America by planners who allowed public transport roads to wither away – replacing them with freeways through the major towns. All that happened was that the motorist drove speedily from one bottleneck to another.

The system in Runcorn, on the other hand, has been devised with the purpose of encouraging people to use the bus. It is an attempt to provide some sort of answer to the increasing urban traffic problem by imposing some control on the use of the car.

The casual onlooker will see the busway as an ordinary two-way road carrying single-deck buses. The appearance belies the fact that for the first time a town of about 100 000 people has been designed and planned around its public transport system. The presence of the busway is apparent in everything connected with the construction of the town from a housing estate to the shopping centre.

The new shopping centre is the core of the town, and the figure-of-eight road system penetrates the very heart of every new residential estate, connecting them by feeder roads to the industrial estates, schools, the town park and the hospital.

(Source: *The Times,* 4 May 1972)

Provision of educational facilities

'The primary schools are fundamental elements of the community structure of the new residential areas . . . . Each 8000 community will have a total of four forms of entry into primary schools.

'The education authority's present policy for secondary education requires a secondary school for each 8000 population community . . . .

'A more flexible arrangement has been adopted to enable more than one school to be sited on a single campus serving two communities . . . . By siting the schools so that they are closely integrated with the local centres and the rapid transit system, it is intended that joint use could be made of playing fields and other school facilities, for recreation outside school hours by children and adults.'

Health and welfare

'The Ministry of Health has approved in principle the provision of a new regional hospital requiring a site of some 40 acres . . . to the south of the town centre . . . in addition local authority clinics in association with group practices for doctors and dentists are proposed. These will serve approximately 16 000 persons, or two communities.'

Churches

'An inter-denominational committee for the area has proposed 12 new churches and these will be built at the local centres.'

Security

'. . . a new district police headquarters will be required, sited in the town centre.'

Surface water drainage

(Predicted levels of run-off from the new town will overload the present stream.) 'Two balancing ponds will have to be constructed . . . in order to reduce the maximum run-off to [the stream] . . . . These . . . would be set in the landscape, informally, so as to provide an amenity for the town for boating, fishing and the creation and preservation of natural life, etc.

'It is intended to provide a completely new drainage system including a new sewage treatment works.'

> Consider the drainage scheme for a linear park in the light of Chapter 10 in **Challenge of the Natural Environment.** *What other schemes could have been implemented?*

Location of utilities

'Except for the main trunk sewer, which would be in the parkway adjoining the expressway road, it is proposed that all service pipes and conduits should be planned in a duct following the rapid transit route. This will facilitate renewals and repairs, and avoid unnecessary complications in built-up areas.'

Improvements for older towns

An undeveloped or '**green field**' site has many advantages. But most urban areas have to make the best of their heritage, they cannot start again from scratch. So how do existing urban networks get a face lift that serves all consumers?

The development of Reading's traffic system shows the problems and solutions well (Fig. 8.10). For the last two decades Reading in Berkshire has been the focus of one of the fastest rates of growth in modern Britain. The catchment population has doubled and with it have come severe problems for central access and traffic flow.

The central shopping area consists of the parallel streets of Broad Street and Friar Street. The natural centre of gravity for shopping is the middle to eastern end of Broad Street. This centre of gravity is strong. An attempt to pull it towards the west by a 1960s development of the Butts Shopping Centre (now called Broad Street Mall) was not the success that had been hoped. The centre of gravity has been the pivot around which the locations for multi-storey car parks, the provision of central access and the traffic flow have been designed.

The problems of improving road infrastructure include a number of conflicting requirements.

 (i) An area with high pedestrian flows cannot be subjected to fast traffic;

 (ii) The physical limitations of the central site (in the angle between two rivers) restrict the number of alternative routes that can be used for through traffic;

Figure 8.10 The main features of Reading, Berks showing the road network and the proposed changes to allow a better flow of traffic

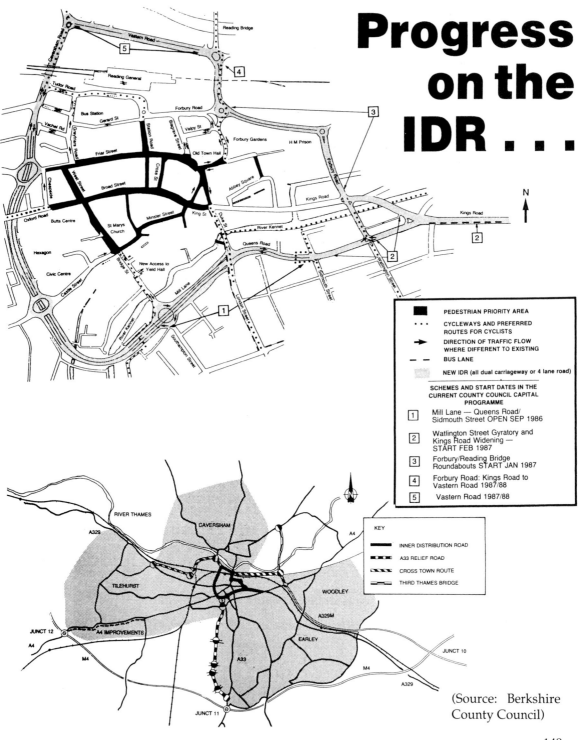

Progress on the IDR . . .

(Source: Berkshire County Council)

(iii) A policy of providing access via public transport must also make the focus truly accessible and this cannot be done by excluding the buses from the shopping area. People with heavy bags will go to car parks if the buses are inconveniently located.

(iv) Traffic flows of four different types have to be accommodated. They are: daily flows of commuters; daily shopping trips; daily flows of delivery and other service vehicles; through route needs of vehicles moving across the region.

Reading is also a major focus of routes. The M4 is effectively a bypass for the town which removes much of the east-west traffic, but north-south traffic between the Southampton conurbation and the Midlands has no satisfactory alternative provision.

In the 1960s the future problems were foreseen and a bold attempt was made to open up the central region by the construction of the Inner Distribution Road(IDR). This is an urban road of motorway proportions, with motorway access points. It is a striking feature of the urban scene.

An inner distribution road has many of the attributes of a railway. It provides fast access within the urban area, but at the expense of considerable disruption to existing communities. As they have limited crossings such roads are as divisive to an urban area as railways. Even ground level roads with fast traffic are divisive.

The solution sought has been to generate traffic flows in three zones:

(i) *An inner zone* which allows people to gain access to the shopping and CBD facilities. Through connections are difficult and this discourages non-essential traffic. The zone is serviced by a number of multi-storey car parks;

(ii) *A gyratory system* for traffic that wants access to the urban area. The intention is to provide a rapid transit system with limited access to the centre and complete connections with the arterial roads; and

(iii) *An outer road system* for traffic which does not require access to the urban space but seeks access to peripheral industrial zones and/or other distant centres (see Enquiry 8B).

Student enquiry 8B

Planning a road system for a growing community in Reading

Reading's schemes show many of the compromises that are necessary when attempting to improve the infrastructure of an existing urban centre.

1. Suggest the main causes of pressure on Reading's transport system.
2. Use Figure 8.10 to identify the major sources of transport congestion. Draw potential congestion areas on a tracing of the Reading area map.
3. The Inner Distribution Road has many effects on the urban space. List the advantages and disadvantages to (a) the elderly; (b) the business community; (c) the wealthy suburban dweller; and (d) the person without private transport. Try to suggest an alternative plan that could have been adopted. Explain the advantages of your proposal.
5. What long term effect will the Inner Distribution Road have on the commercial centre? Where do you expect the future expansion of commercial activities to take place and how will this affect future infrastructure patterns? Draw a likely pattern on a further tracing overlay and suggest how the problems could be overcome.

(a) Inner Distribution Road(IDR)

Reading IDR still a priority for new department

The County Council has formed a new Department of Highways and Planning to face the challenges of the 1990s in what is now one of Britain's fastest-growing areas.

'The IDR is still our top priority road scheme,' says Director of Highways and Planning Bob Clarke, 'and we are keeping on target to complete it by 1989.'

Traffic studies show that every town in Berkshire is suffering from serious traffic congestion and other projects are queueing up for a place in the county's programme, but Reading is still number one with the IDR taking first call on funds.

What happens when the project is finished?

'The County Council is trying to control the rate of development in Berkshire,' said Mr. Clarke, 'but the tremendous growth we have experienced over the last six or seven years, together with the high levels of car ownership and usage which we have in this area, means that road building alone cannot solve the problem. We need to look at a whole range of transportation solutions.

'Yes, we will have to build new roads but we must make better use of the existing ones through wider use of computer controlled signals and other traffic management measures. Public transport must be made a fast and reliable alternative to the car and facilities for cyclists improved. Changes in working hours, even quite small ones, could help commuters to avoid the particularly congested morning and evening peaks.'

The County Council has a number of long term proposals for Reading and central Berkshire and will be keeping the public informed of progress, and asking for comments.

) Friar St with shopping area congestion

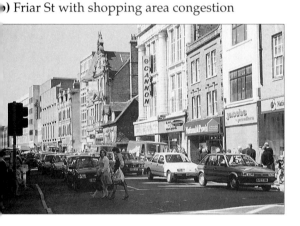

:) Broad St, restricted to buses

(d) New roundabout to ease traffic flows at intersections (4 on Fig 8.10).

. . . AND PLANS FOR MORE SCHEMES FOR THE FUTURE

The above package of schemes is due to be completed by the end of 1989. By that time, there will be more news about the other projects which are planned as part of the Reading Highway Strategy. The map below shows these.

In fact, design work on one scheme is already well advanced and construction will begin in 1988. This is the section of the Cross Town Route from the A329(M)/A4 junction to Broken Brow, which is being funded jointly by the developers of the industrial park in North Earley and the County Council, and which includes a fly-over of the existing "Sutton Seeds" roundabout on the A4.

The future sections of the Cross Town route are intended to link Broken Brow with the roundabout now being constructed by Reading Bridge. This would connect the eastern arm of the Cross Town Route with the IDR. The county Council also has proposals for the western arm of the Route, which would link the IDR to Oxford Road, and include an improvement to the Cow Lane Bridges.

In the future, too, lie the proposals for a third Thames Bridge to the east of the town and for an A33 Relief Road, linking the IDR with an improved Junction 11 on the M4. Also, there are proposals to improve the capacity of the A4 Bath Road.

Student enquiry 8C

How can Liverpool cope with changing demands?

In this enquiry you are given some information about Liverpool. The objective is to examine the pattern of facilities, compare them with the theory explained earlier in the chapter and in particular in the case study of Runcorn (25 km away) and then to make suggestions for future changes to some aspects of the infrastructure.

Liverpool is an established city that has grown piecemeal with the changing demands and fortunes of its industry. Its infrastructure has constantly had to be revised and modified to meet this changing need. Liverpool's problems are immensely complex and represent one of the greatest challenges faced by any planning department. In the enquiry you will find a small sample of the information the planning authorities have at their disposal. Consider all the pieces of evidence before answering any of the questions.

The enquiry objective is given in Q 7. The preceding questions are to provide you with a structured way of gathering the information you will need to answer the main question. You need not write formal answers to all of these preliminary questions, but you must complete Q1.

1. C1 shows the main transport links within Liverpool. Compare these with the pattern for Runcorn, Fig. 8.9.
2. Table C1 gives information about the distribution of people owning cars in Liverpool. Plot this data on a tracing of Map C2 then describe the pattern and comment on the areas most in need of public facilities.

3. Suppose you are able to release land for industrial development. Using the maps in this enquiry, draw up a map showing your priorities for release (consider employment need and available infrastructure). Where would you put land suited to high tech development? A large industrial project having large space requirements? A packaging firm that sends goods via the Red Star rail network and uses large numbers of unskilled workers?
4. The Liverpool structure plan calls for 'an effective public transport service giving reasonable access to jobs, shops, schools and leisure facilities, in particular attending to areas of greater need. On a tracing overlay map the areas of greatest need.
5. Describe the distribution of shops. Explain how you think these groupings have developed and some of the problems associated with their location and pattern.
6. By reference to the social conditions and infrastructure maps try to establish which of the shopping centres would be most attractive for new shopping schemes by large chain stores. What would happen to the others? How would these be affected by out of town shopping developments?
7. **Activity objective**: Suggest some strategies for easing some of Liverpool's infrastructure problems under the headings of:
   (i) improvements to transport systems;
   (ii) improved provision of social services;
   (iii) improved provision of infrastructure that would encourage employment; and
   (iv) improved provision of housing.
   Suggest, by drawing a map in each case, what you would do and which areas would receive priority.

Background information about Liverpool

1. History of employment:

Liverpool is principally a port. Its industries were traditionally connected with the commercial, distribution and processing activities of the port trade. Liverpool did not succeed in diversifying into new employment areas as successfully as many other cities.

Liverpool's workforce is relatively unskilled. It is most under-represented in the managerial and professional group (11 per cent of the economically active population compared to the British average of 19 per cent). By contrast unskilled manual workers were 20 per cent in Liverpool and 13 per cent nationally.

In the lowest income council areas the unemployment rate doubled from 15.5 per cent to 33.7 per cent between 1971 and 1981. Liverpool lost 43 per cent of its jobs between 1961 and 1986 compared with a 5 per cent national decline. This has been particularly severe in manufacturing where 64 per cent have been lost; only 20 per cent of the city's jobs are in manufacturing.

2. Population:

Liverpool grew very rapidly in the 19th and early 20th centuries as Atlantic trade flourished. In 1801 its population was 85 000, in 1851 it was 376 000 and in 1911 it was 746 000. Since 1961 Liverpool's population has dropped by nearly a third, from 750 000 to 480 000, partly because people have been leaving the region and partly because of policies of clearance of older inner city areas and the redistribution of people to outer areas and new towns.

The migrating population has been selectively skewed towards the younger people and thus pre-school populations have dropped by 54 per cent and the school population by 46 per cent. At the same time the population over 75 has risen by 33 per cent.

The groups which place a heavy demand on social and welfare services make up an increasing proportion of the city's residents.

3. Housing, roads and other features of the infrastructure:

The majority of the housing and factory stock was built 80 or more years ago. One of the key elements encouraging economic regeneration is a stock of buildings suitable for modern commercial and industrial use, often on purpose-designed estates. Many of Liverpool's existing buildings were designed for uses no longer required. This is reflected in the high proportion of vacant or partially vacant industrial buildings particularly in the inner city. The sites either have to be refurbished or redeveloped to provide advanced factory units.

The city has been well connected to the rest of the country by the M62, M57 and M58 motorways. Inside the city the mass transit metro city loop and links to Garston and Kirby have considerably reduced congestion. However, car ownership in the city is considerably below the national average, because 62 per cent of households do not have a car (43 per cent nationally). In parts of the city only 1 or 2 households in 10 own a car.

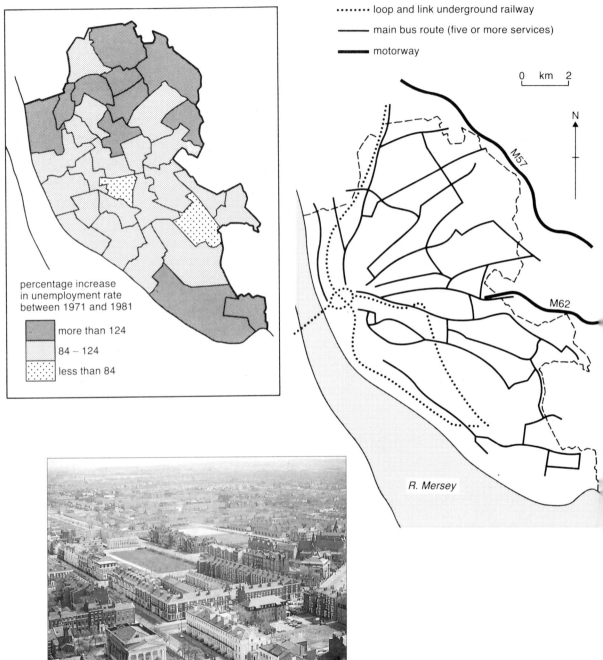

percentage increase
in unemployment rate
between 1971 and 1981

more than 124

84 – 124

less than 84

········ loop and link underground railway

——— main bus route (five or more services)

▬▬▬ motorway

0 km 2

N

M57

M62

R. Mersey

View east over areas where recreational space has been improved

Main road in the east where congestion and poor shopping facilities impair environmental quality

■ main city centre shopping area

● major regional shopping centre

--- City of Liverpool boundary

0 km 2

N

■ major site available for industry (over 5 hectares)

• other large site

0 km 2

N

city centre

R. Mersey

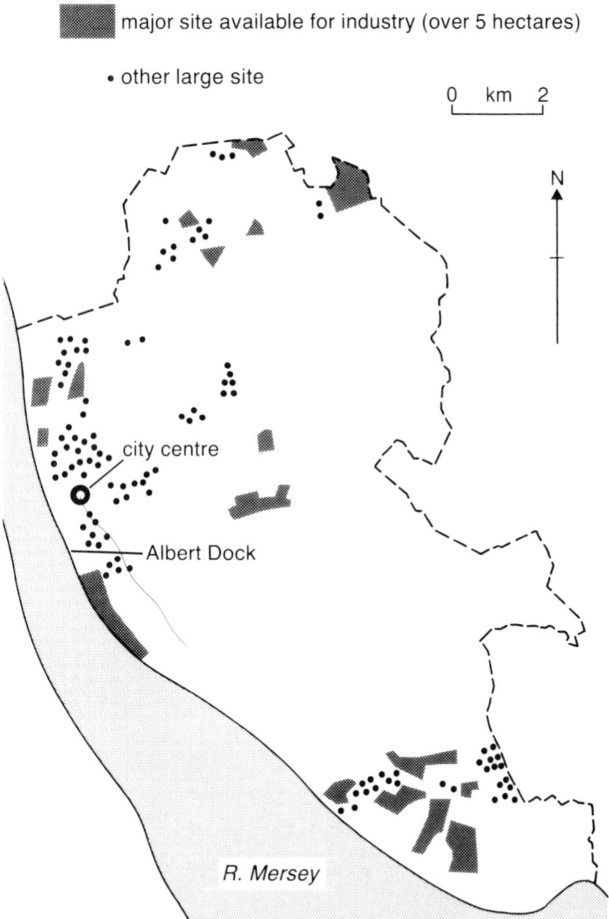

city centre

Albert Dock

R. Mersey

Student enquiry 8C concluded

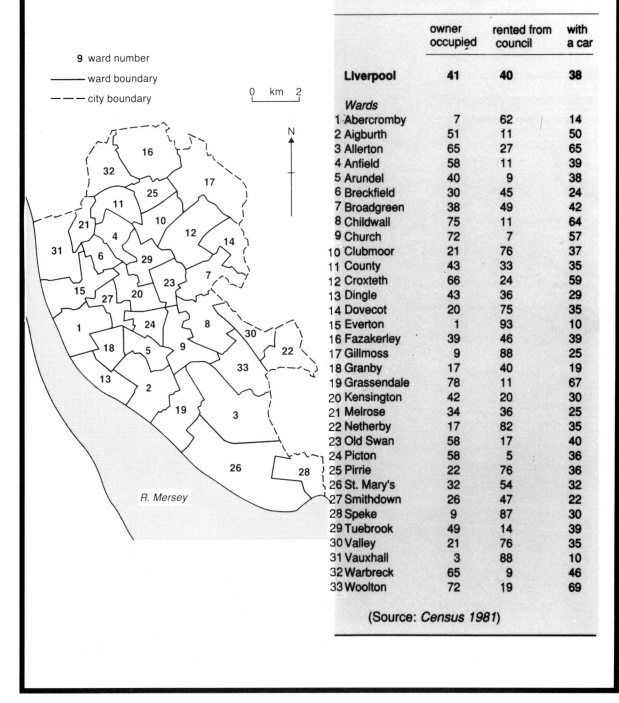

9 ward number
ward boundary
city boundary

0 km 2

N

R. Mersey

	Households 1981		
	owner occupied	rented from council	with a car
Liverpool	**41**	**40**	**38**
Wards			
1 Abercromby	7	62	14
2 Aigburth	51	11	50
3 Allerton	65	27	65
4 Anfield	58	11	39
5 Arundel	40	9	38
6 Breckfield	30	45	24
7 Broadgreen	38	49	42
8 Childwall	75	11	64
9 Church	72	7	57
10 Clubmoor	21	76	37
11 County	43	33	35
12 Croxteth	66	24	59
13 Dingle	43	36	29
14 Dovecot	20	75	35
15 Everton	1	93	10
16 Fazakerley	39	46	39
17 Gillmoss	9	88	25
18 Granby	17	40	19
19 Grassendale	78	11	67
20 Kensington	42	20	30
21 Melrose	34	36	25
22 Netherby	17	82	35
23 Old Swan	58	17	40
24 Picton	58	5	36
25 Pirrie	22	76	36
26 St. Mary's	32	54	32
27 Smithdown	26	47	22
28 Speke	9	87	30
29 Tuebrook	49	14	39
30 Valley	21	76	35
31 Vauxhall	3	88	10
32 Warbreck	65	9	46
33 Woolton	72	19	69

(Source: *Census 1981*)

The issue of improving regional infrastructure

The future commercial success of individual urban areas depends heavily on the regional infrastructure. One of the proposals that aims to make a major impact on the infrastructure of the region of north-west Europe is the proposed Eurotunnel (Datafile 8D). Eurotunnel will be taking advantage of the growing cross-Channel market in

      (i) passengers travelling with vehicles;

      (ii) road freight vehicles;

      (iii) passengers travelling without vehicles by sea or air; and

      (iv) rail freight.

In addition the Eurotunnel is expected to generate new traffic and increase the size of the total market. This extra demand will occur due to ease of movement, reductions in travel time, a reduction in the tariff due to competition, a reduction in the 'frontier effect' and commercial development resulting from the existence of the system.

In 1985 the total cross channel market was 48 million passenger trips and 60 million tonnes of freight. By 2003 the volumes are expected to rise to 94 million passenger trips and 123 million tonnes of freight. It is hoped by the commercial organisations backing the tunnel scheme that it will carry 44 per cent of cross channel passenger traffic and 17 per cent of cross channel freight when it opens.

The system will have two terminals, one near Calais and the other near Folkestone. These terminals will be linked with the existing motorway networks of the two countries (M20 in England and A26 in France). In addition there will be a high speed rail connection between Waterloo in London and Paris and Brussels with extensions to Cologne and Amsterdam.

Student enquiry 8D

Enquiry 8D contains various items related to the Eurotunnel scheme. Taken together the material can be presented either to support the advantages of the Eurotunnel scheme within Britain or to show how it will have an adverse effect on the British environment and jobs elsewhere.

In two separate statements, present the arguments for and then against the Eurotunnel scheme. You should be careful to cover such aspects as national economy, regional economy at the tunnel mouths, impact on jobs, impact on the environment from the national point of view and the impact from the view of the residents near the tunnel.

Student enquiry 8D continued

(Source: *Eurotunnel*)

Tunnel contract worth £700 million could aid region

Around £700 million in orders for the construction of the British side of the Channel rail tunnel should be placed soon.

With construction due to start by the middle of next year, once the tunnel treaty is ratified, tendering will be starting for some complex equipment, particularly the large-scale cutting machines which will slice out the service tunnel and the two main rail tunnels.

This emerged yesterday from the Channel Tunnel Group, whose French partner, France-Manche, is likely to be placing around the same scale of orders. On each side of the Channel the construction companies which are among the founder share-holders will be setting up a new company to carry through the construction of the tunnel and installing its equipment, including the rail rolling stock and signalling.

On the British side, a single company is being formed by Balfour Beatty, Costain, Tarmac, Taylor Woodrow and Wimpey. It will be responsible for total spending of £2300 million at present prices, although inflation is expected to push the value eventually to about £3500 million.

The £700 million in orders will go out to competitive tender, but the TDG says price will not be the only consideration: quality and delivery dates will also be crucial factors.

The British orders will include: reinforcing steel (£15 million); cast iron tunnel lining (£30 million); pre-cast tunnel lining (£130 million); aggregate concrete (£30 million); removal systems (£24 million) construction plant and vehicles (£50 million); steel sections (£60 million); various materials and cement (£100 million). . . .

CUMULATIVE POPULATION WITHIN SPECIFIED DISTANCES FROM THE CHANNEL TUNNEL

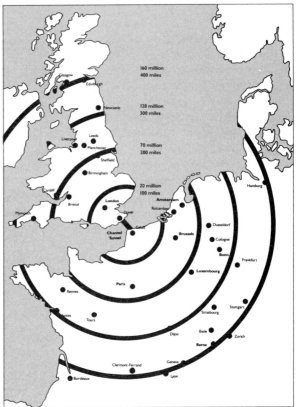

The impact of the tunnel contracts is likely to be widely spread around Britain. Rail equipment could bring work to the Midlands and the North West; pre-cast tunnel linings could come from Midlands factories; there are reinforcing steel plants in the Midlands. North and South East; aggregates could come from areas like Wales and Derbyshire; and there are a number of cement-producing locations including the South East, Derbyshire and Wales.

(Source: Derek Harris, *The Times*, 22 Jan. 1986)

Dover fears Channel Tunnel will block privatisation

Dover, the country's leading port in terms of the value of goods handled, favours privatisation, but believes the Government, after championing the private sector Channel Tunnel Project, is in no hurry to put the seaports for Europe on a private footing.

Like other Channel and North Sea ports which have seen dramatic growth as trade with the EEC countries has gained momentum, Dover fears the Channel tunnel, due to be open Spring 1993, will undermine even the most successful and well-run ports' investments.

While about 40 per cent of the ports are in the private sector, handling 38 per cent of foreign trade, Parliament would have to pass legislation to allow leading non-private ports such as Dover to change their present trust or municipal status to open the way to private ownership . . . .

Dover Harbour Board's turnover last year was a handsome £33 million. The value of goods, passing through the port was £6.4 billion in the third quarter of the last year. It handled 14 million passengers, 2 million cars and 900 000 commercial vehicles. If its trust status were removed there would be considerable scope for new areas of business, such as customs and export clearance systems.

Even with no change in status, the port was being forced by the Channel tunnel to seek a new role, Mr Sloggett said. He fears the fixed link, with strong backing from the French and British governments, will drive down prices for cross-Channel services, dragging the ports with it.

Furthermore, the unfair competition from the tunnel only compounded the competitive disadvantage of a non-private port such as Dover, which has less freedom of movement than private ports.

The uncertainty the Channel tunnel brings for the ports industry is also assessed in the National Westminster Bank's latest Quarterly Review, in which Dr Michael Asteris, the principal economics lecturer at Portsmouth Polytechnic, studies the issues of competition and trans-shipment.

He concludes British ports remain uncompetitive compared with their European rivals leading to Britain assuming the role of an offshore island in international shipping. The gap between British and northern European port costs is largely due to relative efficiency and subsidies.

Countries such as Belgium, West Germany and the Netherlands treat their big seaports as focal points of regional development, while the British Government regards the ports as commercial entities, limiting aid to redundancy funds for dockers or helping ports in financial difficulty, Dr Asteris notes. The BPA estimates that port subsidies in the rest of the EEC amount to about £200 million a year.

Dr Asteris accepts that the concentration of deep-sea shipping on ports close to the main EEC markets, such as Rotterdam, Antwerp and Hamburg, with Britain becoming 'peripheral', is a logical reading of the 'hub and spoke' principle.

But he believes the pivotal role of Heathrow in international airline operations shows that Britain need not restrict its maritime routes to mere feeder services. With a Channel tunnel it would be more appropriate for trans-shipment to be a two-way process, with Britain providing a land bridge to Europe.

(Source: Colin Narbrough, *The Times,* 1 Feb. 1988)

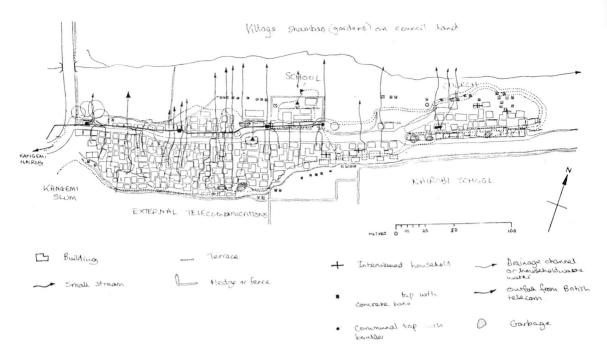

Village shambas (gardens) on council land

SCHOOL

KANGEMI
NAIROBI

KANGEMI
SLUM

EXTERNAL TELECOMMUNICATIONS

NAIROBI SCHOOL

METRES 0 10 25   50   100

N

	Building		Terrace	+	Interviewed household		Drainage channel or household waste water
	Small stream		Hedge or fence	▪	tap with concrete base		outfall from British telecom.
				•	Communal tap with boulder	⊘	Garbage

Water supply in the developing world: the issues

Infrastructure provision in the developing world often contrasts strongly with that of the developed world. We can only touch on some aspects of the problems faced by many developing countries here and we will focus on the supply of clean drinking water.

In Britain we expect to have a constant clean water supply delivered to every household. The network of pipes, dams and purification plants has been established over a long period of time, but even so the cost of providing the water is enormous, and has to be paid for by charging each household a water rate.

Although water is expensive to provide, it would be a great deal more expensive if most people were widely scattered (as opposed to being concentrated in cities), if the population were rising quickly, or if the rainfall were irregular. The primary job of the water supply industry is to maintain and upgrade the system we already have.

The advantageous conditions that prevail in developed countries such as Britain are frequently not found in the developing world. Most people do not earn enough money to pay a sub-

Figure 8.17(a) A field researcher's rough sketch of Kiberagwe. No official map is available

stantial water rate. The populations are also growing quickly and many developing countries are in regions with only seasonal rainfall. Thus many developing world countries are faced with the task of providing this basic infrastructure facility for a rapidly rising population but with no guaranteed rate base. It is an impossible requirement and progress has been modest. Nowhere is this shown more clearly than in Nairobi, the capital of Kenya. The city has an ever expanding need for water, especially to those slum areas which are growing up in previously under-used sections of the city. Population growth in these areas can be 20 per cent a year.

As population grows more rapidly than the gross national product (GNP) there are many stresses on maintaining an adequate water supply. This can be seen clearly in the pocket slum of Kibaragwe, which houses about 3000 people in the north-west of Nairobi (Fig. 8.17). The local stream is too heavily polluted for human use and people must depend on the Nairobi City Commission for their water. A 15 mm water supply pipe (the diameter of a normal domestic tap pipe in a British house) was supplied in 1980 to try to meet some of the needs of the growing com-

Figure 8.17 (b) The main track in Kibaragwe showing the taps; (c) Typical means of carrying water

munity. Four communal taps were fitted to the pipe, spread across the slum area. Concrete platforms for washing were subsequently built. Only one household and the school had 'private' connections.

People have to collect their water from these communal taps using buckets and jerricans. The inconvenience of fetching water influences the whole pattern of life for the residents. For example, many people bring their washing to the taps, making the taps into places of social contact. The small amount of water that can be carried back to the dwellings also affects the way it is used. In Britain 150 l/day is average for consumption by each person. The mean daily consumption for drinking, cooking, washing of utensils and bathing (a private activity not done at the taps) in Kibaragwe is 35 l/day, or about two trips with a jerrican per person per day. In a nearby slum where water is supplied by vendors at a price, residents have cut their water consumption down to 10 l/head/ day.

Figure 8.18 The bay boom keeps out floating waste as well as sharks and boats. Litter on the beaches, a publicity campaign and systems for its collection

Water supply is only part of the responsibility of a water authority. In the developed world the waste water is disposed of using an even more expensive network of large diameter sewer pipes. No such provision can be made in Kibaragwe because the government simply does not have the funds to achieve it. Toilet facilities must make use of dry methods of disposal. The main problem comes from waste cooking and washing water which is generally thrown into the ground outside the dwelling. The lack of drainage can contribute to health problems in the slum.

Consider simple ways in which the public health of the slum could be improved. Is there also a simple way of providing private connections?

Litter: a problem for the island of Hong Kong

People generate mountains of rubbish. Industries create materials that are often toxic: all varieties of materials are mixed in domestic waste sacks,

and a cocktail of chemicals and organic materials is flushed down wastepipes in homes every day. To deal with this requires an army of workers, a fleet of rubbish vans and a complex system of waste pipes below the ground. However, it all has to be treated somewhere and disposed of safely.

In areas with much space there is always the possibility of burying waste in disused dry quarries. In all cases refuse disposal is an expensive business. It is one of the infrastructure advances that can really only be provided in wealthy countries, and even here local authorities often fail to rise to the task. In the developing world refuse disposal is one of the biggest problems many cities have to tackle.

The problems of waste disposal become acute when population pressure increases. This is vividly illustrated in Hong Kong, where the population of 5 million has risen by 2 million since 1971. The island is small, with only 1000 km² of land.

The main effect of intense pressure has been the growth of pollution without the means and infrastructure to deal with it. Of particular concern is the close proximity of sewage water outlets and

the bathing beaches. An example is Castle Peak which is presently unavailable to swimmers due to the poor microbiological quality of the water. The area has to be developed into a residential, recreational and commercial complex because population pressure has already saturated other areas, but before this can happen all the storm water drains which still carry faecal pollution have to be diverted from the beach area.

The dramatic rise in the overall population put pressure on the beaches and caused the urban council to increase its litter collection arrangements. Furthermore the boom laid across the bay is now not just used to keep out sharks and speed boats but also floating waste (Fig. 8.18). In the long term the health and welfare of the whole population depends on an adequate infrastructure to keep the environment clean.

Suggest how sewage can be treated and disposed of in such a high density island.

Pollution puts third beach on the hazard list

The water of another Hong Kong beach was classified as potentially hazardous yesterday as the Environmental Protection Department warned pollution levels at most swimming spots were expected to continue to rise.

Chung Hom Kok beach has joined Silvermine Bay and Castle Peak Bay in Tuen Mun on the blacklist because of an unacceptably high bacteria count.

The popular beach, on the western point of Stanley Bay, was given a 'C' grading, indicating that pollution levels were extreme. The department classifies water quality from A to C.

Principal environmental protection officer for water policy, Mr Paul Holmes, said until there was a major review of agricultural, industrial and sewage disposal outlets in Hong Kong, the beaches would get worse but not to the point of being unacceptable.

> Beaches are graded according to the level of 'E. Coli' from sewage in the seawater.
> *A grade shows the median E Coli count is between zero and 99 per 100 millilitres and the water quality is good.
> *B grade shows the median count is between 100 and 999 per 100 millilitres and the water quality is acceptable.
> *C Grade shows the count is1000 or more per 100 millilitres and the water quality is poor.

'It is not an emergency situation, and although I am not happy with the results of the tests neither am I surprised at the outcome,' he said.

Kwun Yam Wan and Tung Wan also dropped in standard, falling from 'good' ratings to only 'acceptable'.

However, South Bay, St Stephen's and Deepwater Bay beaches showed improvement and went from 'acceptable' to 'good' ratings.

'Naturally I would like to see all beaches rating an 'A' level', Mr Holmes said.

Mr Holmes added that fluctuations in the results of tests for individual beaches were to be expected, and the beaches should only be declared hazardous or closed if low ratings were consistently recorded.

(Source: Wendy Kay in Hong Kong)

Chapter 9
Issues of urban change

"ON A CLEAR DAY YOU CAN
SEE YUPPIES FOREVER"

Introduction

The patterns within a developed world city, such as those we looked at in Chapter 7, capture a static 'snapshot' picture of the urban scene. However, the city is a dynamic place because the needs of the people are constantly changing. This is why the 'snapshot' of a city in one decade will probably be significantly out of date in the next.

A city has shape and purpose that result from the forces acting within the community. In the western 'free market' economy, these are:

(i) market forces produced by individuals striving to improve the quality of their lifestyle through their own endeavours; and

(ii) planning 'sticks' or 'carrots' produced by various tiers of government on behalf of the majority of the community.

Issues of change occur within the city because there is a natural tension between these two forces, and change inevitably brings its winners and losers.

This chapter is concerned with the changes that are occurring in *central* urban areas, and the issues of disadvantage that changes sometimes bring. Issues that arise near the outskirts of the city are dealt with in Chapter 11.

The need for urban change

There is a need for constant change because:

(i) people are always seeking to improve the quality of their lives, perhaps by improving or building new homes, social facilities and open spaces; and

(ii) businesses have to use the latest techniques, and this may mean a change of business location or a change of building design.

Figure 9.1 A selection of planning applications from a local newspaper

The nature of change

Only the grandest of changes ever make the newspaper headlines. The multitude of small changes only make the columns of the local papers under the heading of 'planning application'.

Examine the planning application notices given in Fig.9.1. Devise a scheme to classify them, and then comment on the implications of these changes, assuming 100 are notified each month in a town of 10 000.

The desire of millions of people to improve their quality of life should not be underestimated; the combined influence of their imaginations has appreciable effects on the city shape, both in the structures they improve and the desire to buy new property.

Every scale of change has to be welcomed and accommodated. If it is not, then cities can become fossilised and stagnate. They can even lose people and fade away completely. Many of the cities of the ancient world that are now mere ruins to be visited by the curious tourist were cities that were

```
Applications received for Planning
Permission for development
Q234 Extension and conversion of
existing building to form three self-
contained apartments at 4 Queens Rd
Q235 External staircase enclosing
domestic oil tank at 28, The Gorge
Q236 Conservatory at 19 Elm Rd
Q237 Change of use - retail to estate
agents' offices with ancillary build-
ing society agency at The Arcade,
Market Square
Q238 Demolition of existing lean-to
stores and attached garden wall.
Erection of new 4 bay garage, tractor
garage and new garden wall at Grange
Court, Appleyard
Q239 Double-sided hanging sign and in-
dividual letters at Baileys Butchers,
Mead St
Q240 Change of use - erection of 19
houses on allotment land at Gander St
```

not able to keep abreast of the times (Fig. 9.4). To be successful the inhabitants of a city have continually to find an evolving and important role. They must not struggle on, trying to survive only on the activities that first brought them into being. This is a recipe for unemployment and a lower quality of life.

Figure 9.2 Part of the ruins of a once famous Roman city that did not move with the times

Los Angeles succeeds, at a cost

Figure 9.3 Suburbs of the successful: Beverly Hills, Los Angeles

To help see how change can bring success and problems we can focus on Los Angeles in California, USA. Los Angeles is perhaps the world's most *economically* successful city. It is a classic example of a city spirit overcoming locational disadvantages (Fig. 9.3).

What Los Angeles has achieved is the continual re-invention of its sources of finance. When it became a centre for arable and fruit growing in the late nineteenth century and needed a harbour to export its produce, it made one. Now its exports are $50 billion a year.

In the early years of the twentieth century the entertainment industry made LA its home, largely because there was no restrictive labour legislation. Here it also found the bonus of good weather.

In the 1930s the entertainment industry was overtaken by the aerospace and heavy engineering industry based largely on significant numbers of entrepreneurs in an economy whose main theme was freedom from restriction.

Since the Second World War over a tenth of all new businesses in the USA have been started in Los Angeles because of its spirit of free enterprise and the lack of local government restrictions.

Innovation is the keynote of Los Angeles. It provides a dynamism that its inhabitants feel, that visitors recognise and that entrepreneurs (the future wealth creators) seek to be associated with.

However, there is another side of the coin. Spectacular growth and prosperity has not come to everyone, and the large negro and hispanic populations have mostly been left behind in terms of wages, job opportunities and housing. In the late 1960s the negro district of Watts was the scene of one of the most widespread urban riots in American history. It was a warning that city success must not be allowed to create social divisions.

Los Angeles is still an insecure city, with a level of violence that few cities in other parts of the world would wish on themselves (Fig. 9.4). Growth has been accompanied therefore by a social cost. This is one of the biggest dilemmas faced today. How to get the right mix of growth and social benefits.

Figure 9.4 No room for the poorer people

Processes influencing urban change

1. The impact of industrial change

Business is the economic lifeblood of a city. It produces the jobs and the wages that allow the citizens to prosper. It also indirectly produces the taxes that provide the public services that people require. Thus the needs of business can be regarded as central to the welfare of the city, and they are one of the most powerful driving forces within a city.

It is because industry is so important that its growth, decline, or change in location, has such an impact on a city.

A business will argue that it can only maintain or increase its workforce if it can prosper. In turn this means being given a free hand to choose where to locate and when to move.

In a growing area the residents may feel that the needs of business place an unacceptable burden on their environment, changing its character, its traffic flows, pollution levels and so on.

In an area suffering decline in job numbers (due to the decline of an industry or its relocation) there may be protests at the loss of jobs. The

Fig. 9.5 Protests against housing conditions in the inner city

residents may also try to oppose a change that makes their area look more run down and less attractive (Figs 9.5, 9.6).

It follows that, in order to maintain an employment base, government, through its planning officers, must be as flexible as possible in satisfying industry's requirements. But it rests with government to

(i) decide to allow relocation;

(ii) provide an environment equally attractive to the firm in its present location; or

(iii) attract other industries in to make up the loss suffered by allowing relocation.

As we shall see later, the attempts by government to balance all three solutions have created many issues for local communities.

2. The problems of urban mobility

The dramatic structural change that has taken place within cities in the twentieth century is largely due to improved mobility (see also Chapter 8). The better off can now select a home anywhere in the city and still get swiftly and com-

Figure 9.6 Worn-out buildings without a new use help to create a depressing atmosphere

fortably to any other part. Thus they can choose to refurbish older houses of character near to the city centre, or they can choose to buy newer properties on the periphery. But most of all, increased mobility has caused a rapid increase in segregation of the population and the formation of ghetto areas.

Most people who become wealthy enough to move from the inner city have chosen to do so. This has been greatly to the disadvantage of those who are left behind because they have little political clout and there are few people articulate enough to voice their needs and concerns.

The loss of the more wealthy has also been of considerable worry to the inner city authorities, because it leaves local authorities serving only low income and disadvantaged communities. People with low incomes need more local government help than average, yet at the same time they provide little money as rates, and this restricts the scope of the inner city authorities to help them or to upgrade their environment. The inevitable consequence has been that public

buildings and open spaces have not been improved as much as should have happened. The environment has acquired a run-down appearance and industry has been trapped in a congested environment with little chance of road improvement (Fig. 9.7).

As factories and workshops are relocated to more suitable locations, so the burden of rates falls ever more heavily on the remaining businesses, causing them in turn to look for alternative premises. As a result what starts as a gradual movement becomes almost a flight. And as more and more sites become empty it becomes less desirable for the remaining firms to be seen in such areas. All these are cumulative factors, but the unskilled people have suffered most because they are the least mobile. They cannot keep their relocated jobs because they cannot afford the costs of the longer journeys to work. This has helped to cause a dramatic increase in inner city unemployment.

At the same time as these profound changes in industrial location, the nature and location of shopping has also changed. Increased mobility has affected the viability of many urban shops (Fig. 9.8). As the variety of produce available to

consumers has burgeoned, so the space require-ments of shops have increased. Customers have become used to finding the widest possible vari-ety of choice. In general this cannot be accommo-dated by traditional shops and a new type of shop, similar to a warehouse, has had to be developed. The chances of sufficiently large plots becoming available near the centre are not high. Where they exist the hypermarkets have been quick to step in. However, their more usual sites are on the city outskirts where they can share industrial estates with manufacturing industries and other sorts of warehousing.

The customers of the newer peripheral shopping centres are those with cars and thus higher incomes. It is another example of change that works to the disadvantage of the less wealthy and the less mobile, both by depriving them of the chance to get to the better shops, and by holding down the quality of the local shopping.

Finally, the increase in long distance move-ments that results from people living and work-ing many kilometres apart has put great strain on the urban environment. Central roads in particu-lar are heavily congested. Again the congestion tends to be worst in the inner city regions, putting one more difficulty in the way of improving their environment.

Figure 9.7 There is often little money for home refur-bishment or environmental care in poorer neighbour-hoods

3. Legacies of the past

A city that has grown over centuries shows many examples of compromise. For example, the plots that become available for redevelopment are usually small and the development that occurs has to accommodate itself within the existing urban framework. Many areas in big cities have large numbers of houses over a hundred years old which lack basic amenities such as an inside lava-tory. These properties are often regarded as too small for an adequate quality of life unless com-pletely refurbished.

The majority of inner city houses were built for manual workers with low incomes. They are very small and often difficult to refurbish. However, there are also substantial numbers of good quality and spacious houses, once the homes of the elite. They are, however, too large for most individual families to occupy today and extremely costly to maintain.

The legacy of the past has thus been a situation in which – whether good or poor – housing requires much money to be spent on it if the central city environment and the quality of life are to be improved.

Student enquiry 9A

The changing face of London

The article published in the *Daily News* in 1986, and reproduced on this page and the following two pages, captured the nature of changes that take place over a decade. We can use it to provide a foundation for the issues discussed in this chapter.

1. For each of the changes described or illustrated suggest what impact it had (i) on the losing area; and (ii) on the receiving area.

You should consider both advantages and disadvantages to each area.

2. Of the changes that have taken place what issues have been created in (i) central London; and (ii) the older 'run-down' London?

3. If you had to divide people as winners and losers, which people discussed in the article would fit into each category? Try to suggest some reasons for people winning and losing.

LONDON TOWN TURNED UPSIDE DOWN

In the last eighteen months, London has gone through some of its most violent changes this century. To anyone who hasn't been here for a while, it looks much the same at first, but it soon becomes obvious that drastic things have been happening. In many parts of the capital there's an odd sense of disorientation, a bit like looking at those eerie pictures of wartime Jersey in which Swastika flags flutter over cricket pitches and jack-booted Wehrmacht officers sup pints of bitter in rustic pubs.

The sense of confused unease, of familiar landmarks made meaningless, will force each of us to redraw our mental map of what London is about.

Imagine the culture shock that will face a brain-drained Londoner coming home this Christmas for the first time after a couple of years. His Brymon Airways flight from Paris will start its final approach to a brand new Docklands airport within sight of St Paul's. Coming in to land, a world away from the familiar congestion of Heathrow, he will see, not long-derelict warehouses, but the shiny, crinkled tin boxes that signal sunshine industries and pastel tower blocks put up especially for the BMW-driving classes.

As he sets off for the headquarters of the multi-national bank he works for, his taxi will head, not for the square mile but for Wigmore Street, where the bank has now taken over an old department store.

When he goes to see a couple of financial journalists he knows on the Mall, he'll find the Fleet Street he left behind empty and boarded up. Instead he will go to their new offices in the old Barkers Building in Kensington.

Later that day, if he wants to do some smart shopping, he might well go to Covent Garden, only to discover that the fashionable names are gone, having mysteriously reappeared in converted garages at the end of the Fulham Road. Once London's most irresistible magnet for the style-conscious, Covent Garden has been killed by its own success. The chain stores and taco bars are driving out the one-off fashion shops.

In the evening, he will notice to his surprise that the streets of Soho are sex-free. Vice has moved on from Old Compton Street: the nude massage parlours, dubious cinemas and clip joints have vanished. In their place are modish restaurants with downlighters and silver venetian blinds dispensing Thai food, and fashion shops aimed at refugees from the King's Road.

(Source: *Daily News*, 18 Feb. 1987)

SOHO

Westminster Council's campaign has worked better than anyone expected. Soho's sex shops, strip clubs and clip joints are gradually being moved out by the influx of smart places to eat and drink. The Swiss pub became the Soho Brasserie. Wheelers turned into Braganza, and the Groucho Club has made Soho a Mecca for the media again.

KINGS CROSS

With the red light district of Argyle Square cleaned up, the badly run-down King's Cross area is set for change. The new British Library is going up on the site of an old railway yard on Euston Road, which will bring in scholars from all over the world. There are plans to reopen the spectacular St Pancras Hotel, long derelict but now earmarked for three-star luxury.

Heading west: forget Covent Garden, the smart area to shop these days is SW3

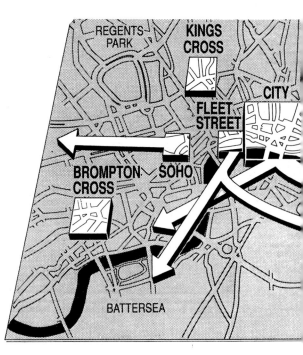

BROMPTON CROSS

Brompton Cross, the name recently given to the stretch where Brompton Road becomes Fulham Road, is London's newest up-market shopping area. But it really took off eighteen months ago, when high fashion retailers bought up garages and greengrocers shops. Now you can find Issey Myiake, Joseph and Katherine Hamnet here and Conran is converting the old Michelin building into a flagship.

FLEET STREET

The newspaper industry's flight from Fleet Street has turned into a stampede. *The Sun* and *The News of the World* were the first to go – and plans have already been drawn up to build offices in their place. *The Mail* is going to the Barkers Building in Kensington next year. *The Telegraph* and *Guardian* are both going to the Isle of Dogs, and the *Observer* is heading for Battersea.

CITY

The Canary Wharf Scheme – 10 million square foot of offices on the Isle of Dogs for the blue chip banks like Credit Suisse and First Boston – is what really panicked the City. Since Canary Wharf was announced, a steady stream of brokers, banks and insurance companies have moved out to Hackney, Tower Hamlets, Southwark, Westminster and even Victoria Station.

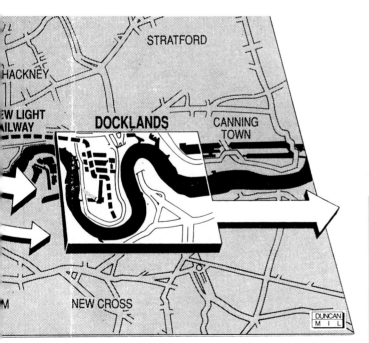

Heading east: who would have thought a decade ago that the Isle of Dogs would become one of the most exclusive addresses in town?

DOCKLANDS

Ten years ago, when the ships had all moved on to Tilbury, The GLC seriously considered turning over Docklands and making it into a park, thinking nobody would build factories or homes there. Now money from the London Docklands Development Corporation has created London's biggest building site. New roads, railways and even an airport are opening soon.

Figure 9.8 Inner city shops find increasing difficulty in making a profit. Those that survive offer only a restricted range of goods and have to stay open long hours

Planning for urban change

The goal of urban change is easy to define. It is to improve the quality of the disadvantaged environments so that all areas in the city provide an equal quality of life for their residents, businesses and visitors. However, as we have seen, the past decades have created a very divided society in which wealthy and poor have become separated; in which business is split between the core and the periphery and in which there is an enormous variation in housing quality and road congestion. Trying to achieve the goal is therefore an extremely difficult problem.

City planning is a very complex activity. It requires sensitivity to the good taste of the public, sensitivity in not putting too many obstacles in the way of enterprise that may bring new jobs, and at the same time it requires that planners have a sense of heritage, help foster civic pride and provide a sound foundation for the future.

The importance of planning can be seen by way of examples. Without some form of planning, the city centre might yield entirely to the forces of bid rent. Thus it would consist of a wide array of offices, in all sorts of odd and conflicting styles, with poor public facilities, no open space, and so on. While everyone would agree that it is very

desirable that there should be parks and libraries, museums and art galleries, none of these land uses could compete on purely bid rent terms. Similarly provision has to be made for civic offices (which also have city centre locational requirements) and effective road networks.

Very often upgrading the quality of the environment can only be achieved by a large public body with sufficient funds (Fig. 9.9). Planning a landscaped industrial estate and linking it with the national road network may encourage new firms to move to the area. All systems work best if they are well designed and linked together in a positive way. A city plan provides the framework within which the market forces of business and individuals can operate. In some cases the plan is produced before the city arrives, but in the majority of cases plans have had to be constructed around the existing urban area.

Planning schemes can be as inappropriate as schemes produced by market forces, sometimes even more so because greater power can be wielded. Socially desirable objectives must be determined before any plan is made. In the next section we shall see how some of the plans turned out, the issues they produced, and what lessons can be learned about the organisation of urban space.

Figure 9.9 City centre with pedestrian only access

The evolution of urban renewal

Urban renewal consists of replacing old, decayed and inappropriate buildings (Fig. 9.10), narrow roads and a congested environment with modern or modernised buildings better suited to present functions, and served by a good road network in a pleasant environment (Fig. 9.11).

> List the factors you think make up a pleasant environment under headings such as (a) comfort; (b) convenience; (c) size and pattern of dwellings; (d) communal space such as parks or private space such as gardens. The photographs on these pages should act as a stimulus.
>
> Now rank them in importance.

1. The ideal place to live in

Defining a pleasant environment is a very difficult task, but lessons can be learned from those with the money to choose their environment. We mentioned earlier that as people became wealthy enough to move from the inner cities they went to the suburbs. So what makes the suburbs a desirable environment?

Developers had been building houses for sale in the suburbs throughout the twentieth century. Because they were for sale, these houses had to match the requirements of the customers. What

Figure 9.10 Inner city tower blocks

Figure 9.11 Private office block set in landscaped grounds enhances the quality of the abbey wall shown on the right of the picture

sort of houses were they? They were small individual boxes, many semi-detached, and of very traditional architectural style. But although many variations of style were chosen, the same theme remained: people were given a private home of their own in a private space they could use more or less as they pleased. The same styles are still the cornerstone of successful private developments today (Fig. 9.12).

A house is a central element of the culture throughout the world, and this is what developers sell along with the bricks and mortar. And if this is the environment people are prepared to pay for when they can buy their own homes, then the chances are that it would also be the preferred choice of those who are not able to buy their homes.

2. The dream of a plan

Urban change has always been a dream to those with the money or the power to cause change. This is a fundamental concept that underlies all the developments within a city. Such dreams may be for prestige or they may be the socialist goal of providing equal standards for all.

The task of planning for change rests largely with architects. For centuries architects have designed grand schemes for new cities, and many of these have been built.

> *Consider the plan for a city shown in Figure 7.6. Suggest some of the advantages and disadvantages of a geometrical plan as the basis for city life. Suggest, and justify, some ways of improving the plan (Fig. 9.13).*

3. Inner city renewal

The Second World War caused the destruction of large areas of Europe's cities. Although the bombing was disastrous, it did have the benefit of releasing large areas of land for urban renewal. These areas for large scale redevelopment – called **brown field** sites – needed to be brought back into use as quickly as possible, because many homes and many business premises had been

destroyed. Most of the property destroyed was small terraced homes which the occupants had rented from private landlords. It was not possible for these private landlords to find the money to rebuild, so after the war the local authorities found themselves having to take on the role of landlord.

The need to rebuild on a large scale opened up a rare possibility for urban renewal, in which housing densities, infrastructure and housing could all be redesigned at the same time. The task the town hall planners and architects set themselves was no less than the replacement of the inner cites. Thus, what had started as a scheme to replace the brown field sites was extended to include the wholesale demolition of older houses in the inner cities, thus cutting out the slums of the nineteenth century and replacing them with modern dwellings with all conveniences.

To achieve these aims millions of people had to be relocated – a task that required many new homes to be built before the older homes were demolished. As a result local authorities from the inner cities sought to build new housing estates on peripheral green field sites (Fig. 9.14). The large housing developments on the edges of many cities are a testimony to this.

> *What were some of the impacts of building housing estates on the outskirts of a city? Refer to the information in Datafile 8B concerning Liverpool and comment on the relationship between outer council estates and the unemployment pattern.*
>
> *When many people are leaving the inner cities and moving to suburban homes, why do you think building housing estates on the outskirts of a city can cause large problems for the tenants?*

Costain have the home for you at Meadow Vale, Lower Earley

Carisbrook One of Costain's top of the range homes. Beautifully designed with luxury features, has two bathrooms, a study, utility room off the fully fitted kitchen and a huge square shaped garage that's a double plus. The generously proportioned lounge has double doors opening onto the rear garden and alongside is the separate dining room. The hall has a cloaks cupboard and cloakroom with w.c. next to the entrance lobby. All four bedrooms have fitted wardrobes and the second bathroom is en suite to the master bedroom.

Stamford A superior four bedroomed detached home with double garage and central heating. The layout of the ground floor has been planned to provide maximum living space. The hall leads into a spacious lounge with a separate dining room. Plenty of room here for really creative furnishings. The kitchen is good-sized with well-fitted storage units and ample worktop space. On the first floor three of the bedrooms have their own fitted wardrobes and there is a super modern bathroom. A well designed family home!

Bembridge This is a superior four bedroomed home with spacious rooms that are well planned to give maximum light. A delightful lounge runs the full width of the house, separate dining room, hall with cloaks, a great study, cleverly tucked away, a fully fitted kitchen plus utility. Fitted wardrobes in three of the bedrooms, bathroom and en suite shower room to the master bedroom. Central heating and double garage.

Choose from six superbly designed houses, planned to make the most of space with maximum light from picture windows.

Beautiful, graceful homes from Costain, with quality specifications for luxury living.

Here are some of them...

∗ Full gas fired central heating designed to N.H.B.C. Grade 1 standards.
∗ Open hearth fireplace to all properties.
∗ Bruynzeel Pallas Prestige - Superb Continental Kitchen Units with Post-Formed worktops in a choice of colour and style. Super NEFF split level hob and oven units with hoods fitted as standard in Carisbrook, Salcombe, Bembridge, Oakham and Stamford types.
∗ High class sanitaryware and fittings and generous wall tiling in bathrooms with a choice from a range of exciting colours.
∗ Generous electrical specification including strip light/shaver point and mirror in bathrooms, T.V. point, telephone point, bell push and porch light.

Figure 9.12 Houses built privately in the 1920s are similar to those shown in an advertisement for a modern housing estate

Figure 9.13 A city plan with strong geometrical lines

Figure 9.14 A housing estate on the city margins

The removal of many people from the inner cities either to housing estates on the outskirts of the city, or even to completely new towns such as Harlow in Essex (see Chapter 11), allowed architects to build homes at a lower density. Thus it was possible to open up the inner city and improve the environment. At the same time it was possible for everyone to see the results of local authority achievements. It was believed that refurbished houses could never have made the same point. New tall buildings could be seen, refurbished ones had too low a profile both physically and politically.

The problems of inner city upheaval

In the last few decades there have been many major upheavals in society. Some of the most important have resulted from changes in the family unit (see Chapter 3). Families have become smaller, there are more divorces and single parent families; there are more old people, particularly older single women, and fewer elderly parents live with their adult children. Furthermore, families have become scattered, perhaps throughout a city, more and more commonly across the country. There have been great changes in employment opportunities requiring people to retrain and often to move to new locations, and also leaving a number of people without work.

Ironically, the problems of inner city refurbishment are compounded by people willing to buy the better housing stock. There is much financial potential in the older housing stock within the city. In the past many of the more substantial properties have been subdivided to provide low cost but poor quality rented accommodation. Now many of these houses are being refurbished to provide town homes for the more affluent. The people moving into these areas are typically caricatured as 'yuppies' (young upwardly-mobile professional persons). Their arrival, which brings the first injection of capital for many decades to such areas, sometimes arouses the anger of the poorer people who do not have the income for refurbishment (Fig. 9.15).

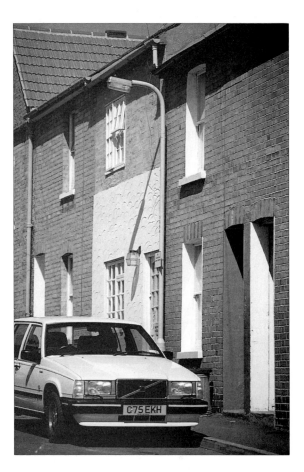

Figure 9.15 Upgraded housing with quality motor cars contrasts strongly with the majority of the housing stock in inner cities

Explain what are the attractions of the inner cities to the upwardly mobile younger element of society.

How has the presence of Yuppies altered the environment of selected inner city areas? On balance discuss whether this change seems to be good for the community as a whole.

All these changes put great stress on social cohesion. The strains can be compounded by great changes in the external environment such as urban renewal. People who are dependent on the local authority for their housing requirements may suffer particularly.

Student enquiry 9B

Problems of inner city estates

The 'brave new urban world' of the post-war planners and architects was to be fashioned out of the old by widespread slum clearance and followed by rebuilding to a new, organised plan. The major problem was how to create a more open environment where there was room for fields and trees. The scheme adopted involved moving people from two storey houses, where they used up all of the land area, into tower blocks.

The scheme was very worthy in its intent, so why did it cause social problems so severe that today no further tower blocks are being built and many of the existing blocks are being demolished?

A. Discovering the problems

1. Refer back to the concept of the ideal home. Identify those features of an ideal home that have been provided in a tower flat and those which are missing.
2. Discuss the contention of one of the most prominent architects of the twentieth century that 'the house is a machine for living in'. As a group contrast the implications of this principle for house design with the 'ideal home' described above.
3. It would have been cheaper to refurbish the old homes than to rebuild in the form of tower blocks. Suggest some reasons why this did not happen.

4. If houses were refurbished how could open spaces have been created?
5. The expression 'high rise blues' was coined to describe the psychological disorder that afflicted many young mothers whose home was a flat high up in a tower block. Suggest what high rise blues might be.
6. Many new developments are daubed with grafitti and are neglected by the same type of resident who used to take good care of a small terraced house. Suggest reasons for this.
7. In recent years government policy has been to allow people to buy their council flats or houses. The government sees this as a way to increase the independence of people and give them a cheap way of getting on to the private housing ladder.
8. Explain why some types of accommodation have been sold more easily than others. What might be the advantages and disadvantages of this strategy both for the environment and the people still waiting for council accommodation?

TOWER BLOCK LIVING BY CHOICE ONLY!

'Tower block living should not be forced upon young families,' says Theresa Shanahan, Chair of the Isle of Dogs Neighbourhood Committee.

Cllr Shanahan who lives very happily on the 13th floor of Knighthead Point is not critical of high rise housing as a concept. But under the right circumstances.

'For couples and single people, high rise living can be fine,' she says.

'It is when young families are allocated such accommodation without option that problems and suffering can arise.'

Cllr Shanahan is convinced that the lack of outlook can create an atmosphere of solitary confinement that is detrimental to the health of young mothers and their children.

'With lifts often out of order, it can literally mean no contact at all with the outside world.'

Mrs K Smith of Glengarnock Avenue is just such a case as she explained recently:

'In April I will become the proud mother of my third child, all will be under four years old.'

'I have 20 flights of stairs to climb daily and as one child is 19 months old I have to haul him up as well.'

The Isle of Dogs Neighbourhood Committee would like to see a housing lettings policy that did not allocate tower block accommodation to young families without their prior approval, especially in flats above the third floor.

But it is frustrating that under the new system of local government in the Borough, the Neighbourhood Committees are given the responsibility for the day to day mangement of the housing stock, but are not allowed a real say in the formation of housing policy.

'We are always being told that the Neighbourhood knows best,' says Cllr Shanahan.

'So why not involve us when it comes to tackling the root cause of housing hardship in our areas?'

Until that happens, Cllr Sha-

nahan believes her Committee will be powerless to help effectively people like Mrs Smith.

'With the homeless now being made a one only offer on a take it or leave it basis, we will find even more young families, who are forced into tower blocks, saying, "Why must we live like this?"' said Cllr Shanahan.

Mrs Smith summed up her feelings: 'I have asked for a transfer and been told I must wait until my third is a year old.

'By that time I will probably be walking up 40 flights as a double buggy does not fit the stairs, and I will have to make two journeys.

'I can't face the thought of climbing the stairs.

'It looks as though I am faced with a severe bout of depression because I am a prisoner in my own home.'

(Source: *Isle of Dogs Neighbourhood News*, No. 2)

Student enquiry 9B concluded

B Case study: inner Manchester

1. The material on this double page spread shows Moss Side in Manchester, an inner city area built in the latter part of the nineteenth century. As a group, try to list some of the advantages and disadvantages of living in this area.

2. Comment on the state of upkeep of the housing. This is an indication of the pride that people feel in their neighbourhood.

3. The adjacent area of Hulme was redeveloped in the 1960s because it was felt that the terraced houses were old and offered too few modern facilities. The estate is shown by photographs. Describe some of the contrasts in living style that might have been produced.

4. What conclusions can be reached by comparing the upkeep of Hulme and Moss Side?

5. In 1985 the residential population of the Hulme estate was 18 per cent lower than in 1981 whereas the population of Moss Side had remained nearly constant. Explain why the experiment in urban renewal did not work and some of the ways in which future progress could be made.

Hulme

Moss Side   Moss Side

Hulme

Moss Side

Renewing the industrial heart of a city

Attempting to renew the housing stock of the older city regions is one important part of city change; renewing the business sector is another. In this section we look at ways in which cities can be revitalised and get the money to rebuild their Central Business Districts (CBDs) (Fig. 9.16).

Most of the major cities in Europe have derelict central areas as a result of the demolition of old factory areas, or dockland and railway goods yard closures. Some of the largest central brown field sites occur around the discarded docklands of London, Liverpool, Manchester and Hull. In London there is a special shortage of inner city space and the opportunity has been taken to use the London Docklands for extending the employment opportunities in these central regions. The examples of Pittsburgh and Atlanta on the following pages help to set the scene by showing two aspects of schemes that have already been tried in America. As Britain develops its own brown field sites it should bear the US experiences in mind.

Figure 9.16 Urban renewal in the heart of Stockport, Cheshire. The upper photograph was taken in 1985, the lower one in 1988

Figure 9.17 Pittsburgh's central cityscape now shows few scars of the past

Figure 9.18 Modern offices dominate the CBD skyline

Pittsburgh, USA

Pittsburgh is one of the great steel making cities in the USA. As industry had to restructure to cope with global recession and overseas competition, Pittsburgh appeared to go into a terminal decline. The steel mills in the city suffered more closures than anywhere else in the world.

Traditional Pittsburgh was an old city, wracked by pollution from its heavy industry. Figures 9.17 and 9.18 show some views of the city today. The CBD is dominated by glass clad towers that house the headquarters of some of the most prestigious companies in the world. The CBD is thriving, and jobs are returning. The secret has been a collaboration between government, industry and universities. The state bought the site of the old steelworks and levelled it. Next they put in modern infrastructure and built high tech compatible offices for lease. At the same time the University of Pittsburgh (UPitt) decided to make an all out drive for software development. It was going to be a centre of brainpower industries, not try to be a second silicon valley.

The unique feature of Pittsburgh is the way the city has been helped to revitalise by the big corporations. They have provided most of the money to support new initiatives, helping small industries until they can support themselves.

Thus Pittsburgh has tried to come through its deindustrialisation by creating new jobs on vacant derelict *central* land. The problem that it still faces is how to keep a community of 'haves' and 'have nots' together into the future.

Figure 9.19 The crystal towers of the CBD are encircled by a dramatically less successful twilight zone

Atlanta, Georgia, USA

Atlanta, the corporate home of Coca Cola, is a city built around the mobility of the car. It is an example of city **ruralisation**. Unlike Pittsburgh there was not a core of heavy industry in Atlanta. With the expansion of the southern states since the 1970s new industry has located directly on peripheral green field sites. This has also encouraged the development of suburban housing development rather than inner city refurbishment (Fig. 9.19).

The main development within the city has been in the CBD. The result leaves the city centre hotels and banks rising from a sea of low nondescript slum buildings (Fig. 9.20). The inner city areas are predominantly populated by black people, the suburbs populated by white people.

Atlanta operated a racial segregation policy until the 1960s. It now operates a bussing policy to try to integrate the various ethnic groups dur-

Figure 9.20 The wealthy live at the city limits. Here there is no opportunity for poorer people except to provide services

ing school times. Until recently relatively little money was put into the black areas.

Atlanta shows how the central areas of a city need to be developed as a unit in order to help social cohesion. In Atlanta community life has all but disappeared – it has become the ultimate in the cellular society.

Student activity 9C

Finding the best way to develop Docklands

Study the information which shows various aspects of the London Docklands controversy.

1. Suggest the ideal environment from the viewpoint of a council house resident.
2. Why do council residents often resent the arrival of both industry and new home owners?
3. Assess the advantages of Docklands for a new resident in the housing developments recently built near the St Katherine's Dock. Explain why such residents can feel that they are a positive value to the area.
4. Prepare the case for development from the viewpoint of central government, explaining why it is impossible to attract jobs for the unskilled unemployed of the area.
5. Tourism is a new growth industry, helped by the Dockland Light Railway that connects the city with the Thames opposite Greenwich. Suggest the ways in which local people could adapt to find employment from this growth sector.

Council tower blocks overlook the new Docklands luxury housing

Part of the new Docklands office developments

With the way the Isle of Dogs is being developed it is not surprising that I am critical of how the LDDC goes about its business.

Filling the Island with luxury homes and office development, especially the proposed Canary Wharf, gives locals nothing.

But at Brunswick Wharf, India Dock Basin and the West Leamouth area there is the chance for local people to benefit, especially younger residents.

There can be homes for rent, local industry and job training schemes for the future.

And goodness only knows it's about time those who actually live in Tower Hamlets started getting some benefits

Roads All Around Them

'Cannons to the right of them, cannons to the left of them' says the famous poem about the charge of the Light Brigade.

But in the case of children at Woolmer Primary School, on the corner of Bullivant Street and Woolmer Street W14, it will be a case of Roads to right and left of them.

That's if road proposals by the LDDC for links into Canary Wharf go ahead.

For school children it will mean being slap in the middle of a main road junction.

Can you think of anywhere better **not** to have a school?

Cllr Christine Shawcroft certainly can't. And as a governor of the school she is determined to do whatever she can to prevent it.

'It's yet another proposal by the LDDC that will frustrate and annoy our community,' she said.

'But this time what they want to do is inconvenient and dangerous and must have a disrupting effect on young children at perhaps the most important time of their lives.'

Cllr Shawcroft is concerned that whatever arrangements are made for crossing these busy roads it will cause problems.

(Source: *Isle of Dogs Neighbourhood News,* No. 2, 1986)

: developments going on around

 Rosehaugh Stanhope were
g their scheme for this area they
hed us with the offer to discuss
ity gain.

se discussions we explained the
e need for local housing, indus-
recreation facilities.

Company listened and agreed to
them, as the front page article of
hbourhood News explains.

e stumbling block, yet again, is
)C. With the Corporation it is a
ake, take, take.

ere's money to be made the
gives that priority over every-

I have tried to explain the needs of our community to Reg Ward, the LDDC's Chief Executive but it is like talking to a brick wall.

And just as frustrating!

He is concerned only with raising still further land values, which are already £3 million an acre. This knocks on the head any hope of developing community schemes.

And yet the LDDC is a Quango set up by the Government. It is unelected and can therefore never be responsible to the people.

Like those living on the Isle of Dogs.

Believe it or not – when it was first set up the LDDC was told it must consider the needs of local people.

Nothing could be further from the truth.

Even when a developer is prepared to provide the homes and industry Tower Hamlets so badly needs the LDDC says No!

The Isle of Dogs Neighbourhood Committee will fight the Brunswick issue to the bitter end.

As for the residents I suggest you use your vote at the next election to make your feelings known..

(Source: Theresa Shanahan, *Isle of Dogs Neighbourhood News,* No. 2, 1986)

Future assured by imaginative approach

At the beginning of 1981 London's Docklands bore the scars of 20 years of decline and neglect. Dock closure had led to the disappearance of related industries. New industry did not take the place of the old and 8500 jobs were lost between 1975 and 1980. A shrinking, and increasingly elderly, population found itself isolated among wide tracts of derelict land and buildings.

Conventional local government solutions failed to halt the accelerating decline. A new approach was needed. The London Docklands Development Corporation was created in July 1981 and charged with the regeneration of the area. The Corporation is a single purpose statutory body appointed and funded by Central Government and accountable to Parliament. LDDC's entrepreneurial role in the development of the area has produced impressive achievements over the last five years under its two chairmen, Sir Nigel Broakes and now Christopher Benson.

A comprehensive programme of land acquisition, reclamation, infrastructure provision, community support and marketing has transformed Docklands into a major growth point in Central London. Over 300 companies have moved into the area since the formation of the corporation and private investment commitments to date exceed £1100 million.

This is an impressive record but the future shows even greater promise. The Docklands light railway, which has been jointly funded by the Corporation and London Regional Transport, is due to open in the middle of next year. Almost 10 km of new roads have already been opened with more on the way. A wide range of major developments are taking place and more are at the advanced stage of planning.

These exciting results stem from a single minded and imaginative approach to urban renewal, combining the best of both private and public sector approaches. The future is now very bright with the promise of yet further growth utilising the current technological revolution, just as the construction of the docks provided the impetus for the economic growth of London in the last century.

Nicholas Ridley
Secretary of State for the Environment

(Source: *New Civil Engineer,* 4 Sep. 1986)

High-priced docklands property to subsidise inner city regeneration

An ambitious scheme to provide high-priced homes in London's Docklands which will help to subsidise the lower priced shared ownership houses and rented accommodation is being considered by the Docklands Development Corporation (LDDC).

The scheme could be applied in all parts of the country which have a problem with urban or inner city regeneration. It would involve the public and private sectors combining in a way that both the government and the Prince of Wales, after his comments on housing last week, would approve.

Known as SHARE, Social Housing Asset Renewal Exchange, the proposed scheme for the London borough of Tower Hamlets is the idea of Assured Developments, a non-profit making organisation which is a co-adventure by a team of architects and professionals.

The concept has the full support of Mr John Patten, the Minister of Housing; Tower Hamlets also favours it, and it is being put out to tender with four other schemes by the LDDC.

Under the plan for a prime riverside site on the Isle of Dogs, a total of 275 flats would be built at full market value, with the generated surplus, forecast in the region of £5 million, used to fund the rehabilitation of 1000 run-down inner city homes without cost to the local authority. It already has the backing of a leading building society.

The essence of the scheme is a balance, on a four to one ratio, of low and high cost on homes.

That is based on the shared ownership properties being sold at a price affordable by those on average earnings in Tower Hamlets, about £7000–£9000 meaning properties at around £20 000–£21 000.

(Source: Chrisopher Warman, *The Times*, 13 Nov. 1986)

A stop for the light railway

St Katherine's Dock by the Tower

The ups and downs of Docklands

There has been much controversy over the success or failure of the London Docklands scheme and many extravagant claims have been made about how it will solve many of the capital's problems and also those of the local community. For example, it has been suggested that Docklands will play a major part in the predicted tourist boom as London regains its position as the world's leading finance centre in the light of the City's Big Bang and Canary Wharf project. Experts are predicting tourist figures to double in the next few years – particularly in the field of business visitors.

Business visitors represented 23 per cent of the domestic and overseas tourist market to London in 1985, accounting for 44 per cent of all tourist expenditure – a total of over £950 million. However, visitors are still complaining of inadequate hotel facilities. If these problems can be put right by developments in Docklands, then future business visitors to London may never need to go to the West End. Businessmen from neighbouring EEC countries will also be able to avoid lengthy delays at London's major commercial airports by using the the new London City Airport in North Woolwich.

Tourism is expected to be part of the permanent regeneration of Docklands. With this in mind, the LDDC has set about creating a new environment that will act as a counterpoint to the traditional tourist facilities that exist in the West End of London, but on a scale unparalleled elsewhere in Europe.

The rapidity of achieving a financial return in the mid 1980s convinced hard-nosed City and property investors that putting money into the docks is not the high risk venture it was once believed to be.

Mr Ward, chief executive of the LDDC, identifies six factors in the LDDC's success: the changed views about Docklands, the advent of the Dockland's Light Railway and its extension to Bank Station in the City, the creation of the Isle of Dogs Enterprise Zone, the agreement to locate the London City Airport in the Royal Docks, the sitings in the docks of the London Earth Satellite Teleport and the massive proposed development of a new financial district at Canary Wharf.

However, the Docklands scheme has recently fallen on harder times, illustrating how the success of an area depends on long-term geographic factors rather than short-term speculation by financiers. One of the main problems confounding further development into the 1990s is the fluctuating property market. In the peak of the property market in 1987 people were falling over themselves to buy and lease properties for residential and commercial uses. This meant that all looked fair for the development of hotels and entertainment facilities and the growth of tourism revenues. With this came the prospect of more jobs for local people. But the collapse of the market the year after has left many property owners in difficulties and now there is less confidence about whether Docklands can really compete, as it aspires to, for West End shoppers and eaters-out, and the residences of the smart traditional areas of London.

Whether the LDDC succeeds in convincing the sceptics that it is a viable alternative to the West End and City depends partly on aspects of development which the LDDC has until recently not made an absolute priority – transport.

The equivalent development in Paris – La Defense – saw the planning of the infrastructure first and the commercial properties later. It was a paced out development which, in the political climate in Britain, could not be matched. In the case of Docklands, the pace of development was such that the two had to try to go hand in hand. It has not quite worked out this way and, although Docklands sports a bright new Light Railway, this is insufficient to carry the numbers of people who will want to use it in just a few years from now. At present the Light Railway carries only 4000 people an hour as far as the Tower of London – it does not connect with the heart of the City. As a result it can take nearly an hour to get from the City to Docklands offices, and this makes recruiting very difficult at the secretarial level and also restricts the free flow of people wanting to move easily about the city. In practice, Docklands is discovering that it cannot develop successfully as an independent island but must become an integral part of the city.

(Source: *Based on an opening address to a schools audience by a geography lecturer,* 1989)

CANARY WHARF: a man-made monster

Canary Wharf is an artificial peninsula about the length of The Mall which juts out into the West India docks on the northern fringes of the Isle of Dogs. Dotted about are the little successes of the London Docklands Development Corporation – fragments of slick architecture erected by companies eager to exploit the financial and planning incentives available for dockland revivers.

In 1976 the Chicago Financial Futures Market was born and, since then, financial services have been exploding in all directions. Vast, open-plan floor areas are now required to provide instant visual and personal communication between dealers. In addition, massive computer and air-conditioning requirements mean that the floors have to be deeper – 15ft against 11 or 12ft in the usual office building.

The significance of the Greenwich Meridian is that it indicates Britain's ancient role as the centre of the world. Today it makes sense because we lie in a time zone between New York and Tokyo. The new financial markets have to be in action 24 hours a day, so a centre in Western Europe is essential. With its language and a history as a financial capital London is the obvious choice.

So Canary Wharf was born. The overall plan, put together by the banks – and including some 20 schemes – is so big that it justifies its own telephone, electricity, water and rail systems. Potential customers will buy a freehold and have their own building designed, although it will have to meet with the approval of the consortium's architects, Skidmore, Owings and Merrill, the biggest firm of its kind in the world.

No planning permission is necessary as the area is designated as an Enterprise Zone and customers will get a six-year rates holiday as part of the package. And the promised benefits seem staggering: once the holiday ended, the rate income for the borough of Tower Hamlets would double instantly; 57 000 permanent new jobs would be created; the Chancellor would receive £340 million extra in tax and national insurance, and so on.

(Source: *The Times,* 2 May 1986)

Chapter 10
Environments in developing world cities

Introduction

The rise of the developing world city is one of the main features of twentieth century urbanisation. Its origins and circumstances of growth often give it a distinctively different appearance from the developed world city. However, it should be remembered that there is a whole spectrum of cities within the developing world and they can only be briefly sampled in a single chapter.

This chapter looks at some of the issues raised by rapid growth – particularly of megacities – and investigates some of the possible solutions. Because of the wide variety of circumstances of growth there is often no single model that can be used as the basis for explaining the pattern of development. This makes planning all the more difficult.

The statistics of city living

At present over 40 per cent of the world's 5 billion people and 80 per cent of the developed world's population live in cities. Between 1925 and 1950 at least 100 million people in the developing countries – about 10 per cent of their rural populations in 1925 – permanently migrated from rural to urban areas; between 1950 and 1975 the number rose to about 330 million – about 25 per cent of the rural population in 1950 (Fig. 10.1). These figures do not include the countless millions who migrated on a seasonal basis or just for short periods. In the developing world today the number of people added to cities each year is equivalent to adding the people of a country the size of Spain (about 40 million).

Most of the urban population increase is taking place in the biggest cities. This is because people bypass the smaller towns and cities in their exodus from the countryside. If this rate of city growth continues, then by the year 2000 twenty

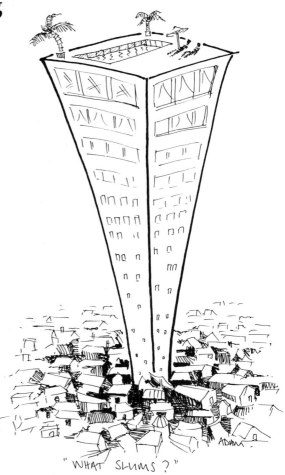

"WHAT SLUMS?"

of the twenty-five major conurbations of more than 10 million people will be in the developing world (Fig. 10.2).

However, migration is not the prime cause of expansion in many of today's megacities. This early cause for expansion has been eclipsed in many countries by the growth generated within the cities themselves. Of a sample of 29 developing countries, 60 per cent of urban growth was found to be from within the cities, with 10 per cent more increase due to reclassification of suburban areas or small towns from rural to urban status. Even so, the 30 per cent that is due to migration can often be overwhelming in terms of the city's ability to provide an adequate infrastructure.

Problems with megacities

Cities serve basic functions of service, and for services to be maintained there has to be a reasonable degree of mobility. In general mobility is inversely related to city size throughout the world. Thus, by the time cities have about five million inhabitants there are signs that mobility is becoming severely reduced. Characteristically this is seen in the interminable traffic jams that haunt such cities.

When cities have grown and contain over 10 million people, each person can often only sensibly reach one sector of the metropolis each day (Fig. 10.3). At this stage the whole urban system begins to break down. Thus city problems are related to absolute size rather than proportion of a country in urban areas. In the developing world the problems are often accentuated by the lack of capital to provide adequate mass transit systems, or to improve the road infrastructure to aid traffic flow.

Most developing countries see their degree of urbanisation as 'excessive', even though on average cities contain less than 40 per cent of their populations. As a result, over three quarters of

Figure 10.1 These photographs show scenes from Jakarta, its skyscrapers locating the formal business district (a, above), set in a sea of low rise workshops and dwellings (b, below)

developing world governments are actively pursuing policies either to slow down or reverse internal migration. In centrally planned economies such policies can be effective: in China, for example, residence permits are used to control the movement of people. In more liberal societies this is not a practical solution.

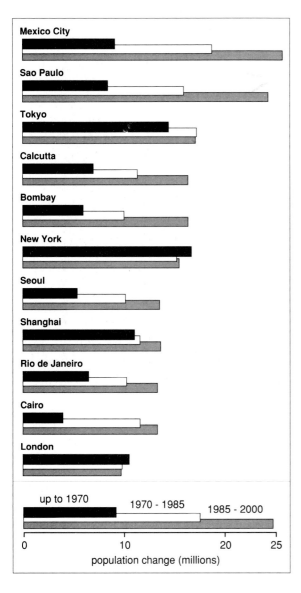

Mexico City

Sao Paulo

Tokyo

Calcutta

Bombay

New York

Seoul

Shanghai

Rio de Janeiro

Cairo

London

up to 1970   1970 - 1985   1985 - 2000

0   10   20   25
population change (millions)

Figure 10.2 The world megacities

Criticisms of developing world cities

People have criticised developing world cities in the following ways:

A. Confusion
1. There is no clarity of organisation in planning.
2. Most urban plans state too many objectives.
3. There is no clear set of priorities given for the plan objectives.
4. The plans fail to appreciate the relationship between urban and rural planning.

B. Apathy
1. The rich and powerful elites have strong motives for maintaining the status quo.
2. The ownership of land is the key to planning, but the wealthy are unwilling to give it up.
3. Schemes to raise the living standards of the poor are developed with little understanding of the initiative and community pride which exist even in poor areas, or the social and financial penalties that might be produced.

C. Symbolic schemes
1. Urban plans are based on western ideas indiscriminately transferred by planners trained in developed world institutions.
2. Plans rely on big prestige schemes or grand designs which use resources ineffectively.
3. Public participation in decisions is usually only a formality.
4. The needs of the poor are frequently misrepresented.

One solution often put forward by planners is to encourage people to move to the smaller centres. However, making small and medium sized towns an attractive alternative to major cities is a hard task. This is because people perceive that they can maximise their job opportunities by seeking work in the largest possible city. They argue that they are more likely to find an employment niche even if the unemployment rate is high. A large city is also more likely to contain other people from migrants source regions who can support them, find them work and share experiences on how to survive in an urban world.

The attraction of people to small and medium sized cities has really been successful only in South Korea and this is probably because the economy is growing so fast that job opportunities exist everywhere.

Student enquiry 10A

Problems of megacities

These pages contain extracts from an article in *The Times* which gives some first hand information about living in Cairo, one of the developing world's great cities. Overleaf is a photograph of part of central Cairo.

1. Using the information, write down some of the major problems facing the city.
2. Comment on whether these problems seem to relate only to Cairo, or whether there are parallels with developed world cities such as London.
3. Assess how far Cairo matches the criticisms listed on the previous page.

Crowded Cairo

You cannot find a map of all Cairo these days. The city is simply growing too fast for the cartographers. Even the modern maps show fields where there are now tenements, canals which have long ago turned into open sewers, cemeteries which now contain more living inhabitants than dead.

At Giza, new housing now runs almost to the Great Pyramids. In many inner city slums, the poor do not often know their exact address. The old centre of Cairo is surrounded by a thick belt of poverty. The tenements of Imbaba on the west bank of the Nile eventually face the square miles of misery in Chobra and Bulaq and the big rail yards behind Ramses Street station. To the east lies the City of the Dead, the acres of Mameluke tombs in which, so recent estimates suggest, there live more than three million of Cairo's poor.

The few oases left in this desert are confined to the rich or to the foreign residents of the city that once called itself Mother of the Earth.

Abdul-Rahim Abdul-Sayeh lives with 25 dead men and 27 dead women. He says this with a sort of affirmative nod, as if daring us to disagree. He sells soft drinks from a battered ice-tub outside the flaking walls of an Ottoman mausoleum. He has lived in the cemetery all his life.

Behind him, in street after sweltering street, between graves and mosques of mourning and beside sarcophagi of white marble, live the people of the City of the Dead – three million of them, if conservative estimates are to be believed – a whole community, perhaps a fifth of Cairo's entire population, who have sought sanctuary from homelessness by cohabiting with the dead.

They eat in the little rooms reserved for prayer and sit in the cool of the evening below tablets which record the passing of Cairo's former, but infinitely wealthier, inhabitants. Around the cemetery of Mukater alone there are three primary schools for the children of the City of the Dead. On hot afternoons when even the dust acquires a distinct, fetid smell, they can be found on the door-

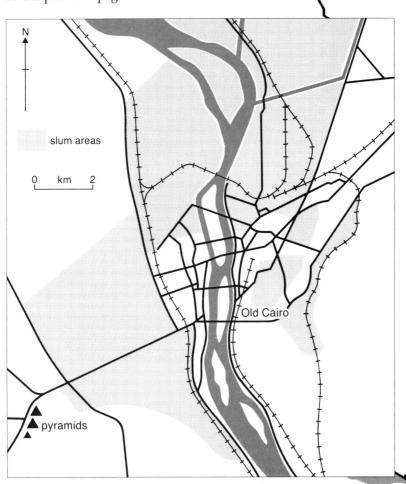

N

slum areas

0   km   2

Old Cairo

pyramids

steps. Some of the men work as drivers or soldiers or garbage collectors. A whole community specialises in the recycling of rubbish, brought to its shanty town on the railway tracks below the Mokkatam hills by the 10 year old scavengers who cart their broken metal, old wheels and offal up from the muck of the city centre in wagons.

'Yes, you can come in,' Zakkiyeh Mohamed says with domestic politeness, and she pulls aside a tattered curtain to lead us into her little tomb. It is not *her* tomb, of course. The grave in the back garden is clearly marked 'General Abdul Rahmeh Beik Fahmi, Died 1928'. It's a fancy affair, with an inscription in classical Arabic and a military coat of arms.

'We live here. What else can we do?' she asks. 'My neighbours and I – we came from Beni Sueff 40 years ago. We have nowhere else to live. We are better off than those who live in the centre of the city.'

Is she? Sultan Ahmed Mabrouk used to be a grave digger in the cemetery. 'We sleep with the dead,' he says. 'There is no fear. But the government does nothing for us.' He is an old, old man – 'I am 75 or 80, I think,' he says – and he falls half asleep as he talks, almost one with those who lie beneath the floor of his house. From the crumbling mosque outside Sultan Ahmed's funereal home, you can just make out the smog above Chobra and Bulaq. It takes three quarters of an hour to negotiate the traffic jams down to the Nile, through streets of dilapidated tenements. A boy of perhaps eight whips two donkeys hauling a wooden cart of trash up to the Mokkatam hills. I try to take a photograph of him and a policeman runs up. 'Go away – you are not allowed to do this,' he screams. 'Go and take pictures of the Pyramids. You have other things to do.'

Below the broken Turkish aqueduct a fruit market is wedged between piles of garbage. 'No pictures!' an urchin shrieks when he catches sight of my camera. In an alleyway of hovels, each built atop the other, the shattered balconies draped with old washing, a man cries out: 'Why do you look at us? Who are you? Are you a spy?' There can be no dignity amid this squalor.

Chobra stretches for miles up across the rail tracks and over the groaning iron bridge across the Nile, where old men sleep beside the fuming buses, where the dust settles on your perspiration until you find your body enveloped in a kind of grey, greasy film. But the worst is at Bulaq. Bulaq is not its real name. Years ago, the French residents of Cairo built their gracious mansions here, on the very edge of the Nile. They called the place 'Beau Lac' and the breeze of the river cooled their spacious rooms at night.

But the Nile slunk away westwards, leaving only a swamp for the poor to live in around the abandoned mansions. The houses were replaced by cheap tenements and the poorest of the poor built homes on top of their tenements. Their children built shacks on top of the homes on top of the shacks on top of the homes on top of the tenements.

Bulaq expanded upwards as well as sideways, a contusion behind the new corniche where tourists in the Ramses Hilton Hotel have no conception of the endurance that goes on a few yards from their air conditioned rooms. All Bedrooms face west, towards the Nile, and the fertile island of Gezira. Sometimes, across Cairo, the tenements simply collapse under the weight burying their occupants in ancient lift shafts, stone and muck. The Egyptian papers routinely call these events 'tragedies', reporting them like some natural phenomenon, an earthquake or an act of God.

The statistics are as awesome as the slums. A national population of 51 million, a new baby every 24.4 seconds, a city that may have at least 14 million people living in it, clinging to the wiry river and its waterways: more than 99 per cent of the population lives in only 4 per cent of the total area of the country, living off the fertility of the Nile, yet daily cutting into its clay to make bricks for houses for people who need more food.

Now the World Bank and International Monetary Fund want to call in

their loans; they want President Mubarak to withdraw subsidies on basic foodstuffs. Foreign capital is drying up in Egypt as surely as – does Mubarak realise this? – the patience of Cairo's poor. 'Not long ago, I went around the city and saw something I had never seen before. The speaker is Mohamed Heikal, the Egyptian writer and journalist whose expansive, eloquent assessments are perhaps too often sought out by foreign journalists. But he is not expansive now. He has been doing a little street reporting of his own, trying to find out why the Egyptian security police rioted earlier this year.

'I found something extraordinary,' he says.

'I came across a whole series of cancerous new communities around the city, 200 communities that no one has registered, in places that weren't even on the map. How many people live in Cairo now? How many people will live there in the year 2000? Twenty-three million? Twenty-five million?

'There will be a thousand of these cancerous, unknown communities then, surrounding and preying on the jungle of the old city. For all God Knows, the rest of Cairo will collapse into rubble . . . .'

Cairo, of course, will not disappear from the map, even if it redefines our notion of a 'city'. It may become a place from which people ultimately flee. Yet in Egypt, there is nowhere for them to go.

An American aid official put it grimly enough a couple of months ago. 'You think things can't get worse, but they can. And in the end, there will be some kind of upheaval. Maybe the Army will hold things for a while. Maybe religion will sustain the people. But it's going to get worse . . . .'

(Source: Robert Fisk, *The Times*, 4 July 1986)

Student enquiry 10A concluded

Figure 10.3 Traffic flow in Bangkok. Although this city has a network of wide roads, the absence of a mass transit system for the 10 million inhabitants means that traffic is almost permanently congested and cross-city journeys can take several hours

Cities without models

In the previous chapter we focused on developed world cities and the way in which a certain combination of economic and planning policies had given the cities their common characteristics. It is, however, very difficult to apply developed world city models such as those of concentric zones to a developing world situation.

The developed world city model rests partly on an assumption of rapidly increased mobility, a graduation of wealth and the ability of people easily to improve their quality of life by, for example, buying a better house. In the developing world there is not the same spread of wealth. Only a relatively small part of the population is able to earn enough money to enter the formal housing market, and there is an almost un-

bridgable gap between these people and the majority who have limited financial resources. Further, the the majority of the population are not mobile. Most people still walk to work rather than use mass transit systems because they cannot afford the fares. As a result the majority still need to be close to their place of work.

There is often a vast difference between the wealth of the few 'haves' who make up a strikingly conspicuous elite (Fig. 10.4), and the vast mass – the 'have nots'–, who are equally strikingly poor (Fig. 10.5). It is for this reason that people have dubbed developing world cities 'cities of peasants'. There is little opportunity for many of these people to span the enormous gap from initial poverty to a stage where they can join the middle class and begin to advance along the improvement ladder that is taken for granted in the developed world.

Unlike the developed world city, which receives much of its services either on a do-it-yourself basis or through mobile service companies, virtually all middle class families in the developing world will have domestic servants. Sometimes these will be residential, but more often they will have to find their own accommodation. Low wages and the cost of transport makes people want to live close to their work. Thus the developing world city often has modern spacious housing cheek by jowl with a collection of shanty or slum dwellings (Fig. 10.6). This often gives rise to issues of where people should be allowed to stay.

Figure 10.4 A view over the wealthy suburb of Haus Khaz in Delhi

Figure 10.6 Middle class and shanty dwellings side by side in Bombay

Figure 10.5 A shanty development by the railway line in Calcutta

Planning issues

Administrative pressure

With a limited financial 'cake' to share out, and with power firmly in the hands of the elite, there is a quite distinctive form of planning and control both in terms of employment and housing opportunities.

Most developing world governments try to find money to supply services to the city. They give the city preference over the country for several reasons:

(i) it requires less per capita expenditure because people are close together and services are more easily connected;

(ii) city improvements allow greater productivity for industry and therefore greater output. In turn this allows local products to be substituted for imported ones and saves

on foreign exchange. It may even produce considerable potential for export. Service improvements to the country are, by comparison, often thought to be less cost effective; and

(iii) the city is more politically aware and civil unrest is more likely to come from the city than the country where people are poorly organised politically.

Because there are so few wealthy people the amount of money raised by tax in the developing world city is quite insufficient to provide the range of services and the infrastructure always taken for granted in the developed world. People in developed world cities may complain because their leaking taps have not been serviced recently; in many areas of the developing world cities there are no taps in houses to complain about!

Coping with the speed of growth

Part of the contrast between developed and developing world cities can be found in the smaller amounts of revenue they have at their disposal. But part can also be found in the speed with which people have migrated from country to city and the nature of employment opportunities. A growth of population which took over a hundred years to achieve in the developed world cities has,

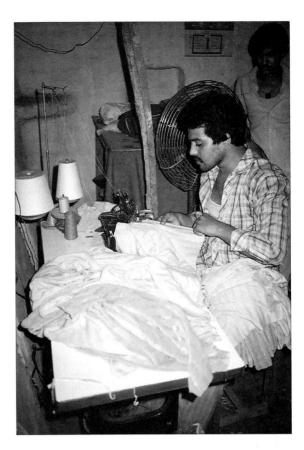

Figure 10.7 Informal tailoring in a hut within a shanty settlement. The electricity to power the machine comes from an illegal tapping from the overhead power cables

for example, been completed in a mere couple of decades in many developing world cities. It is doubtful whether even the wealthiest developed world cities could provide the infrastructure or the housing stock for a population that doubles itself every 15 years.

The problem is aggravated further because the people migrating from the countryside have largely been engaged in a subsistence farming economy. They have not had the advantages of education that we take for granted and they probably do not have the skills (even as basic as reading and writing) required for many new city activities. As a result they cannot gain well paid jobs and begin to improve their status.

With no chance of government support and no money, many people either have to sleep on the streets or begin to build a home with materials discarded by others. Indeed, for example, Mexico City's largest 'suburb' the 'city' of Netza, is at the site of Mexico City's largest rubbish dump, and has been largely constructed from its chief resource – rubbish. Because there is no chance of government help people do not expect assistance as is the rule in the developed world. Here survival depends on self help and most people intend slowly to upgrade their shacks for themselves. None of this will happen quickly and allowance must be made for the time involved. In the meantime the city is going to look a mess – from a developed world viewpoint, that is.

Employment

During the rise of many developed world cities manufacturing industry was very labour intensive and jobs were relatively easily had, even if the pay was poor. By contrast people seeking work in a developing world city today find unskilled jobs in modern industries very hard to find. For the mass of unskilled people the only way to make a living is to accept jobs with very low wages outside the modern factory system (Fig. 10.7). Alternatively they have to share out the demand for personal services – and services provided for the poor cannot give high incomes

(Fig. 10.8). As a result, alongside the modern (or **formal**) form of earning a living (e.g. in an office or registered factory) lies the alternative small scale form of employment, known as the **informal, unorganised or bazaar system**. Many products used in the modern formal economy were made at least in part by the informal sector.

People in high rise modern flats who work in offices can look down on the clusters of people living in shacks and engaged in the production of simple products or providing basic services, using the street as their shop (Fig. 10.9). They may even employ some of the people as guards or domestic servants. Jostling among the morass of modern cars is a bewildering variety of hand and animal drawn carts, rickshaws and other unmotorised means of getting about. Because of the wide gulf between these alternative forms of urbanisation, neither shows any signs of decreasing, rather, they are increasing together, perhaps even in step and they are certainly heavily interdependent.

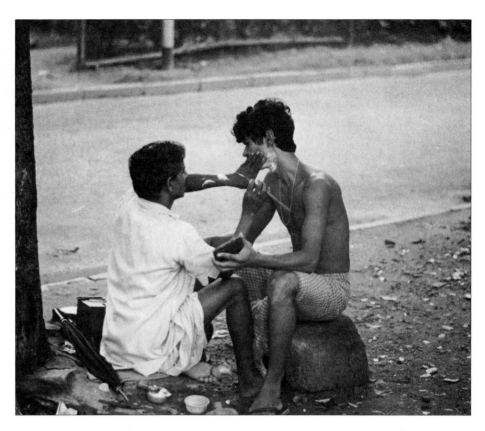

Figure 10.8 Informal services: this man is offering the personal service of shaving

The main problem faced by people in the informal sector is that it is extremely hard to earn enough money to rise above or even reach the (official) poverty line. Most people are in debt. This debt, which is often transferable to their heirs and other family members when the debtor dies, is little short of a modern form of slavery.

Housing

Different types of housing

If you have enough wealth there is no problem finding somewhere to live in a developing world city. Usually you can pick something that is low rise and in an area of low density. But you don't have to go out to the peripheral suburbs to find this – bid rent (which operates for the formal sector only) will ensure that you can achieve a good quality of living fairly close to the centre. And while very expensive areas of housing exist in all developed world cities in select areas such as London's Hampstead or Los Angeles' Beverly

Hills, they still form a minor part of the city scene. By contrast, in the developing world city such minorities often own the majority of the land.

Normally the middle and upper classes of society have a choice of location within the city. However, because of poor mobility, and because many of the more wealthy people are involved in the central business sector, a central location for living is often preferred to a peripheral one. Alternatively, people will choose a peripheral location near to a good communication line. In small cities, such as Nairobi in Kenya where the population is less than 2 million, the more wealthy occupy a wedge of land stretching out from near the centre and along a good access route. This area of spacious housing and gardens contrasts with other parts of the city where people are very tightly packed together. In large cities, such as Bombay, the wealthy sections of the population occupy large 'islands' within the city.

For the majority, however, somewhere to live consists of either a slum or a shanty settlement.

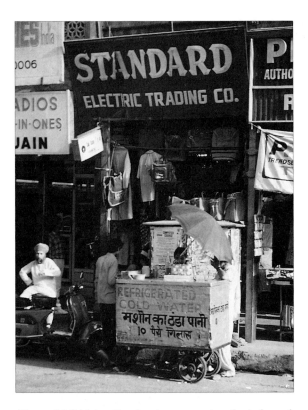

Figure 10.9 Using the street as a premises for informal trading maximises the use of space but alters the whole perspective of the urban scene

(*Note: First you must get used to looking at this kind of settlement. In each of the shanty and slum photographs in this chapter look at the general scene but then look in more detail. Do not judge everything by western norms. Rather, ask the question: does this provide a start on the housing ladder, does it satisfy at least some basic requirements? Also remember the climate may be quite different from that experienced in most developed countries.*)

A **shanty** settlement is occupied by squatters, i.e. those in illegal occupation of land who have to build their homes from available materials such as corrugated iron and pieces of cardboard box or rags (Fig. 10.10). A **slum** is a legal dwelling which is sub-standard (on a developed world scale) due to age, neglect or because it has been divided up into tiny living spaces. Most slums are dilapidated conventional dwellings in the older sections of the city often close to the CBD (Fig. 10.11).

Because squatter settlements (shanties, spontaneous settlements) are illegal most of them are

Figure 10.10 These are shanty huts because they do not have the right of legal land possession. They have been built of old tins that used to contain cooking fat

ignored by the city authorities and provided with no form of infrastructure such as water, sewage, electricity or roads. They are therefore very little burden to the local authorities. Most of the inhabitants are forced to become masters of innovation and most squatter settlements do have an intricate network of both water and electricity supplies taken illegally from nearby city service lines.

The nature of acquiring somewhere to live varies with culture. In Latin America, for example, squatting and establishing a new shanty settlement is often a highly organised operation by a relatively large group of families who arrive overnight to stake their claim. They operate on the principle that it is much harder to evict large numbers of people. This overnight occupancy has given such people the nickname 'parachute troops' in Mexico City, for example. However, in Asia the movement is more of the style of individual infiltration and marginal growth around existing settlements, working on the principle that a few more won't be noticed.

In all cases of settlement the most important location requirement is to be near to, and preferably next to sources of employment. In some cases this may be on the city periphery because the city rubbish tips may be the resource that enables people to earn a living, but most often it is near the centre of the city or near the elite regions. This is because it is here that the greatest opportunities

Figure 10.11 Slums in Calcutta's central area. Here tiers of housing rise above the shops with tents perched on the rooftops

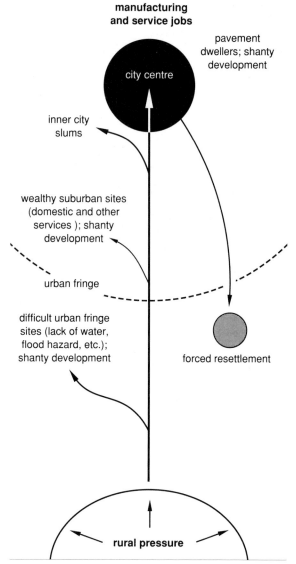

Figure 10.12 Suggested movements of low income people within a developing world city

for employment lie. Some people hope to work in domestic capacities, others perform public services such as sewage collection (e.g. India's notorious night soil people who collect the waste from the outside privies) and others work in the informal industries that supply part-made products to the formal factories.

The draw of work is stronger than the draw of somewhere to live (the opposite to the developed world philosophy) and so people are prepared to live on the pavements if this means they can earn a living (Fig. 10.12).

Planning for low income housing

City authorities are faced with a planning dilemma. If they want to continue to build part of the city to the equivalent of western standards, then they must evict squatters and even pull down slums. The occupants will then need re-

housing. Planners are under extreme pressure to pull down and bulldoze away the shanty settlements in order to improve the quality of the area for those in good accommodation. The pressure is to do this irrespective of whether or not building will soon start in that place. At the same time planners do see that the people existing in these conditions need a place to live.

One of the ways in which many authorities have tried to solve this problem is by **resettlement**

Figure 10.13 Resettlement colonies that are operated on a self-build basis. To begin with they had a high failure rate; now people are coming to terms with them

schemes. In this system squatters are forcibly evicted from their sites, but at the same time given an entitlement to a concrete pad in a resettlement zone or colony. This pad will form the base for the house they will be required to build for themselves. Pads are organised into patterns that allow roads and services to be introduced as the money becomes available (Fig. 10.13).

Unfortunately, whereas in western cities people would be pleased to be relocated to the peripheral suburbs, in the developing world city such relocation may spell economic disaster. Most job opportunities are in central city locations, near to elite districts or formal industry. Relocation divorces people from their source of employment and forces them to spend a large proportion of their income on transport. Even charging very low rents adds an additional financial burden because these people were used to paying no rent at all. Extra payments on transport and rent may well force them so far below the poverty line that they are compelled to sell their entitlement to the resettlement plot to lower middle income families (for whom it offers the prospect of a real and affordable improvement in living standard) and take their chances back in the city.

Many of the resettlement colonies of Delhi, for example, have return rates of over 15 per cent when they are first established, although with time most people come to terms with their situation. The major wage earners often now stay in the slums or shanties in the city centre, leaving the rest of the family to live in the colony. This is not a good way to retain family unity.

Self-help for low income families

The problem of slums is even less adequately dealt with largely because slum demolition cannot even be considered while there is an overall housing shortage. As a result much of the money made available to the low income sectors of the cities has to be used either to relocate squatters or to help provide some basic services. As soon as this is done the authorities tacitly agree to recognise their permanent situation.

Basic improvements of shanty settlements have many advantages over conventional housing projects:

    (i) they eventually provide adequate accommodation at much lower cost because the occupants are responsible for the upgrading of their own properties;

(ii) squatters often build their dwellings at greater densities than would be possible with formal high rise blocks and this allows smaller sites to be used in central areas;
(iii) the urban poor can match housing need to other priorities such as family size and income; and
(iv) it also gives the urban poor a more definite and acceptable role within the wider community.

There are also many reasons for the regular organisation of dwellings within a shanty. Most important is that plots that are more or less rectangular and uniform in size and have a front on to a street area can carry future urban services. These are more likely eventually to be registered as legal freehold properties. The 'official' requirements are well known to settlers when they share out the land and it strongly encourages them to follow the requirements when they first arrive. In effect they are doing their own urban planning.

Case study: Delhi, India

Chausat Khamba was a squatter community behind a hospital in Delhi. Hemmed in by high rise flats it was inconspicuous from the road, but it was complained of by the residents of the flats and targeted by Delhi's policy for demolition and resettlement. Chausat Khamba was a community of about 600 households, a total of 3000 people, many of whom had migrated from the south of India. Because many people were recent immigrants, there were about 100 men to every 44 women but the community still had a considerable number of families with children of school age. One day the demolition squad gave notice that the next day the people would be forcibly resettled and the land cleared. The resettlement would take place to a colony peripheral to the city, called Sundar Nagar. The facilities at Sundar Nagar were promised to be very much better than those they had to suffer as squatters.

During the move the people in each squatter hutment were given a ticket allocating them a piece of land 20 square metres in size on which they could build a new dwelling. At Sundar Nagar there was room for dwellings to have two rooms and a separate kitchen, as opposed to

Chausat Khamba where there was space for only one room. Sundar Nagar was well laid out and would be provided with services so that, for example, sharing was reduced from 1 water point for 200 families (at Chausat Khamba) to 1 point for 10 families (Fig. 10.14).

To an outsider it would seem that the temporary mud huts (known locally as **jhuggies**) with thatched roofs of Chausat Khama would have little to offer in comparison with the chance legally to own a large site. Near the hospital there was no electricity, no drainage and only four public lavatories. But the community was centrally located, close to a wholesale market which sold cheap food and close to all the institutions that employed the people. Some pulled rickshaws, others worked as government sweepers, some were painters, some pulled carts, some worked in textile mills, and others worked as mechanics in garages and repair shops. All these are central functions. Everyone could walk to work, and those with irregular hours and split shifts could come home and look after the children between working periods. And no one had to pay rent. They had also invested considerable time finding and scrounging the mud bricks of which their huts were made.

There were a number of problems during the move: the bulldozers moved in to Chausat Khamba very quickly and gave little time to recover the building materials which would be needed to start the next dwelling; when the people arrived at Sundar Nagar the public facilities had not been built and there were, for example, no lavatories (although they were later installed).

Most of the local logistic and infrastructure problems were solved within a few months of the move. However, some deep seated problems remained. For example, the local school near Chausat Khamba taught in Urdu, while the one available at Sundar Nagar taught in Hindi, and so the displaced children could not understand the class work. But even more important than this is that the colony is far from the source of employment and a long way from a market. As a result the people have to buy food from hawkers who visit their colony and this is more expensive than the market. In addition, 10 per cent of the income has to be spent on transport costs, while over 2

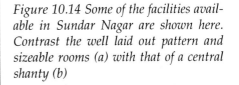

Figure 10.14 Some of the facilities available in Sundar Nagar are shown here. Contrast the well laid out pattern and sizeable rooms (a) with that of a central shanty (b)

hours a day in travelling time is needed. Furthermore, parents are no longer able to get home from work frequently to supervise their children, nor are there any child minders in the area.

People are thus better off physically but worse off financially and socially as a result of the move. On balance people put financial and social considerations above physical ones. Many have sold their rights to the plots and gone back to shanties nearer their work. In this way they have also made a profit on the move.

The municipal authorities are reluctant to continue with this form of resettlement. On the one hand this is because the middle class people complain that poor people misuse the land given to them and only move in order to be able to sell the land and make a profit. At the same time the

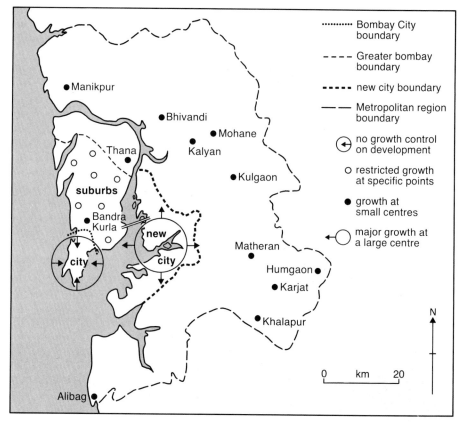

Figure 10.15 (a) The development plan for Bombay

Legend:
- Bombay City boundary
- Greater bombay boundary
- new city boundary
- Metropolitan region boundary
- no growth control on development
- restricted growth at specific points
- growth at small centres
- major growth at a large centre

Map labels: Manikpur, Bhivandi, Mohane, Thana, Kalyan, Kulgaon, suburbs, Bandra Kurla, new city, city, Matheran, Humgaon, Karjat, Khalapur, Alibag

N

0 km 20

Examples of city planning

1. Bombay

Bombay has a problem. It is the most successful city in India. As such it is the main magnet for a whole range of rural people who seek to make their fortunes. At the same time, the indigenous population is increasing rapidly.

The city has never developed an infrastructure to deal with the expansion. In its plan for the period between the 1960s and 80s only about a third of the proposals were ever put into effect, and most of these have been overwhelmed by the rapid rise in the population, lack of finance and bureaucratic delays. So the new plan aims to stop the rise in job opportunities in the most over-crowded region near the old port and direct it elsewhere. Can it succeed?

The plan for Bombay in the year 2001 proposes multiple growth centres (Fig. 10.15(a)). It plans for a metropolitan region 80 km by 70 km. In effect the plan seeks to achieve rational distribution of

middle classes complain that the squatters in the city are eyesores and should be removed. The people of Chausat Khamba wanted to be re-housed centrally because their wages are so marginal they cannot afford the transport cost involved in coming to work from the peripheral areas, but there is no room in central areas for such rehousing. These are the almost unmatchable conflicts that confront Indian and other developing world cities.

There are other strands to the argument. It is said that squatters are used as human tractors. As one of the settlers complained:

'The government policy is to send squatters to marshy land that has no value. In order to survive there they will have to raise it up; fill it in, even it up. Then by these improvements they will make the land valuable. Then, of course, it comes to the notice of the architects and planners, the developers and the builders. They say: "How come this valuable land is occupied by the poor? It is worth far too much for them." So you are pushed out.'

jobs, facilities and amenities and it proposes to achieve this by land use zoning, controls on population and a good transportation system. Thus it is intended that the northern suburbs of the city should take the strain away from the island city in the south.

The multicentred city requires strict prohibition of new industry on the island and the setting up of a port at New Bombay to act as a counter-magnet. Even offices and commerce must be diverted to New Bombay by prohibition on new office building.

However the plan suggests a population of about 10 million by 2001, whereas projections based on the 1981 census suggest a figure of at least 15 million. The reason for the provisions being directed at the low end of the scale is, as the planners state, there are not even sufficient financial resources to pay for the improvements required for a city of 10 million, let alone 15 or more million. Thus there is every prospect that the

Figure 10.15 (b) Mexico City, now the greatest urban area in the world

plans will be overwhelmed by events and that there will be sporadic improvements in a sea of slums whose numbers will be swelled by 5 million by 2001.

2. Mexico City

Mexico City is the world's largest city. Already having a population of 18 million, it is certain to have at least 25 million people by the year 2000 and possibly as many as 32 million (Fig. 10.15(b)).

Consider the difficulty that London, one of the world's richest cities, is having in supplying homes and jobs adequately to its population of a little over 6 million. This gives some idea of the staggering task facing a city authority with three times the population of London. Furthermore, the majority of the people are very poor. Mexico

Figure 10.16 Mexico City sprawls across an old lake floor

City now sprawls out over 50 km across a dried up lake bed; its suburban tentacles stretch out to twice that distance.

It took London 130 years to grow from 1 million people to 6 million; Mexico City did it in the 30 years from 1940 to 1970. London then stopped growing as the middle classes moved out to the countryside; Mexico City spent its next 15 years doubling its population again.

Mexico City has many infrastructure problems. There is no surface railway system for commuters. The railway was designed for long distance travel and has few stops that can be used by commuters. The grand central railway station handles less than 20 services a day.

Overcrowding on the roads means that people must live as close to their work as possible. Even then city workers spend on average two and a half hours travelling at an average speed as low as 4 km/hr.

Each day about two and a half million private cars crowd on to the streets bringing traffic chaos from early morning to late at night. The pollution generated by this traffic and the nearby industry is trapped by the surrounding mountains, causing an all pervading pall of pollution (Fig. 10.16).

The director of the urban development programme in Mexico City has remarked, 'We are breaking our heads over what to do about the motor car. It is killing the city. There are 2.5 million cars yet 90 per cent of them solve only 20 per cent of daily trip requirements. In contrast a mere 7000 buses carried 80 per cent of the 20 million trips a day'. The 80 km of underground system is a great help. It was opened in 1969 when the city was still only 9 million in population. Today it handles 3 million people (twice that of London's underground) on a network a seventh of the size of London. Fortunately for the mass of people the charge is only 1 peso (1/100th the cost in London) and this may help compensate for the phenomenal crush in the compartments.

Figure 10.17 Illegal shanty settlements in Mexico City

The city has a fifth of the country's entire population but it accounts for nearly half the industrial output and receives most of the educational and social opportunities. Even the 1985 earthquake, which shook the city and killed as many as 20 000 people (*see Challenge of the Natural Environment*, Chapter 1) has not disturbed this trend. It has merely shifted the focus. The headquarters of many administrative and financial institutions, which suffered the collapse of many of their buildings, have taken the opportunity to decentralise to the less crowded south and south-west of the core area. They have not been relocated in other parts of the country.

Half of the housing in Mexico City is illegally settled. A typical squatter settlement has a density of 75 000 in each square kilometre, seven times the density of London's densest borough (Fig. 10.17). Nearly a third of families live in one room. Nevertheless, conditions here are better than in the countryside: only 1 in 10 dwellings in the city lacks a water supply, compared with rural areas where it is 5 in 10. Only 3 in 10 homes in the city are not connected to a sewer against 5 in 10 in the country. One in ten lacks electricity in the city compared with 7 in 10 in the rural areas, and in the villages education is almost non-existent. Conditions are made even worse by the low prices forced on farmers for their food produce in order to achieve political stability in the city.

For all these reasons, and despite its problems of housing, pollution and traffic, about a thousand people a day migrate from the countryside. There is little sign yet of Mexico City slowing down its growth.

Socialist cities

China, the largest socialist country in the developing world, contains a quarter of the world's people and its housing problems are formidable. The Chinese have chosen a unique political philosophy to work under and this causes a very different city geography to those in the 'west'. Can it cope any better than India or Mexico?

As a socialist developing country China is often supposed to show the combined characteristics of the socialist and developing world in its cities. However, this is too simple a generalisation because the political system in China, although socialist, operates in a unique fashion (Fig. 10.18).

As in all socialist countries the state plays a decisive role in urban form through central planning. The state is much less prone to interference from market forces and bid rent is not a determinant of city pattern. However, as we have seen, market forces can provide an urban form which is acceptable to the majority, it can provide a ladder of opportunity, and people can see a way of progressing in their lives. A state run system adds

Fig. 10.18 Chinese cities have developed a unique style. This is the great Tiananmen Square near the forbidden city within Beijing

a layer of bureaucratic uniformity, a downward levelling. In the developed world state control has often led to drab uniformity, to depersonalisation of homes and streets. The great slab blocks of many local authorities, and the equally depressing slab blocks of Moscow and Warsaw show the effects of planning for large numbers.

In China the change from a feudal to a socialist society was an immense step. In the heart of Beijing, China's capital city, the Forbidden City still lies, a reminder of the imperial past. Here the new order stands clearly against the old. Grand new squares were built soon after the revolution of 1949. The enormous Tiananmen Square is the new focal centre of Beijing, a memorial to the unity of the people. It is also a memorial to the grand design and corporate identity of a socialist way of life.

The grand squares of a city tell little of the real way it works. Whereas the cities of many coun-

tries function independently of the countryside, in China countryside and city are welded together. This has been a matter of considered policy because it has been the intention, wherever possible, to make the countryside near a city the supplier of its foodstuffs. It is a realisation of a practical problem of a large developing country. In a city where fridges are uncommon and fuel precious, unnecessary transport of perishable foodstuffs should be avoided.

There is a general symbiotic relationship between the city and the countryside (Fig. 10.19). It is seen not only in the way food moves to the city, but also in the way in which waste from the city is taken back to the countryside and used as a fertiliser. It is an attempt at a truly self-sufficient relationship, much the way the world was organised before the industrial revolution.

The city region consists of the urban **shi** and the surrounding rural **xian**. Within the xian lie a

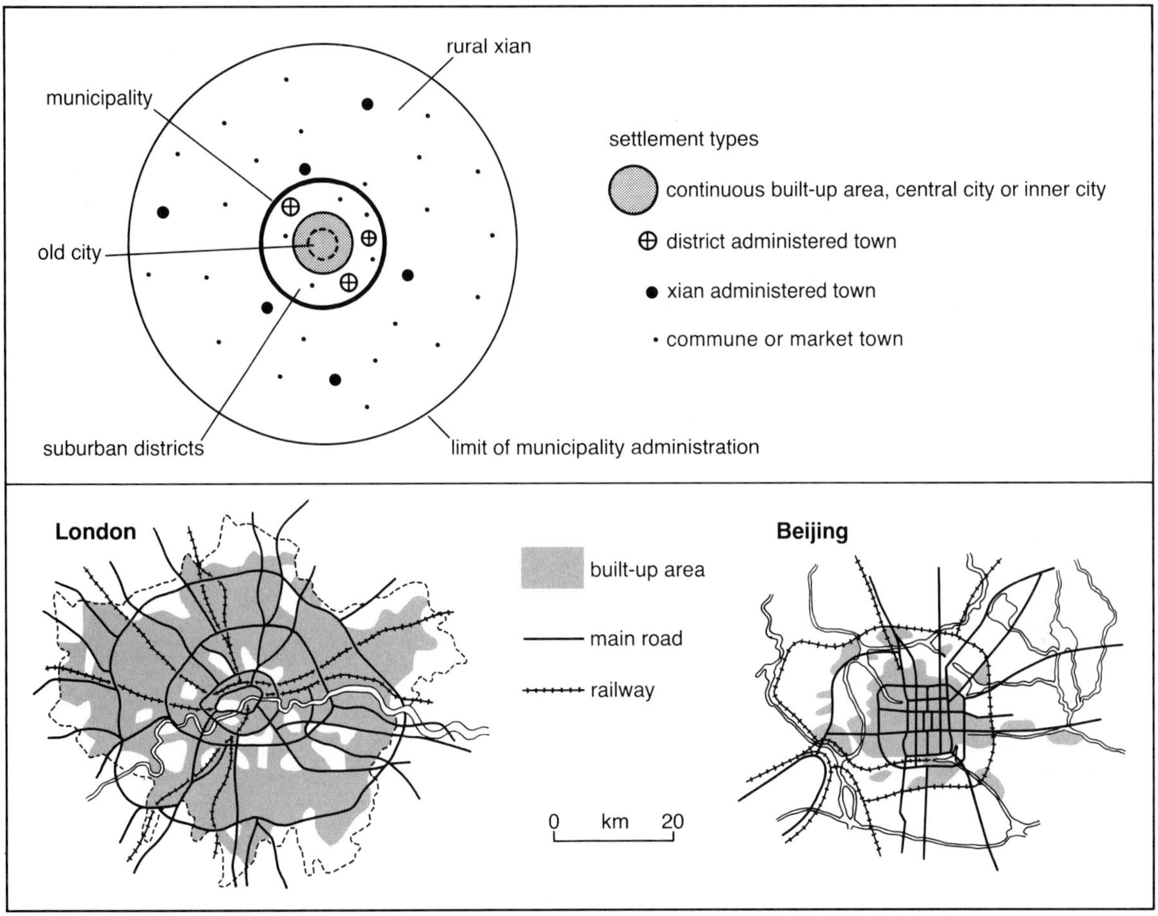
rural xian
municipality
old city
suburban districts
limit of municipality administration
settlement types
continuous built-up area, central city or inner city
district administered town
xian administered town
commune or market town
London
Beijing
built-up area
main road
railway
0 km 20

Fig. 10.19 The structure of a Chinese municipality

number of administrative towns as well as a multitude of villages, laid out and organised much as Central Place Theory would suggest. Within the city neighbourhoods are organised much like rural villages, each designed to be self-sufficient with both service facilities and industry. This is another reflection of planning to turn a natural inadequacy to advantage. In this case an inadequate level of transport has been a guiding light in promoting strong neighbourhood units.

Despite a state policy of disseminating services uniformly over the country, there is more advantage to being in the city that the countryside. This has led to a tendency to rural–urban migration. However, within a tightly controlled socialist state such migration can be held in check. This is achieved in two ways: first by controlling permits that allow movements, and secondly by controlling the location of new industrial projects. For example, so great has the population pressure on Beijing been that it is now policy not to locate any new industrial projects (and thus job opportunities) in Beijing. Those that have been required in the area have been redirected to the satellite towns. The policy is thus to keep Beijing at its current size until at least the end of the century.

As you can see, the problems of shanty development and suburban growth can be contained, but only at the price of restricting individual freedom of action. It is a trade off that only brings some advantages when it is strictly enforced. Because of the difficulties of enforcement, the Chinese pattern of development is not an easy model to copy in the rest of the developing world. Political changes within China have now resulted in a slackening of central control and insensitive blanket directives. It will be interesting to see how this new pattern of control will influence the growth of Chinese cities.

Student enquiry 10B

Comparing cities of the world

Although it is easy to talk about a developing world city, it is sometimes less easy to know what standards of living really are like. This chapter and Chapter 7 provide the basis for making such comparisons.

1. The diagrams on page 215 give standard of living profiles. Suggest the criteria that could be used to compile the profiles.
2. Describe, and attempt to account for the standard of living profiles for a capitalist city, a socialist city and a developing world city.

3. Draw the profiles, placing them side by side in such a way as to show how the standard of living may be compared on a world basis. Justify your decision.
4. Study the article 'Chinese critics of small cities ...' which discusses the way in which the state is trying to cope with popular pressure for change. In the context of patterns in other countries throughout the world, discuss the advantages and disadvantages of small cities.

Chinese critics of small cities lose debate

A Chinese conference on urban growth has decided to push ahead with a policy to develop more small cities to house the 350 million peasants who are expected to leave the land over the next 15 years.

This follows a lively debate in the press, in which some have said that small cities are costly and waste China's diminishing amount of arable land. Many have argued that large industrial conurbations are the key to modernisation.

But the conference has concluded that the country must concentrate on developing small cities of between 50 000 and 200 000 to prevent mass migration to the big cities.

China will spend about eight billion pounds on urban development during the late 1980s as the number of cities grows from 324 to 400, said Mr Feng Shixiu, head of the financial department of the Ministry of Urban and Rural Construction.

Population experts are predicting a momentous transformation to take place by the year 2000 when the number of urban residents will have more than doubled.

Under chairman Mao the Communist Party, which chiefly consisted of peasants, harboured a deep mistrust of the big city, and regarded urbanisation as an evil consequence of capitalist production methods.

In contrast to much of the Third World, strict controls prevented the rural drift to the cities and restricted their growth.

Instead there were forced transfers of urban residents to the countryside. From Shanghai alone nearly four million people were evicted, particularly during the Cultural Revolution, and many of these are still trying to get back.

Since the launching of the economic reforms, 55 million peasants are reckoned to have moved to the cities in search of work, some of them effectively second-class citizens. They often provide cheap labour as domestics or on building sites and are not entitled to grain coupons

The Shanghai-based *World Economic Herald* had argued against the development of small cities.

Between 1984 and 1986 the registered urban areas in China tripled to 730 000 square kilometres, and by the end of the century, it has been estimated that there will be only 0.16 of an acre of arable land per person left.

(Source: Jasper Becker, *The Guardian*, 7 Nov. 1988)

INDICATORS	average of the fifteen largest Chinese cities	Tokyo	Singapore	Hong Kong	Taibei	Bangkok
population (millions)	2.9	11.6	2.4	5.1	2.2	5.1
area per 10 000 people	6.1	1.9	2.5	2.1	1.2	3.0
percentage of employed population in manufacturing	53	23	30	41	23	19
percentage of employed population in wholesale, retail and restaurants	6	29	22	19	32	22
motor vehicles (per cent of population)	0.0	23	16	6	25	5
number of doctors (percent of population)	0.45	0.18	0.09	0.08	0.14	n/a

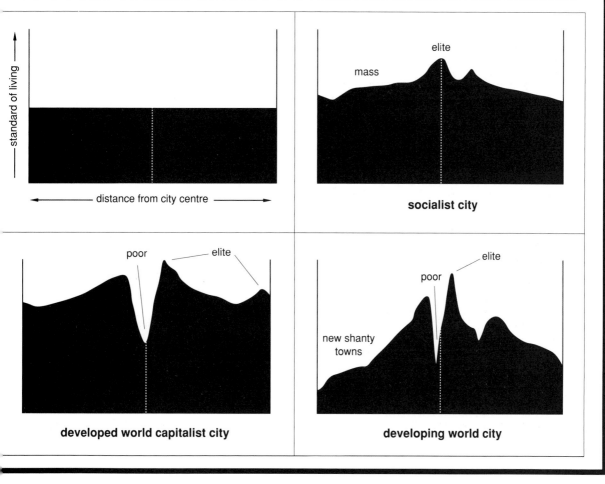

Student enquiry 10C

Improving the urban environment of Calcutta

In this enquiry you will use the experience provided by the case studies of developing world cities to consider the challenge of a city that was once described as 'the worst city in the world'.

Background file 1:

History

There could be few less promising places for the location of one of the world's great cities. About 160 kilometres from the sea and set on a levee surrounded by rice paddy fields and marshes, plagued by malaria and hurricanes and flooded by the annual monsoon, and with no adequate place for expansion.

From its foundation Calcutta was operated as a commercial/administrative/service centre protected at the downstream end by a fort. Two parallel cities grew up which today stretch some 80 km along the banks of the Hoogly and yet are linked by only three bridges. Each has a high density of population (750 persons per ha average in Calcutta city, 1961; New York 400; Los Angeles, 40). Thus, unlike New York or London or Los Angeles, where improvements in transport led to a rapid sprawl of the city, Calcutta has remained hemmed in by its marshes, containing ever more people at ever higher densities.

Towards the end of the nineteenth century the jute industry began to grow quickly. The locations of the jute mills were on the outskirts of the city, where there was room for production. They grew particularly along the east bank of the river because the jute is mostly grown in East Bengal. By contrast, the main railway lines and the proximity to the coalfields gave rise to the dominance of engineering at Howrah on the west bank, while the river barrier largely prevented one bank sharing in the manufacturing of the other.

For a million people in Calcutta, there is no alternative at present to living in the disease-ridden tenement slums. The congestion that this brings is amongst the worst in the world and widely regarded as intolerable.

The CBD of Calcutta extends from the Hoogly bridge to the area of the colonial fort. The upper class residential areas occur in the south and south-west. The rest remains a sea of two and three storey buildings, interspersed with squatter huts. The proliferation of high rise flats, so typical of bustling Bombay, are not much in evidence here.

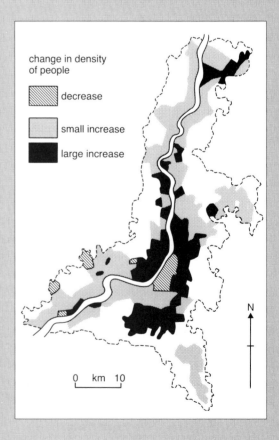

change in density of people

decrease

small increase

large increase

0   km   10

N

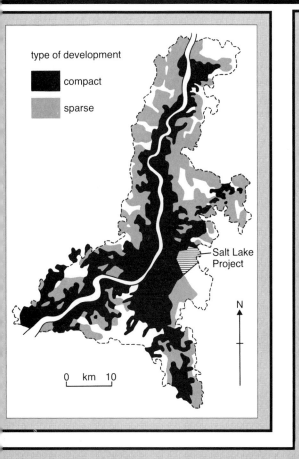

type of development

■ compact

▨ sparse

Salt Lake Project

0 km 10

N

Background file 2:

Calcutta slums

There are two categories of slums. Those in the central area have sewers and are small in area with little open space and very high density. Those beyond the sewered area have a much lower population density, sprawling over large areas with much area unused or covered with lakes. Further, there are at least 70 000 (and possibly 200 000) people with no homes at all, no matter how primitive: these are the pavement dwellers.

The official slum areas occupy about a twelfth of the Calcutta metropolitan area, with unofficial slums bringing the total to about a quarter. Half of these slum areas are on the eastern margin of the city. Within the slums many people live in rented accommodation under absentee landlords. Areas dominated by this form of ownership are called **bustees**. They are particularly geared to single migrants who have come to the city in search of work and opportunity. Most of these people are young single males.

A bustee is defined as an area of land occupied by, or for the purposes of, any collection of huts. A hut means any building , no substantial part of which is constructed of masonry or other building material. The tenure is distinctive. The land is owned by a landlord who rents it to people who build huts on the land and then rent these to people who live in the bustees.

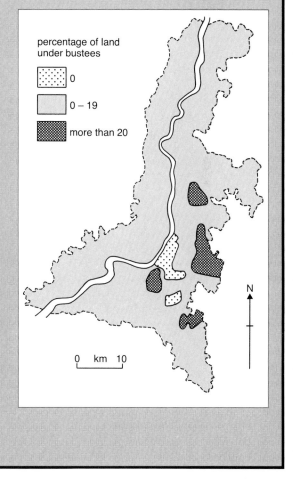

percentage of land under bustees

⬚ 0

☐ 0 – 19

▨ more than 20

0 km 10

N

Background file 3:

Calcutta public health

Calcutta lies in part of the great Ganges delta. Great barrages are causing reductions in discharge of the Hoogly River and are resulting in its sedimentation and salinisation, so that the surface waters are becoming even less suitable as a source of water. Nevertheless this water, after chlorination, is a major part of the city water supply. The main aquifer consists of alluvial sands at a depth of over 50 m below the city and represents the most promising water supply for the area. This is accessed through a network of tube wells. Because the accessibility of water is limited, and people may have to fetch it from a tap in a shop, large numbers use the readily available surface waters of ponds and lakes or streams. These are all polluted.

The extremely flat topography of the city, with a maximum elevation of 10 m above sea level, makes gravity drainage of sewerage extremely difficult. The municipal sewerage system is very limited and relates only to a small part of the city. Only half of Calcutta city is sewered; Howrah, the part of the metropolis on the west bank of the Hoogly, has no sewerage at all. For the most part raw sewage is discharged to the major rivers by means of surface ditches. Only new towns such as Kalyani have an adequate sewerage system. This means that the vast majority of the people have to rely on the dry conservancy system of night soil disposal; that is the periodic collection of night soil from service privies by municipal trailers (a service privy is a small shed with a platform over an earthenware bowl sited at ground level: in the monsoon floods such arrangements present a particular health hazard). Such polluted water infects and pollutes the tanks in which people bathe and wash their clothes and utensils.

The low lying nature of Calcutta, combined with the high rainfall during the monsoon season from June to September, makes drainage extremely difficult. It is virtually impossible to remove sewage through even the open ditches during this season. With refuse lying uncollected and sewage not removed, the health situation of the area is nothing short of a nightmare. In the monsoon season streets are quickly flooded and water reaches knee level, making life in the shanties and slums even more miserable as raw sewage spills from the drainage ditches over the streets and into the houses.

Cholera and many other diseases are endemic to Calcutta. The only way to correct the drinking water problem is to manipulate the river flow yet further, as is now achieved by the Farakka Barrage, a diversion barrage on the Ganges, and a diversion canal linked to the Hoogly system.

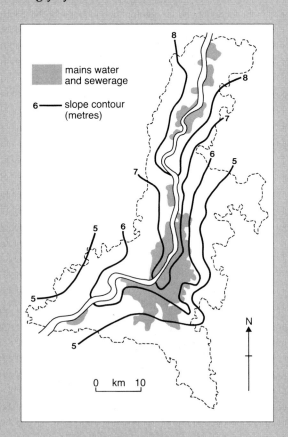

mains water and sewerage

6 —— slope contour (metres)

0   km   10

N

Questions for Student enquiry 10C

1. Look at the diagram which shows the population pyramids for Calcutta and a sample of migrants. Describe the differences and try to account for their causes. Explain why the migrant population is more likely to be found in the bustee areas than in other slum or shanty housing.

2. The population density of just under 5 persons per dwelling unit is not especially high, but the dwelling units are very small, so that three quarters of the population have less space than 2 m x 2.5 m each. What are some of the problems of getting rid of the bustees? Why might solutions be different in the crowded central areas where bustees are fragmented as opposed to the more suburban regions?

3. Describe and explain the pattern of changes in population density within the Calcutta district between 1951 and 1961.

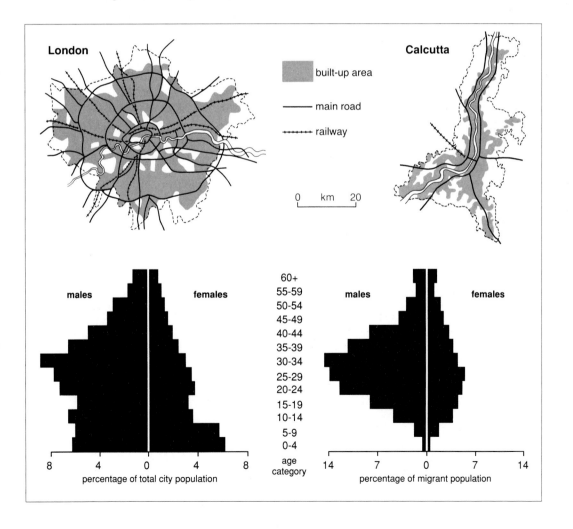

4. Table 10C1 shows the populations of the major urban areas of India and their growth rates between 1961 and 1981, the period projected by the Calcutta Metropolitan District (CMD) when they were preparing their plan for the city. Use the figures to make a comparison of the urban growth of Calcutta with the other major centres of India. Try to explain, using information in the text, why there is a contrast.
5. Starting from the population in 1961 of 6.72 million people, make projections for the population based on the figures from the plan.

Projection 1
Declining rate of natural increase from 2.2 per cent per annum to 1.4 per cent per annum; no migration into urban areas.

Projection 2
Urbanisation at the rate current in 1961 of 13.1 per cent per year.

Projection 3
Urbanisation rate will reach India's 1961 level by 1986 (i.e. 1.9 per cent per year).

Projection 4
Urbanisation rate will equal the level for India by 1986 (4.64 per cent per year).

The formula for compounding increases is

$$Pi (r/100 + 1)n = Pf$$

where Pi is the initial population; r is the rate of change, n is the number of years in the projection and Pf is the final projected population.

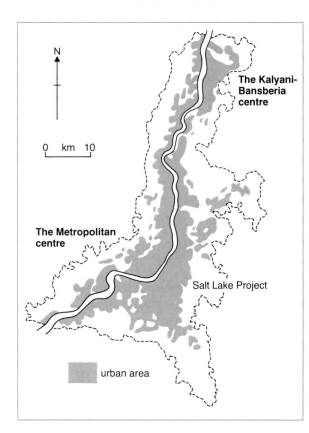

Growth rates of India's largest cities

city	1981 population (millions)	Average growth rate (per cent)	
		1961-71	1971-81
Calcutta	9.1	2.0	2.7
Bombay	8.2	3.6	3.2
Delhi	5.7	4.4	4.5
Madras	4.2	4.9	3.0
Bangalore	2.9	3.2	5.7
Hyderabad	2.5	3.6	3.4
Ahmedabad	2.5	3.6	3.6
Kanpur	1.7	2.7	2.8
Pune	1.7	3.6	4.0
Nagpur	1.3	3.0	3.4
Lucknow	1.0	2.1	2.1
Jaipur	1.0	4.4	4.6

6. The regional plan envisages concentration upon the centre of the metropolitan area and the Kalyani/Bansberia (K/B) centre 40 km to the north. The K/B area is a new urban centre, far enough from the metropolitan centre to discourage daily commuting but close enough to enjoy some of the external economies available in the metropolis. This centre has a much better infrastructure than established centres. The plan states that it is important to concentrate on specific centres rather than to spread the money available too widely. Explain why this might be so.

7. Look at the map of mass transit desire lines that was prepared by the CMD as part of their planning process. Discuss the types of system that should be developed and whether some alternative form of planning might be used to reduce the central focus on journeys.

8. The CMD commented in 1961:
   'The results of the present failure to provide for adequate and sanitary housing, even at minimum standards, to keep pace with population expansion, are visible throughout the cities of Calcutta and Howrah, and in every municipality

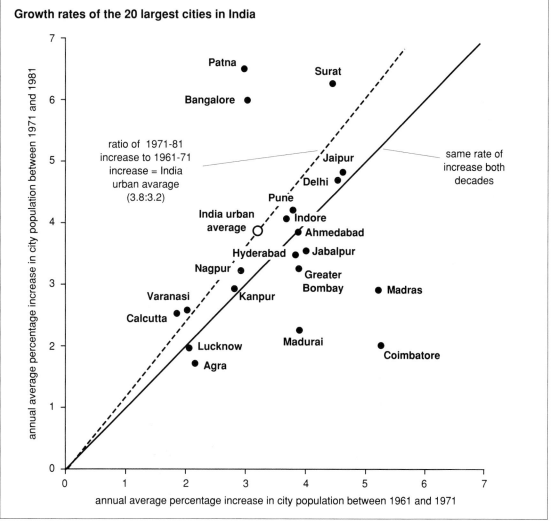

Growth rates of Indian cities

of the CMD. *Everywhere the picture so far as housing is concerned is one of congestion, insanitation, inadequate water supply, extensive bustee areas, high rents and premiums. Everywhere there is a great deal of illegal occupation and squatting on public and private lands – whether of refugee colonies built out of necessity on the vacant lands of absentee landlords, or of pathetic clusters of squatters in tattered and improvised shelters on public pavements, on the municipal refuse-dumps, and indeed on any vacant site. The urban environment in metropolitan Calcutta is probably deteriorating faster through the sheer inadequacy of housing, with its attendant evils, than through any other single cause.'*

Discuss some of the ways the city might try to correct this situation. Examine whether any of the schemes discussed earlier in the chapter could be used effectively in, say, the unused area called Salt Lake (see map).

9. The Salt Lake redevelopment has gone ahead largely to provide for middle and upper income families rather than for low income developments. Suggest some reasons why this might be so.

10. In the light of the information on Calcutta, discuss whether the criticisms of developing world cities stated earlier in chapter seem well founded.

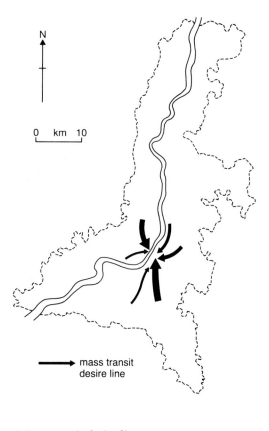

mass transit desire line

Mass transit desire lines

Chapter 11
Alternatives to the megacity

Introduction

The growth of the megacity has brought problems of congestion and accommodation throughout the world. Cities have often become magnets for people migrating from less advantageous regions, creating problems that most governments find impossible to solve. Even without this problem there is a constant need to upgrade the environment available to those already there. This chapter looks at some of the attempts which have been made to improve the city environment by redirecting people to other places and some of the issues that such action has raised.

Reasons for decentralisation

Because sites within a city normally only become available for redevelopment in small units, change is usually slow. This is the main reason that cities remain congested and infrastructure often inadequate. Many people would like to speed up this process of change.

At the same time, many inner city areas are too densely populated. An improvement to the inner city environment therefore requires the transfer of some people to other parts of the city or to places away from the city (Fig. 11.1). Furthermore, many people have also argued that cities should not be allowed to grow in an uncontrolled manner and that the total population and the area of land used should be contained.

Figure 11.1 The opening up and revitalising of inner Liverpool has been achieved by encouraging people to leave the city for new towns such as Runcorn and thus reduce the housing demand. The density of this housing is lower, and the environment more attractive, than the housing it replaced. The objective is not only to provide better housing for the local population, but to upgrade the environment and make it more attractive for new businesses

The problem has been to find an effective way of achieving standstill in growth while upgrading the environment. Local authorities have sometimes relocated the inner city families in housing estates on the periphery. This was the case in Liverpool (Chapter 7) and also Delhi (Chapter 9). However, people can only be moved about within a city to a limited degree. For all these reasons, therefore, many city authorities have been in favour of planned decentralisation.

The economic pressure to decentralise

Local authorities are worried about the welfare of the population; companies are worried about the continuing success of their businesses. The main economic forces for businesses considering re-location can be considered as push factors. They are supplemented by both location neutral and pull factors:

(i) **Push factors**: firms often find a combination of congestion and high rents a powerful force for relocation from a central city site whether or not there are attractions of new town facilities. These problems are compounded by the lack of physical space for expansion and the very high house prices and poor environmental conditions for the workforce (Fig. 11.2).

(ii) **Pull factors:** for most production processes and office activities that deal with routine matters, a peripheral location near to bypass roads and motorways is better for transport. Green field sites can also be adapted to allow horizontal work flows to occur. Furthermore, factories are mainly designed as single storey units because they are heavily dependent on conveyor and robotic systems (Fig. 11.3). This means that they must seek locations with low rents per square metre.

Figure 11.2 Few central sites contain parking space and the nearby streets are very congested

Fig. 11.3 A single storey warehouse designed for the distribution of goods. A large car park is required for customers to this wholesale cash and carry as well as a substantial site for the building

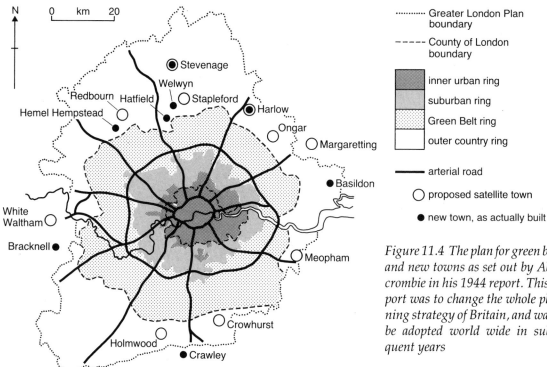

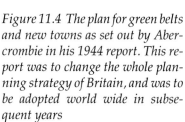

Figure 11.4 The plan for green belts and new towns as set out by Abercrombie in his 1944 report. This report was to change the whole planning strategy of Britain, and was to be adopted world wide in subsequent years

(iii) **Neutral factors:** rapid improvements in communications have been the most important neutral factor. Computer, telephone and other information technology systems make the location of most production processes, either factory or office based, a less important factor than in the past. Transport costs are often a minimal part of the total product cost and the extra distance imposed by a peripheral site is only important if the market is heavily concentrated at one central location.

The concept of new towns

As we have shown in the previous sections, there are two separate forces for decentralisation. One is a perceived problem of deteriorating environment, as seen by the planners. The other is a specific problem of survival of a business.

The problems of cities and their growth has been a concern throughout the century, and an improved environment was first suggested by

Ebenezer Howard in his Garden City concept (see Chapter 9). However, the first major integrated scheme for decentralisation had to wait until after the Second World War when a combination of large areas of bombed land and a severe shortage of homes required some drastic action.

Professor Abercrombie (who worked as adviser to the government during the war) calculated that new homes for 1 million people would be needed for the London conurbation alone, if he were to meet the objectives of rehousing the homeless and providing for a more open environment in the inner city. Until this time it had been accepted that the way to deal with this problem had been to build new housing estates on the edges of the cities, but Abercrombie wanted to end the sprawl. He therefore proposed a **Green Belt** around the existing urban sprawl of London in which further development would be discouraged (Fig. 11.4).

At the time mobility was much less than it is today, and people living beyond a green belt only 30 km wide would not conveniently be able to work in London. It was therefore essential to construct totally new and self-contained communities called **new towns**. It was a scheme

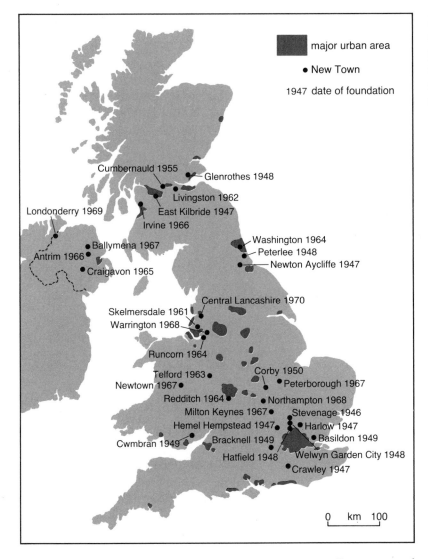

Figure 11.5 The established new towns of Britain and their date of foundation. Notice the early new towns were situated much closer to the conurbations than the later towns

major urban area
● New Town
1947 date of foundation

Cumbernauld 1955
Glenrothes 1948
Livingston 1962
East Kilbride 1947
Irvine 1966
Londonderry 1969
Ballymena 1967
Antrim 1966
Craigavon 1965
Washington 1964
Peterlee 1948
Newton Aycliffe 1947
Central Lancashire 1970
Skelmersdale 1961
Warrington 1968
Runcorn 1964
Telford 1963
Corby 1950
Newtown 1967
Peterborough 1967
Redditch 1964
Northampton 1968
Milton Keynes 1967
Stevenage 1946
Hemel Hempstead 1947
Harlow 1947
Cwmbran 1949
Bracknell 1949
Basildon 1949
Hatfield 1948
Welwyn Garden City 1948
Crawley 1947

0   km   100

which could offer opportunities to satisfy both planning concerns and also benefit businesses trapped within congested cities.

New Town development

Abercrombie's plan envisaged eight new towns for London, each with a population of about 50 000 and built at a distance of 40–50 km from the centre of the city (Fig. 11.5). Similar schemes were proposed for many of the other major British conurbations. Together they set the scene for the transformation of Britain's urban and rural environment and provided the lead that would be followed throughout the world.

To ensure the new towns got underway effectively and quickly, they were separated from the normal system of local government, and each town was put under the control of a **New Town Development Corporation** until it had matured (which turned out to be the 1980s).

The first group of new towns were built in the late 1940s and early 1950s. They housed businesses and people from the inner cities where the bombing had been most severe. However, as the new towns grew, so their pressure on the countryside caused considerable opposition (see also Chapter 12). For a decade opponents to the new town plans successfully restricted further developments, but this put intolerable pressure on the

Figure 11.6 The environment of the new towns depended on the decisions of the planners and architects. In some places economy in housing design led to a faceless new town that did little to encourage a community feeling. These photographs are from Peterlee

cities because it restricted large scale urban renewal programmes.

By the mid 1960s stock had been taken of the successes and failures of the first group of new towns. It had proved easier and cheaper to weld a 'new town' into a town with an existing infrastructure than to start from scratch. Thus the next wave of new towns were primarily designed as major expansion schemes.

The 'South-East Study', published in 1964, was a major proposal to build houses for a further three and a half million people in the south-east of England before 1981. Because mobility had increased and many of the original new towns were now used partly as commuting centres, the second wave of new towns were to be built at greater distances from the centres of conurbations.

Milton Keynes, designated as the first planned new city, was built 80 km from London and projected to contain a population of 250 000. The others were really expansions of existing towns, such as Northampton, 110 km from London, Telford (based on a collection of old coal mining villages) and Redditch. These towns were developed to take the overspill from the West Midlands. Runcorn, Warrington, Skelmersdale and Central Lancashire were built to take pressure from Merseyside and Greater Manchester in the north-west. Washington and Cramlington were built near Newcastle, and Livingstone and Irvine

were built to take the overspill from Glasgow and Edinburgh.

The real challenge of this relocation policy was to make each community work, to build in a sense of belonging and a sense of place. In many futuristic housing designs this was very difficult to achieve (Fig. 11.6).The reason was that planners were concerned with accommodating people from an 'architectural' standpoint and were unaware of the social impacts of such large scale planning. Indeed, many people found themselves suffering from a sense of isolation, a phenomenon that came to be known, in the early years before the towns developed into mature communities, as the **new town blues**.

Student enquiry 11A

Problems of a new town

New towns form part of a great social experiment. In this enquiry we try to see how the experiment has fared and what lessons can be learned for the future.

Background file 1: Harlow

Harlow was designed for a population of about 60 000. However, the population estimates were soon revised to 80 000 as planners changed the master plan to give a greater housing density. The plan defined four neighbourhood areas for housing, each with its own shopping and social centre. Industry was segregated from the housing in industrial estates, and the whole town arranged in such a way that it focused on the town centre.

The master plan for Harlow, showing the four housing neighbourhoods and the town shopping centre

The main roads were designed to service these separated communities by following routes through landscaped country 'wedges' within the town and so houses and main traffic flows were separate. Furthermore, the road pattern was designed to prevent central congestion and it does not follow a radial pattern. The whole town was then surrounded by a green belt on which no building was to be allowed.

In the late 1940s Harlow was dominated by younger families with small children. As a result it came to be called 'pram city'. Harlow was also dominated by people with a restricted social and locational background: they had mostly come for skilled or unskilled manual jobs as overspill from London's inner city areas. The town consequently had a lack of maturity, and it proved difficult to attract professional and managerial people to the area because it provided few facilities that these groups wanted. As a result these groups worked in Harlow but lived in more mature towns such as Bishops Stortford.

Legend:
- residential area
- industrial area
- town centre
- major neighbourhood centre
- neighbourhood sub-centre
- **P** primary school
- **S** secondary school
- **FE** college of further education
- major road
- minor town road
- railway

N

0 km 2

Student enquiry 11A concluded

1. Read the article 'How fares the brave new town' and describe the developments that have taken place in Harlow in the forty years since its birth.
2. New towns come in many forms. Basingstoke, in north-east Hampshire, could be called an expanded town, although the original town has been completely swamped by three decades of expansion.

Information about the growth of Basingstoke is given in this enquiry. You will also find information on the population structure over

How fares the brave new town?

Here they designed a town, rather than merely planned it: its visionary, the late Sir Freddie Gibberd, walked the fields for weeks before laying out its streets and homes to preserve the hummocks, valleys and copses. Here were built Britain's first ready-to-rent standardised factories, Britain's first integrated homes for the elderly, Britain's first sports centre.

All that achievement has to be set, too, against the remark in his later years of Lew Silkin, Minister of Town and Country Planning in the 1945 Attlee government, that the only way he got the new town scheme through Cabinet was that the Treasury were convinced it would never cost a penny – because this 'socialist pipe dream' would never be built.

But for every voice raised in praise at birthday parties, there will be another somewhere in the background booing. Harlow is a town that prompts fierce reaction. It did so at the beginning from the Essex folk up on those ridgelines, gazing down on refugees from east London slums now placed in their Tory midst with all the neighbourly warmth with which the Iceni used to spy on Roman encampments hereabouts.

Forty years have made these neighbours no more fond. But most criticism of Harlow has nothing to do with politics. It is aimed rather at the mood of the town, and especially the perception of its people, in their small, neat and varied houses. Harlow is felt to be boring.

Which much wounds men like Ben Hyde Harvey. Now 78, he was finance officer when Harlow was launched, and later the Development Corporation's longest serving chief executive: the shopping complex is named after him. It was he who made that remark about Harlow being a beacon for a brave new world.

'We were wrong in some things. This was to have been a town where people walked or cycled to work. We allowed for one car for three families. But no one in 1947 dreamt it would be like now – sometimes three cars per house, clogging the streets.

'We were right in other decisions. Bringing in dozens of different firms of architects to give us every conceivable sort of housing. We were lucky in others: we didn't want homes for grannies at first. We gave in and it became one of the best things we ever did ... fitting in those little blocks on the corners imported not only baby-sitters and part-time workers for the community, it imported wisdom.

'Luckiest of all though, were the people we attracted. Britain's mistake was not setting up idealistic and practical development corporations like ours to rebuild the inner cities. We took all the best people, left them with the worst. Today's inner city problems began then.'

And Harlow today? 'Those pioneers have all gone. Now I'm afraid it has become just another place to live, a normal town that used to be special. But no, not boring as so many critics say. There is little in this life to do that cannot be done in Harlow.'

That is the view, too, of Harry Platt. 'I know outsiders don't like us. They see the sameness, the newness of the place and make their judgement. But it is a town of high standards of living and high expectations.

'Harlow has survived cutbacks and swings, changes of fashion and governments. Some things have not worked. The idea of a self-contained living-and-working town' – 30 per cent of Harlow workers commute to London, while 30 per cent of the town's labour travels from without. 'The idea of managers and workers living side by side has not succeeded.There are good homes in Harlow. But a posh part of town? No, we certainly wouldn't want that.'

The sentiment might well lie at the heart of Harlow thinking and thus, perhaps, of outsiders' dislike of the place. They avoided uniformity in the place, but perhaps not in the

the past three census periods. Represent the information as population pyramids and discuss the changes that have taken place, making comparisons with Harlow as appropriate. Could the term 'pram city' reasonably have been applied to Basingstoke at any stage?

people. Standing around its shopping mall can be chilling. There is a uniformity in dress, in speech, in first names (Wayne and Tracy are legion) and a chain-store stylelessness about the shops.

Seeking a grip on the spirit of Harlow, I asked a long-serving local journalist. 'Harlow is my proof that character is more moulded by genetics than environment,' he said. Meaning? 'Meaning that this is a town of apathetic oicks. They had a mass meeting to discuss the great birthday celebrations. Only 25 turned up.'

Let us agree that his is a jaundiced view, though he was not alone in expressing it. Let us agree that with its fields and fresh air, its services, Harlow is holding fast to its founders' belief in a place to bring up healthy children.

Yet I found it depressing that in a town where was created the nation's first sports centre, a town now striped by manicured playing fields, the district council recently found it necessary to appoint a Sports Motivating Officer – to get the 14 year olds currently riding bikes up and down outside chip shops to take up a sport.

If Harlow was seen 40 years ago as an attempt to knock up a temporal heaven on a truly green and pleasant land, the verdict is that paradise is at least postponed. Before the next attempt we need, perhaps, first to breed the Paradisians.

(Source: Brian James, *The Times,* 13 Mar. 1987)

Year	Population
1951	16978
1961	26021
1966	34470
1971	49922
1981	71368
1986	74707
1991 (est)	75774

Basingstoke population

Age	Males	Females
85+	111	367
80-84	719	484
75-79	504	793
70-74	797	1082
65-69	1081	1312
60-64	1227	1356
55-59	1694	1656
50-54	1790	1719
45-49	2091	1906
40-45	2344	2227
35-39	2738	2808
30-34	3330	3432
25-29	2907	2986
20-24	2682	3033
15-19	3367	3380
10-14	3683	3452
5-9	3208	3056
0-4	2904	2713

Basingstoke population structure 1981

Student enquiry 11B

Issues of relocation

Most companies decide to relocate for commercial reasons, but the success of new towns depends on satisfying the needs of the people who come to this new environment.

In 1987 Sun Life of Canada plc, a major assurance company, decided to move its British Headquarters Office (BHO) from Cockspur St near central London's Trafalgar Square to the new town of Basingstoke, 70 kilometres away in Hampshire. It was typical of those firms that felt the costs of staying in central London outweighed the benefits. Relocation gave the benefits of moving to a purpose-built office with on-site parking, but it also involved a considerable amount of disruption for its workforce.

Sun Life spent two years relocating its staff and preparing for the move. During that time staff were encouraged to move to Basingstoke and take advantage of the free staff coach service into London each day. The experiences of the staff moves were reported in the company newspaper. Extracts from some of the articles in the paper are given here.

1. On a map of South East England, locate the homes of the people described in the articles. Suggest some of the possible reasons for their locations (perhaps refer to Chapter 6 on city patterns) and the nature of their journeys to work.
2. Comment on the size of the catchment area for the staff based in the London office.
3. All the people involved in relocation had some fears of the move. Explain what these fears were and try to categorise them. Use the information about the refuseniks to help.
4. Relocation has an impact on the whole family, not just on the person employed by the company. Discuss some of the ways in which this impact has been felt and overcome.

The new offices in Basingstoke

The refuseniks - what they cost

The refusal of thousands of workers to move home to another part of the country – often in spite of promotion and salary increases – is currently costing British industry £500 million a year, according to a recent survey. Two thirds of firms which have moved, or considered doing so, report 'strong opposition' from the workforce.

Neil Culliford, general manager of Homequity, the Swindon-based relocation consultancy which commissioned the survey, says: 'House prices are a problem. People moving from the south fear they may never be able to afford to come back again, while people moving the other way find the prices to be simply too high.

'This is also a time when there are often two wage earners in a family and if one moves the other has a choice between job and marriage. But most of all it is just a fear of an unknown locality.'

The cost to an employer of one refusal to move is estimated at between £3000 and £4000 a head – made up of advertising for a suitable replacement, time spent interviewing and the absence for a while of the right person in the right job.

'The best answer is for a firm to start its plans at least two years in advance, set up permanent exhibitions of information about the new area, arrange frequent fact-finding trips and generally ease both the shock and the burden,' Culliford says.

The public as well as the private sector have to face the problems of relocation as the process of decentralisation continues – it was announced last week that the Customs and Excise and the Ministry of Defence will be among a number of government departments leaving their London premises.

(Source: *The Times*, 11 Jan. 1988)

Semi-rural housing in villages near to Basingstoke

NO WAY!

By Mandy Bowskill
'Certainly not!' was my reaction to the proposal that as a family we might consider moving to Basingstoke so that we might be nearer Bob's job. I was very happy in Guildford, where we had been living for nine years. The girls were happy at school, I had lots of friends and there was plenty to do – we felt very much part of the community. However, I felt it only right to have a look at Basingstoke and then at least I could say I'd been!

Predestined

Have you ever had the feeling that someone has a plan for you despite what you would prefer to do? Well to cut a long story short we moved to Basing-stoke on the 11th September, into a rather old rambling house which needs a lot of attention. We are near the town and eventually Bob will be able to walk to work instead of the long train journey he has at present! The girls have hap-pily settled into their respective schools at Fairfields and have made lots of new friends and been to lots of parties. Generally we have found the 'natives' very friendly, and as Bob said earlier the warm welcome we have received at our local church has helped us settle in.

The Challenge

I am not pretending it's been easy, it hasn't. There are days when I miss Guildford and the friends we made there very much and I wonder whether we have done the right thing. Neverthe-less I now look forward to becoming part of the community and meeting the challenges ahead. After all, to some extent settling into a new town and home is always what you are prepared to make it.

The Dewers

The move to Basingstoke seems to have produced a new sporting Mrs Marion Dewer. Apparently she is frequently to be seen jogging around the streets of Chineham, that is of course when she is not partaking of an aerobics class in Chineham village hall. And as if this isn't enough, Marion and Ian have regular games of squash at the Basingstoke Sports Centre. Perhaps the fresh Hampshire air is having an invigorating effect or maybe just keeping up with their two and a half year old twins Patrick and Ryan, and their five year old son Jamie, is demanding even greater levels of fitness.

Minders

The Dewer family are definitely enjoying their new home. 'We have a lot more in common with our neighbours than we did in High Wycombe,' comments Ian. Chineham seems full of young couples with children of pre-school age. Indeed a 'baby-sitting circle' has been established in the Dewers' road whereby all the parents take it in turn to mind each others children. A cheap and mutually beneficial arrangement. Also an ideal way to break the ice in a new area.

However the move wasn't without its worries. Both Marion and Ian were, like all trail blazers, apprehensive about leaving friends behind and setting up home in a new area, but things seem to be working out quite well. The early move was necessitated by young Jamie starting school for the first time last September.

Talk to me

On the subject of moving, Ian has some advice to offer. 'Talk to people who have already moved. Naturally they know much more about the area than you do. It's amazing how misleading the impressions gained on short visits can be. I am always happy to talk to anyone considering relocation.'

'It's not

Confirmed city boy Larry Berry, from Computer Information Serv-ices, was absolutely determined not to move to Basingstoke when reloca-tion was first announced. After all, he was a North Londoner born and bred and he was scared of open spaces, particularly of fields. It was bad enough having to go south of the river occasionally, let alone south of Lon-don; but as time pressed on Larry

The Creightons

Don's family were a little worried about moving to Hampshire: the Creighton children Julia (aged 13) and Catherine (aged 10) were not happy about leaving friends or changing schools, and Don's wife Anne, was anxious about giving up her job. But after a great deal of thought and discussion, Don and Anne decided that an early move was the best thing. Indeed as both Julia and Catherine were settling down well in the Richard Aldworth School and Kempshott County Junior School respectively, it seems the right decision was made.

House Prices

Commuting from Basingstoke is not a serious problem for Don as the distance from London and the cost of travelling are comparable to Milton Keynes. A serious difference however, was in the disparity of house prices between the two towns. In an interesting experiment Don discovered, through the Basingstoke estate agents, that his house in Milton Keynes would have been worth an extra £11 000 in Basingstoke!

So the move has meant a bigger mortgage but Don, despite the extra financial burden, is still enjoying his new environment. Indeed, with his characteristic tendency to overstate the case Don went as far as to say 'It's not a bad place!'

The Smiths

Vera Smith, from Premium Collections, thinks she timed her move to Basingstoke perfectly, as she says 'I'm really enjoying being the first person to live in my house and it was particularly satisfying having the final say in the interior decor.'

Vera has two daughters – Joanne (17 years) and Melanie (14 years). Joanne has had to remain in London to finish a training course and will be following the family in a few weeks, while Melanie started school in Brithton Hill only three days after the move. Vera thought it would do no harm for her to be 'thrown in at the dep end' and luckily she seems to be right as Melanie is enjoying her new school.

Overjoyed

Vera's husband Keith is a contracting electrician and was overjoyed about the move to Basingstoke. 'He was probably more excited than I was,' says Vera. 'All the new buildings in Basingstoke ensure that there will be no shortage of work for people like Keith.'

as bad as people think'

began to weigh up the options and his determination faltered.

His parents had moved to America in 1982 so Larry's main alternatives were to emigrate to join them, to remain with his sister (Janis Angus from Premium Collections) in Tottenham or relocate. To everyone's great surprise, particularly his own, Larry chose Basingstoke and the opportunity to establish his independence.

Having made the decision Larry didn't exactly rush things. He found his one bedroomed house in Chineham in January but didn't move in until May. Even then he was only living there at weekends and staying with his sister midweek. Gradually his weekends 'in the country' got longer until in June he moved down there 'lock, stock and barrel'.

Student enquiry 11B concluded

The Thomsons

Although they have only been there a few months Pam Thomson and her family are settling down very well in Basingstoke. Pam is very proud of how quickly they managed to set up home in their three bedroom house in Popley. 'Within a fortnight we had the carpets laid, the curtains up and most of the necessary redecorating done, it's a real home from home now.' This is the first time Pam and her husband Joe have invested in property and she says: 'We couldn't have done it without the Company's help.'

Job prospects

Joe is equally happy about the move. Having spent the past three years on the dole in London, Joe hopes that his job prospects will be better in Basingstoke; with the unemployment figures well below the national average and ever decreasing as more companies move into the area, his hopes are well founded.

Pam's children, Mark (15) and Denise (13) are less enamoured of the move. They found it very hard leaving friends and schoolmates behind. However after some initial problems, they are now beginning to enjoy their new school 'The Vyne'. 'It's always difficult for kids of their age to change schools but I think they are doing it very well,' said Pam.

Counting the cost

Pam's relocation has not been without its problems; the increased fares and the longer travelling times are taking their toll. Pam's annual British Rail season ticket from New Cross (where they lived previously) cost £200 last year while the pass from Basingstoke is costing £1,038 this year on top of which she has to pay 80p a day bus fare. Inevitably, with the increase in travelling expenses and her new mortgage repayments, Pam is financially worse off.

Even so, Pam is very happy to be in Basingstoke and is enjoying her new environment but she can't wait for the days when the office is a ten minutes bus ride away!

Availability of alternative office employment

Figure 11.7 Low cost rented accommodation

Housing for management

'A saner way of life'

When David Arnott, Media Resources Adviser, decided to relocate he had two definite types of property in mind. He either wanted to buy a run-down cottage in need of a lot of renovation or a new property that needed no work whatsoever. Older properties are in short supply in the Basingstoke area so David settled for a new terrace house in Linford (twenty miles from Basingstoke).

Like Larry Berry, David was a Londoner born and bred. So he initially found it difficult to settle into a 'country life'. This wasn't helped by the fact that his job took him all round the country (and to Monte Carlo) so that he only spent 4 nights out of the first month in his new house. It was nearly Christmas before David had met his neighbours let alone settled in.

To start with, David found himself making social trips back to London at least twice a week but now he feels less inclined to leave Linford, particularly at the weekend. Simultaneously his London friends seem increasingly keen to come and stay in Linford. Slowly David is getting to know the locals and the more he does the more he likes it there. 'In London you feel very much at the centre of things; I was very unhappy about leaving, but now I love it. Life is much saner and friendlier here and I've even got ducks and swans at the end of my road.'

Although David is now happily settled in Linford he did have one slight setback. David opened his door one morning to find that all the wheels had been stolen off his car and that the body was lying flat on the driveway! For a brief moment he must have felt like he was back in London.

World New Towns

The great resettlement experiment has not been confined to Britain. Customised versions have been forged by many governments throughout the world. However, the reasons for doing so remain the same.

1. Moscow

All great cities, no matter what the political system that runs them, are centres of attraction. Moscow, the hub of a centralist system, has developed as rapidly as any in the west. By 1960 a general plan for the reconstruction of Moscow showed many of the elements familiar in all western cities. In this case an inner suburban zone has been designated as green belt, isolating the city centre from the outer 50 kilometre suburban zone.

The green belt is only about 10 km wide, and is seen as an open space within the city rather than as a containment. It is the lungs of the city and a place where recreational facilities can be focused. Its resident population, accounting for about a fifth of all the people in the Moscow region, was to be held constant.

The outer suburban zone includes 25 cities and contains about 40 per cent of the Moscow region's population. A large part of the industrial base for the city is also located there.

Moscow has a very pronounced radial communications pattern and a large number of satellite towns have grown on the axes of the radial routes. The growth of Moscow beyond its existing population of 3.6 million was seen as a problem as early as 1935 when a city plan prohibited the construction of new industrial enterprises. Later, the prohibition was extended to the 50 km outer suburban zone. Nevertheless, in the 25 years after this first plan the city had still managed to grow to 6 million people, mainly depending on service, research and educational jobs.

The planners of Moscow between the 1960s and 1980s were thus presented with a dilemma. Either expand the city by peripheral growth or choose to develop new towns and expanded towns at least 50 km from the city. In the case of the Soviet Union, the problem of attracting new industry to the new towns did not exist. Central

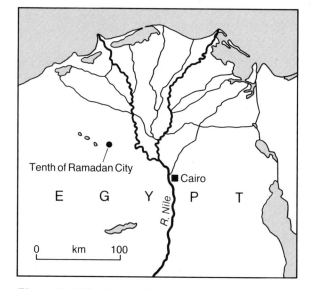

Figure 11.7 The Tenth of Ramadan city occupies a part of the desert and does not conflict with use of the precious Nile valley agricultural land

planning determined the location of all institutions and these could readily be moved to new towns so that people could have local workplaces.

2. Cairo

New towns are an increasingly attractive solution to pressing demographic problems in developing countries. However, the resettlement colonies of Delhi show how difficult it is to resettle people permanently when they are close to an existing city and there is no satisfactory means of local employment. Egypt has the problem of containing the 10 million people of Cairo and it already has massive new peripheral housing estates stretching out into the desert.

The prospect of new towns is especially attractive to Egypt because it has a large amount of undeveloped land. Currently Egypt only uses 4 per cent of its land area, and although the remainder is desert, there is no reason why future cities should not be built on such land. The Nile valley farmland is far too valuable to be built on. The Tenth of Ramadan City, some 80 km north-west of Cairo, is an attempt to create just one of nineteen new towns (Fig. 11.7). Since its foundation in 1977, over £200 million has been spent on this one city, a very considerable sum for a country so heavily in debt. Egypt has been forced into this position

Figure 11.8 Examples of prominent locations offered by decentralisation include prestigious buildings set in unconfined spaces

simply because it had become impossible to provide a reasonable level of service in Cairo. Now businesses are attracted out to the new towns by offers of low cost building land and a tax free 'holiday' of ten years. For the workforce the bonus is a reasonable home in a place that is less crowded and overbearing.

The difficulty Egypt now faces is how to keep provision of homes in step with its exploding population. Each of the present nineteen new towns will have to absorb 500 000 people by the end of the century and thus become new cities. There will need to be a further ten more new cities just to absorb the extra people, and even more than this if the government is to achieve an improvement in the overcrowded environment of Cairo.

The expanded town

New towns are expensive to create, especially in densely populated areas. Even when the first wave of new towns were being built in the late 1940s and early 1950s to house 400 000 people, the British government was trying to find homes for 600 000 more people by enlarging existing towns. The British experience was that expanded towns were much easier and cheaper to construct. In recent years this expanded town policy has virtually replaced the idea of a new town.

New towns are a government creation. They are seen primarily as a way of improving the urban environment rather than as a way of causing industry to relocate. But the attractions for decentralisation provided by the new towns are only too real. Firms will therefore often try to seek decentralisation whether or not the government is providing a suitable framework.

The corporate firm is sometimes large and influential enough to generate a new town environment. Corporations all experience the lack of pull by the city and the neutrality of the communications factor. As a result other factors can rise to prominence for deciding future locations. One of these is the image of the corporate firm.

It is possible, by judicious choice of location, to go from a fairly anonymous central city location to a prestigious location which associates the corporate identity with a town. Thus a decentralised location becomes a pull factor. Towns offering a high profile site, especially if it is on the main road most often used by visitors, will have an attraction for the corporate firm anxious to present as important an image as possible (Fig. 11.8).

The search for suitable towns to act as corporate headquarters (either national or regional) focuses on the ability of each town to meet certain requirements :

(i) there has to be a site suitable for the proposed development and further expansion. This often means a prestigious site with a suitable drive, lawns or parkland environment;

(ii) the town has to have the capacity to absorb a large proportion of the workforce, providing high landscape quality environments for executives;

(iii) it has to have some form of supportive infrastructure, such as local services; and

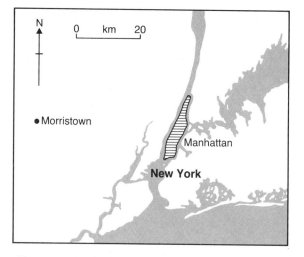

Figure 11.9 The location of Morristown

(iv) it has to have some form of prestige, such as a historic core, historic connection, high landscape quality, be associated with industrial dynamism, etc.

Morristown, New Jersey, USA

Morristown began as a 'European' farming settlement in 1710 (Fig. 11.9). The town grew as a service centre around the 'green', where the church stood and where a courthouse was built in 1755. But the most important historical factor was perhaps when George Washington, Commander of the Continental Army, chose Morristown as his winter headquarters in 1777 and 1779 during the lull in fighting against the British.

Morristown slowly slipped out of the public eye over the next centuries and into rural insignificance. A rail link allowed it to experience a period of 'Victorian' glory as it was chosen as a retreat centre for wealthy city people. They built large villas and developed parkland estates(Fig. 11.10). However, it became impossible to maintain these villas and estates through the depression of the late 1920s and the tax base was lost. As a result the town's fabric started to decay.

With the possibility of decentralisation of industry the local city hall had the foresight to establish an **Urban Renewal Agency**. Its job was to refurbish much of the older town. Behind this programme was a strategy aimed at attracting industry to choose Morristown as a corporate centre. It could offer advantages beyond the heritage association. It lies in a pleasant hill-lands region of New Jersey, and it is within a hour of Manhattan via the turnpike (toll motorway).

This strategy has been successful and the town is now the corporate headquarters for AT & T, one of America's largest information technology and communications companies. The injection of capital that this has brought has made a major difference to the region. One complete site redeveloped in the centre (Fig. 11.11) and known as 'Headquarters Plaza' is largely occupied by AT & T offices, but also contains a 260 room hotel for visiting businessmen and 10 000 sq m of retail commercial space.

The importance of the corporate move was, however, even more profound. AT &T has produced an **agglomeration effect**, attracting further industries. These are not necessarily providing AT& T with services or products, but are coming in under the umbrella perception created by AT&T of Morristown as a prestigious and dynamic place to be.

Morristown is now a prosperous town with enough money to be able to enhance its environment yet further. It has benefited greatly from the corporate image, as has AT &T benefited from being associated with the refurbishment of one of America's heritage sites. In effect Morristown has become a revitalised town thanks to the forces that have drawn industry to decentralise.

New villages for developing countries

In the sections above we have considered how the pressure on large cities can be relieved by a system of new or expanded towns, each set away from the city and with its own self-contained industries. The objective is to redistribute the existing urban population in ways that lead to an improvement of the environment for all. In this sense it is very much the product of developed world thinking, based on slow population growth. Cairo is now leading the way in showing how the concept can also be applied to the developing world.

In many parts of the developing world, much of the population increase in a city is due to

Figure 11.10 *Older central houses of Morristown*

rural – urban migration (see Chapter 5). Where this is a major factor, governments have the alternative of trying to stem the flow of people to the city in the first place.

Many countries have tried some form of **new village** scheme: that is, the controlled movement of households from one area to another, often with a large amount of administrative control both in the moving process and in the activities of the households once the movement is complete. Creating new villages is not the same as finding city people new homes. Rather it attempts to improve the economic basis of the rural areas and

Figure 11.11 *Headquarters Plaza*

reduce the incentive for migration in the first place. However, its effect is to cause the growth of population away from the centre and thus act as a mechanism for decentralisation.

Developing new nucleated settlements also has several advantages for the administration: it is easier to plan and control the activities of the population; to provide medical assistance and education; to build useful roads and to export produce; to give expert agricultural help, and so on. Furthermore, when a new village scheme occurs roads and houses are built, people move in, new irrigation facilities are created: everyone can see that something is being done. This has considerable political attractions for a developing world government and especially immediately after independence. Foreign donors also favour new village schemes, because they can be seen as prestige aid projects: foreign governments are seen to care.

New village schemes do have disadvantages, primarily in the break up of the social structure of the communities they are focused on. Concentration is directed towards monoculture of new, often hybrid crops whose pattern of nurture may not be fully understood and this may lead to soil degradation; they rely heavily on foreign inputs and continuous subsidies. Major new village schemes include the Gezira scheme in the Sudan, the Volta project in Ghana, the Assam project in India, new villages in Zimbabwe, Alto Beni in Bolivia, Transmigration in Indonesia, Villagisation in Tanzania and the Nueva Ixclatlan project in Mexico.

Chapter 12
Urbanisation of the countryside

Note to the reader: This concluding chapter is concerned with some of the most complex challenges of the human environment. Because the information required for decision making is extensive and also needs detailed knowledge of the culture of a people, this chapter deals only with Britain at a regional and local level. To demonstrate the principles involved example material is drawn from the area to the west of London. For the same reason, this chapter also contains more extensive datafiles than other chapters. The material can readily be paralleled with local information from the reader's own area.

Introduction

In the early parts of the book we discussed the ways in which population changes were driving people from the countryside. We then saw how these pressures took their toll on city life. In the developed world today, many city people are moving back to the countryside and the pattern of movement has almost come full circle.

Today there is a three-way flow of people between rural and urban environments. Those who leave the countryside do so for the economic benefits that the city brings; those who leave the city for the countryside do so largely for relaxation and a quieter pace of life; and those who leave the city for business, do so to enjoy the benefits of green field development. As these flows take place they produce pressures on environments and conflicts between people. The conflicts in the city are described in Chapters 9 and 10, the conflicts and issues raised due to the urbanisation of the countryside form the basis of this chapter.

Why there is conflict in the countryside

Only about 2 per cent of the workforce of Britain is engaged in some form of agricultural activity. A smaller percentage still is paid to protect wildlife or to conserve the countryside. Most people live in urban areas and have little practical idea about how to manage the rural environment other than from the paintbrush image gleaned

Figure 12.1 This green and pleasant land. Who should have the right to determine its future?

from programmes on the television and in the newspapers. Nevertheless, many people have a concern for the countryside and are keen to contribute to the dialogue on how it should be managed (Fig. 12.1). One difficulty that arises is, instead of understanding the countryside as one of the most complex systems in the world (see *Challenge of the Natural Environment*, Chapters 12–14) there is a tendency to see the countryside in very simplistic terms and to develop equally simplistic proposals. The conflict in the countryside results from:

(i) those who would work the land for the crops it will grow;

(ii) those who would conserve or fossilise it in some way that they see as an ideal; and

(iii) those who would use it as some form of non-agricultural recreational, living or business resource.

Today there is, coincidentally, even more reason for conflict, at least in Western Europe. Traditionally, the need to be as self-sufficient in staple foodstuffs as possible has been a basic plank of national strategy in case there should ever be a conflict with overseas countries that would put national survival at risk . This has led to government legislation directed at using land within existing urban areas rather than new green field sites. However, the green revolution, so talked about for the developing world, has produced just as important an impact on the developed world's farming outputs. The increase in farm output that has led to mountains and lakes of surplus food and drink in the EEC. This has allowed people to challenge the *a priori* assumption that as much land should be kept free from development as possible.

There is no longer a need for so much land to be used for commercial production. European governments are actively planning to take millions of hectares out of commercial food production in order to reduce the agricultural surpluses that will otherwise grow ever larger. Thus the question facing the nation now is: what should happen to the 'surplus' land?

Priorities in the countryside

The main reasons for preservation of the status quo come from:

(i) an individual desire from people already established in the countryside not to see their environment become more urban;

(ii) the desire for protection of wildlife, natural ecosystems and pollution free water supplies;

(iii) the desire to protect distinctive and treasured landscapes and country environments for the benefit of future generations; and

(iv) farmers want to go on maximising production in order to capitalise on the Common Agricultural Policy and its guaranteed high prices.

The main reasons for change come from:

(i) the desire to improve the environment of many people now trapped in high density urban environments;

(ii) the wish to distribute industry in locations as commercially effective as possible;

(iii) the wish to adapt the countryside for the uses of a population at present largely excluded from most of it; and

(iv) the desire of millions of people to improve their personal quality of life either by moving to the countryside, or by buying second homes so that they can get the benefits of both town and country.

As the arguments for and against the urbanisation of the countryside show, there is not an obvious wrong to be righted as is the case with the inner cities. This is why there is so much difficulty in coming to a satisfactory resolution of how to plan for the future of the countryside.

The issue of green field development

Most people agree that there has to be economic expansion, that the country must prosper, and that people should have an ever improving environment in which to live. But if these things cannot all take place in the existing cities, where else can the desires be satisfied? There are three options:

(i) allow development in the countryside of the green belt;

(ii) make development by-pass the green belts and force it into the existing villages and towns beyond; and

(iii) decide to allow development on green field countryside sites beyond the green belt.

Each of these solutions has its problems. Because people don't like living at high densities, they cannot all be persuaded to live in the cities. If development of existing villages and towns is allowed, eventually these settlements display the same disadvantages that developed in the major cities. If the green belt is used, the major cities simply sprawl in an uncontrolled manner and the cities face strangling themselves to death. If green field sites are chosen, this means starting ever more new towns (see Chapter 11) or extending the existing market towns and villages with peripheral estates (Fig. 12.2).

In general the pressure to develop means that all of these options may be taken up in time. The

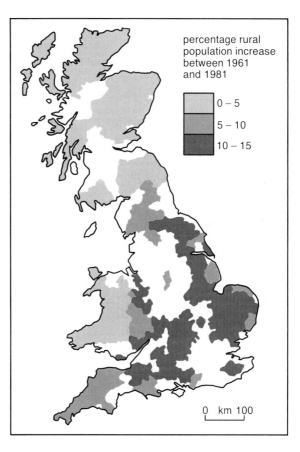

Figure 12.2 The changes in rural population density between 1961 and 1981. Many areas already suffer pressure, with the most severe pressure being to the west of London

pressure for development is immense. For example, it is estimated that 400 000 new homes will be needed in the area surrounding Greater London in the decade before the turn of the century.

The change of country lifestyle

Urban people often think the countryside is a place of little change, of backward ideas and slow pace. However, the pace of change has been so rapid that widespread hardship has been created among the least advantaged members of the rural community.

A person who has lived in the countryside, worked on a farm, and has now reached retirement age has seen almost revolutionary changes

Figure 12.3 This country cottage has been gentrified with the provision of modern utilities. A farm based lifestyle could not, however, provide the income for such refurbishment

in the rural environment. They would have grown up in the years just after the First World War in countryside where the village and small market towns were still inhabited primarily by those who worked on the surrounding labour-intensive farms, who milked cows, walked with the horses as they ploughed the fields and made up stooks as the harvest was gathered in. They would have become used to the local services consisting of carpenter, blacksmith and horse breaker. There would have been many local shops, grocers, butchers, bakers, coal merchants, milkman and outfitter.

The Second World War was almost as traumatic for the people of the countryside as for those in the bombed cities. Every last hectare of land had to be used for production. But, perhaps more significantly, many people left the farms and were conscripted in the forces. As a result young people from the countryside began to experience new lifestyles, and their expectations changed. When the war was over many did not return to the countryside, partly because there was progressively less work in the mechanised farming systems, partly because they had experienced and been educated for alternatives.

The changing circumstances brought about by the agricultural and educational revolutions produced a countryside where there was less work. As a result more dwellings remained unused and continued a century-long slide into dereliction and decay. At the same time the standard of living in the cities continued to rise faster than in the countryside. Being a farm labourer had never been well paid, now it was all people could do to make ends meet, let alone buy the new consumer goods that were flooding on to the markets.

The first signs of a change in the fortunes of the countryside occurred as personal mobility increased. By the 1960s the village was changing dramatically. No longer was there a decline to decay. Instead, the cottages were bought up and refurbished and the gardens tended for the first time in decades. But the people who bought the houses were not those from the countryside. Rather they were people from the city, searching for some tranquillity in the countryside to balance their hectic business lifestyle (Fig. 12.3). These newcomers were the most mobile sector of the community, those with sufficient disposable income to afford the cost of daily *personal* travel.

Figure 12.4 Henley in Arden was a self-contained market town. Now within reach of Birmingham's commuters and on the tourists' trail to Stratford, its shops cater for a new range of clients, with basic provisions very low down on the list

And so the labourer was replaced by the sales manager, the computer programmer, the doctor and the supermarket executive.

The increasing desire to become part of the rural landscape also brought demand for country housing where before there had been little. But demand also brought a rise in the price of houses. The final twist for those born in the countryside has therefore been to see house prices move out of their reach. With low salaries paid to rural manual workers, and demand high from the better paid members of society, the village that was once a unified community has become a split society.

Shops have also changed character to suit those with the higher disposable incomes. In many villages dominated by commuters, the butcher mainly sells the best quality cuts of meat and the village store is a supermarket whose sales range is almost equal to that of a delicatessen. The pub has a restaurant tacked on the side and there are aspirations to be on the good food lists. The market town shops sell more and more high fashion clothes (Fig. 12.4).

The new villagers find their way of life comfortable and satisfying. With a population shift to the wealthier and older section of the community, there has been a vociferous movement for conservation of the rural heritage. These lobbyists are a powerful political group who have in their midst all the skills required to defend and win battles with local planning authorities. At the same time, the rural manual worker cannot now find a council home to rent because there is a limitation on building. Jobs are ever harder to come by unless the factories conform to stringent requirements to blend in with the landscape and not cause any form of disruption. The same people who lobby for rural conservation also stifle any entrepreneurial ideas the rural worker may have wished to develop. This restricts the employment developments to high tech research or professional consultancies. There is little chance of a manual worker finding a job in such an environment. Clearly the countryside is destined to be available only to the better off if market forces alone are allowed to prevail.

Student enquiry 12A

Pressures on a rural village

This enquiry contains information about the village of Sonning Common in South Oxfordshire.

1. Study the list of retail and commercial activities in the village and the photographs of the village. What is the evidence for suggesting that the village functions have become oriented towards those with a higher disposable income?

2. Show, by means of a graph, how the characteristics of the population have changed in recent decades.

3. Study the information relating to occupations. Describe how the nature of the occupations and their locations might affect the character of the village. In the long term how might this affect the composition of people in the village?

4. In 1985 there was an attempt to change the boundaries of southern Oxfordshire to bring several villages, including Sonning Common, into the county of Berkshire, and particularly to make it more or less a part of the expanding industrial town of Reading. In a petition to the Boundary Commission, over 90 per cent of the residents said they wanted to stay in the rural district of South Oxfordshire. Suggest some reasons why the residents might have wanted to stay separate from Reading.

5. The newspaper extracts highlight the fears about changes in the village scene. Using this material, summarise the fears and explain why they are not shared evenly through the village population.

Plague

'Of course estate agents need premises in very desirable areas but the amount of offices seems disproportionate to the need when we are losing more and more essential shops.'

South Oxfordshire District Councillor Tony Lane said of the plague of estate agents: 'The problem is getting worse in Henley and around the area.

'A town or village needs first and foremost to look after the essential needs of its inhabitants with shops for food which people need every day.

'A house is extremely important of course but it is something which people may buy just a few times in their life or not at all.

'We are resisting more estate agents' offices being set up where they change the use of premises from retail shop.'

Functions within Sonning Common	
public houses	7
leisure centre	1
motor showroom	2
research lab	1
garage	3
accountant	1
newsagent	2
electrical appliance	1
bank	2
garden machinery	1
building supplies	1
building contractor	1
general stores	3
post office	1
security systems	1
sports club	1
school	2
garden buildings mfr	1
health centre	1
pet supplies	1
hardware	1
building society	1
estate agent	3
architect	2
dentist	1
fish and chips	1
hairdresser	2
vet	1
agricultural merchant	1
baker	1
wine merchant	1
wool shop	1
stationery shop	1
supermarket	1
chemist	1
butcher	2
village hall	1
police station	1
churches	2
library	1
old people's home	1
herb farm	1
graphic design	1

(NB many other services are offered by professional people using private houses as their trading premises and based on computer/fax/modem communications)

Part of the shopping centre, Sonning Common

The Village Hall, Sonning Common

Shopping habits survey

length of residence in survey area	total households	households shopping in Sonning Common for			households shopping regularly elsewhere			means of travel		
		food	other	majority of needs	Reading	Henley	Slough	car	bus	other
less than 15 years	695	592	422	274	473	178	11	433	218	11
over 15 years	381	300	252	263	271	55	0	126	196	4
Total	1076	892	674	537	744	233	11	559	414	15

Vehicle ownership

length of residence (years)	households	1 car	2 or more cars
under 1	133	92	7
1-2	215	152	33
3-4	128	89	11
5-6	63	30	15
7-10	100	48	15
11-15	56	33	11
over 15	381	189	63
Total	1076	633	192

Student enquiry 12A concluded

Travel to work

Place of work	Means of travel						total
	car	bus	cycle	walk	rail	other (coach etc)	
Sonning Common	67	30	74	96	0	7	274
Henley	130	4	7	7	0	22	170
other Oxon	41	0	0	0	0	4	45
Reading	396	218	33	0	0	37	684
Slough	15	0	0	0	4	0	19
other Berks	89	0	0	0	0	4	93
Bucks	30	0	0	0	0	0	30
London	52	0	0	0	37	0	89
Southern England	30	0	0	0	0	0	30
Total	850	252	114	103	41	74	1434

Country folk 'in urgent need of cheap homes'

New ways of providing low cost housing in rural areas must be sought as a matter of urgency, a report by the London and South-East Regional Planning Conference says.

Villages in the south-east have become the new suburbia for many whose work is unrelated to agriculture, it points out. The lifestyle of these inhabitants is heavily dependent on wealth and the motor car.

But traditional village residents still exist. They include agricutural workers, local service workers, those employed in small industries and many elderly people who find it difficult, if not impossible to compete for local housing. Prices are high, the right to buy is depleting the small stock of council housing, and rented accommodation is decreasing.

The evidence indicates that these problems cannot be solved simply by the provision of small numbers of additional private houses. Even a disproportionate, and therefore environmentally unacceptable increase in housing is unlikely to have more than a marginal effect.

The only approach to this problem is to open up new housing opportunities for those unable to compete in the market, the report says. Otherwise government policies to stimulate rural enterprise cannot be sustained.

(Source: John Young, *The Times*, 1 Feb. 1988)

What estate our villages are getting in!

The centuries-old villages and quaint little towns around Berkshire face a new threat . . . the invasion of the estate agents.

You may not be able to find a cobblers or a bakery in some of the villages in the area, but you'll have difficulty avoiding the estate agents packed into the narrow streets.

Councillors in the Reading area are worried about the invasion spoiling the village and town life-style. And there are attempts to resist estate agents taking over shop premises in some places.

Berkshire County Councillor for Tilehurst West, Jean Gardner said: 'It is ridiculous with the limited facilities available in the old village of Tilehurst that there are s[o] many estate agents.

'I know it's a growth in[dustry] but there are only s[o] many houses to sell in sma[ll] towns and villages, an[d] people who live there mig[ht] be better served sometim[es] with a shop.

'We had an applicatio[n] recently for a fish and chi[p] shop in Knowsley Road i[n] Tilehurst which was turne[d] down and now another es[tate] agents has gone u[p] there.

'I am not saying that [it] should necessarily have bee[n] a fish and chip shop, but th[at] sort of thing might be of mor[e] use to the local people tha[n] yet another estate agents.'

Residence and origin of households

Place of origin	Length of residence in survey area (years)						
	1	1-2	3-4	5-6	7-10	11+	total
Henley	15	22	44	22	33	19	155
Reading	37	36	30	22	22	22	169
Berkshire	22	30	7	4	0	4	67
London	9	33	9	6	3	6	66
SE England	24	75	13	9	23	1	145
Midlands	15	4	11	0	4	0	34
Other UK	7	11	7	0	15	4	44
Overseas	4	4	7	0	0	0	15
Totals	133	215	128	63	100	56	695

'The estate agents must be fighting each other on the doorstep to find so much business.'

And villagers in Pangbourne are worried about the effect the estate agent fever is having on village life.

Pangbourne Parish council clerk Dennis Jones said: 'We are not against estate agents as such, but we do lament the loss of retail shops which is harming village life.'

'It may get to a stage where there may be no shops left and just a whole street of estate agents and building societies.'

(Source: (Reading) *Evening Post*, 1988)

Villagers press ministers for more homes

Ministers are being urged to introduce measures into housing legislation to make it easier for people, especially the young and the elderly, to buy homes in rural areas.

The Housing Corporation and the Development Commission for Rural England, will again point out that commuters and second home owners are pricing local people out of the market and that the sale of council houses is compounding the problem.

Limited exceptions to the right-to-buy policy, which permit rural councils to exercise a buy-back option or limit house sales to local people, are ineffective.

Both the commission and the corporation are expected to demand that housing legislation should include provision to make it easier to provide equity sharing schemes and houses for rent.

Mr John Williams, chief executive of the commission, revealed the initiative yesterday as a consortium of rural organisations launched a new strategy for housing, jobs and services.

The strategy document from Rural Voice, an alliance which spans the National Farmers Union, the Council for the Protection of Rural England, and other interest groups, says that rural house prices are forcing young people out of the countryside in ways which reduce family care for the old and infirm, and reduce the variety of skills needed for an integrated economy.

It urges planning authorities to rethink their policies of rigorously limiting rural housing to 'key settlements'. Instead councils should be allowed to spend much more of their house sales income on new housing, and to rent vacant properties for local use. The report makes proposals for ensuring the survival of schools, libraries, health services, village shops and other services.

Rural Voice leaders will press ministers for an integrated approach to rural needs. They will go on to list four crucial factors: the rush of firms and families from cities to small towns and villages; Common Market and Government measures to cut farm surpluses; the growing demand for rurally-based recreation; and growing concern about the quality of the environment.

(Source: John Ardill, *The Times*, 1988)

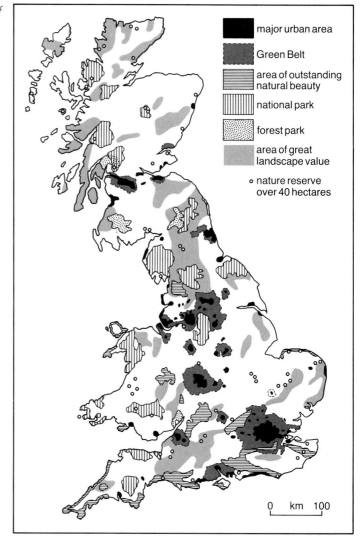

Figure 12.5 Green belts and other areas of rural importance in Britain

Legend:
- major urban area
- Green Belt
- area of outstanding natural beauty
- national park
- forest park
- area of great landscape value
- nature reserve over 40 hectares

0   km   100

Conflict in the Green Belt

The changes that have taken place in Sonning Common are typical of those affecting the countryside within commuting reach of urban areas. The reasons for developing protected zones have been explained in Chapter 11. Figure 12.5 shows the extent of the protected areas in Britain. However, the reasons for restricting planning permission do not always find favour with those in urgent need of housing, nor those seeking a place to set up a business. Nowhere is this pressure to develop and to restrict development more intense than in the green belt.

The London green belt is by far the most threatened. Because London urgently needed a ring road permission was given for the orbital motorway M25. Three lanes wide and hopelessly overcrowded from the day it was opened, this ring motorway is a symbol of the latent business that would gobble up the green belt given half a chance. In 1983 a consortium of some of the biggest builders in the country lobbied parliament to release enough building land to satisfy the demand. The lack of land was, according to the developers, one of the major reasons that house and business rent prices were shooting through the roof in the south-east. Not only was this crippling to business, but it was stopping people from the north moving to the south where there were more job opportunities.

The bid to burst the Green Belt

Tillingham Hall is a new town in the middle of South Essex between West Horndon and Bulphan on a 760 acre, flat, rather boggy site four miles off the M25. Or, at least, it will be, if a proposal by a consortium of housebuilders receives outline planning approval to go ahead with its plan to build the new town complete with road, sewers, schools, shopping centre, and community buildings – all with private money.

In ten years Consortium Developments, which include Barratt, Wimpey, Beazer, Christian Salvesen and Tarmac, hopes to have built 5100 homes, and provided 2000 jobs through the 810 000 square feet of offices and industrial accommodation, as well as shops, pubs, a filling station and everything else needed to turn a building site into a town. They lodged their planning application with Thurrock district council on Wednesday, and are now awaiting the response which they assume will be unfavourable.

Consortium Developments expect the whole thing to go to a public enquiry and be eventually settled by the Secretary of State. The group are prepared to put up £500 000 to back their case for the building, not only of Tillingham Hall, but of a dozen more new country towns, as they call them, predominantly in the south-east.

The consortium's glossy brochure seems to meet just about every criticism head on. The town is designed to be a self-contained unit with a raised embankment planted with shelter trees to suggest that the town is fen woodland from a distance. The boundary will also define and limit the town to prevent future sprawl. An inner loop road will be the main access route. The present drainage problems will be used to provide an urban landscape of parks and lakes.

The architect's visualisation suggests a pleasantly wooded and landscaped new town on the Milton Keynes model, with a babbling brook running down the middle of the shopping centre. Little architect people indulge themselves in country walking along a boundary dyke, feeding the ducks in the high street duck pond, and sailing their Laser dinghies and windsurfers on the lake.

Why have the builders decided to risk so much money on such a scheme? The answer is shortage of land and the perennial battle between developers and conservationists, with the Green Belt the chosen battleground. The developers point to the increasing mismatch between the demand for housing in the south-east and the shortage of land which is driving up the price of new homes. They argue that the regional structure plan for the south-east is only estimating 540 000 new households in the region by the end of the decade, whereas the consortium's own estimate puts the need at some 884 400 new homes. Andy Bennett, executive director for the consortium, says 'The scale of the problem is such that we cannot solve it by relying on the redevelopment of London's inner city areas and new estates tacked on on to existing towns.'

(Source: Tim Roberts, *The Guardian*, 11 May 1985)

The first major attempt at development in the green belt was at Tillingham Hall (see above). This proposal was turned down. However, developers are not permanently discouraged and their schemes are progressively more environmentally sensitive and therefore less easy to turn down. Nevertheless, one of the fundamental objections to the addition of new housing or business remains that it will change the character of the environment.

Leapfrogging the green belts

If green belt development is not allowed, the next obvious development proposals will affect the areas beyond. In the case of London, as with many other major cities, Areas of Outstanding Natural Beauty (AONB) are to be found (Fig. 12.5). Clearly, to direct the development away from such areas and into those places where the development would be less environmentally sensitive requires a regional strategy. This is one of the reasons for the introduction of **regional structure plans**. Under this system, each county decides on the future allowance of housing, business and so forth, based on guidelines given by the government. Eventually these are approved as targets for expansion over a period of about a decade. The Cambridge structure plan was used as the basis for student enquiry 6C, earlier in this book.

The natural environment determines that some counties with areas of outstanding natural beauty will lie alongside areas where rapid expansion is planned. One of these areas of conflict lies in the region of South Oxfordshire and central Berkshire.

Peril to

A lobby far more powerful than Mr Arthur Scargill's militant miners' union is putting Britain's whole industrial future at risk. Although its stance will cost the country tens of thousands of new jobs and homes, the hardliners, who are fighting for a hopelessly uneconomic status quo, strike fear into the Government.

Their battle for their existing rights and privileges has been fierce. They care not whether they impoverish others. They are the modern embodiment of the 'I'm all right Jack' mentality. The power of these 'barons' has left successive Ministers shaken and impotently raging at their immense behind-the-scenes influence.

I refer, of course, to those doughty campaigners who defend the Green Belt against encroachment. There are few strikes or demonstrations in these costly leafy lanes. But the cosy villages in the Tory heartland that surrounds the M25 orbital motorway are proving a far greater barrier to Britain's hopes of growth and industrial success than our now-cowed unions.

Shopping centre tests green belt

A shopping centre has been designed in the style of a huge Palladian mansion to try to overcome Green Belt objections.

Plans for the £150 million centre, about three miles west of Heathrow Airport, are to be submitted to South Buckinghamshire council on Friday.

The architect, the Chapman Taylor Partnership, has set the porticoed design in a landscaped park.

The developer, County and District Properties, proposes to provide the one million square feet of shopping space on two levels. There would also be some leisure amenities such as woodland nature trails and picnic sites adjoining a lake nearby.

According to Mr Roger Taylor, a director of County and District, the scheme includes some £12 million for road improvements, including widening of the M4.

The 100-acre site is a former gravel pit, which for about ten years has been used as a refuse tip. Much of it at present is a sea of mud, and it lies close to an industrial estate within site of the M4 and M25 and the tower blocks of Slough.

In spite of the site's present lack of visual appeal or amenity value, the scheme is certain to be vigorously opposed, not only because any intrusion into the Green Belt is seen as the thin end of the wedge.

At least two rival schemes for similar shopping centres, at Wraysbury and Staines, have been submitted by other developers. A public inquiry into the Wraysbury plan starts this week.

The need for any such centre, which would almost certainly take the trade away from the West London suburbs and from towns in the area, is being questioned, quite aside from its architectural attractions.

Mr Taylor said he had written to Mr William Waldegrave, Minister of State at the Department of the Environment, suggesting that all the applications should be considered at a single enquiry, but that had been rejected.

There is also a strong possibility that the Department of Transport will oppose the scheme.

Although it is empowered to intervene directly only when a development encroaches within 67 metres of a motorway, it has made known its concern at the extra congestion and safety hazards that could arise from the provision of direct access to and from the already overcrowded roads such as the M25.

An official said that the department would study any scheme very closely before deciding whether to give evidence to a public enquiry.

(Source: John Young, *The Times,* 23 Nov. 1987)

Britain from semi-rural Luddites

To put it quite simply, the modern Luddite occupies a £350,000 country house, holds a distinguished professional job, and is chairman of the local conservation society. In particularly hard cases – and he may tell you that, like the Bishop of Durham, his telephone is being tapped – he may be the local vicar himself.

No one should doubt the intentions of these good people – any more than we doubt trade unionists who proclaim they are fighting for fairness and justice. These semi-rural campaigners are palpably sincere in their desire to save the village way of life, just as Mr Scargill fought valiantly to save the Yorkshire pit 'communities'.

And yet the failure to develop new villages, new towns and new factories along the M25 could be the next twist in Britain's remorseless industrial decline. Why should, as these campaigners wish, good managers, good skilled workers and, most of all, entrepreneurs be sent into exile in a rundown inner city or hopeless northern New Towns? Sadly, after a few early sallies by Nicholas Ridley, the Environment Secretary, the Government seems to have given up the struggle.

Mrs Thatcher has convinced the country that you cannot expect prosperity if you tell businessmen what to do. She has ended the myriad of controls that stifled enterprise – with one crucial exception. Planners still expect to tell businessmen where they can take things.

As the success of the Boston Route 8 has proved – and the new high-tech businesses that have sprung up along the M4 in Britain confirm – companies want to cluster together along great arterial roads. It's good business, it's good economics. The whole state of Massachusetts has boomed as a result of Route 8 and the companies which have flourished alongside it. Yet British planners, frightened of middle class protest groups, go for the easy option. Factories, shopping centres and housing estates that are desperately needed go unbuilt.

Our latter-day Luddites have already enjoyed the benefits of the new motorway. They boast of how quickly they can reach distant parts of the country and both the airports. They are very happy that their house prices immediately rose by 25 per cent as soon as it opened. They have done very well out of the M25, thank you. It is the rest of the country that has still to receive the benefit of this huge national investment.

(Source: Graham Paterson, The *Daily Telegraph*, 28 Aug. 1987)

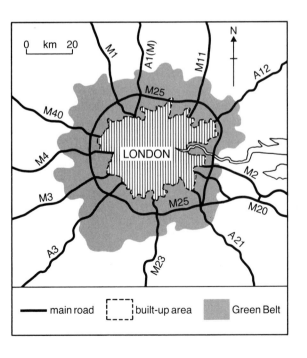

Resisting change

1. Read the article 'Peril to Britain from semi-rural Luddites'. List the main reasons the author puts forward to explain the need to open up the green belt and the reasons such development is opposed by green belt residents.
2. Examine the article 'The bid to burst the green belt' earlier in this chapter and describe the reasons for the development. Comment on how important the 'Luddites' view may have been in a final decision not to allow the development.
3. The article 'Shopping centre tests green belt' describes another form of development. Suggest the strategic reasons behind the development location. If this development were allowed, forecast where development proposals would soon follow. Mark these on the map of the London region provided.
4. As a group, argue for and against some of the consequences of such developments.

Development pressures in rural South Oxfordshire

The rural area of South Oxfordshire is mostly an Area of Outstanding Natural Beauty on the western margins of London. As such it is one of many protected areas in Britain (Fig. 12.5). However, it is especially vulnerable to urban pressure because it is flanked by the M4 and M40 motorways and is very close to the most rapidly growing part of Britain. South Oxfordshire extends to the fringes of both the city of Oxford and Reading. Both urban areas impose development pressures on South Oxfordshire. The city of Oxford is ringed with a green belt, while London's green belt extends close to the eastern boundary of Reading. Thus South Oxfordshire acts as a wedge of preserved countryside in an area that is otherwise experiencing much development.

Regional planning policy, under the umbrella of the *Strategic Plan for the South-East*, identifies certain growth points to which development will be directed. South Oxfordshire's position close to 'Area 8', the Reading–Basingstoke–Wokingham triangle, makes it vulnerable to development pressures arising from major growth taking place in this area. As the M40 is extended from Oxford to Birmingham, additional traffic from Area 8 to the M40 can be expected, especially if a third bridge over the River Thames at Reading is built. All this extra traffic will be channelled through South Oxfordshire.

The primary objective of the planning authority is to protect the attractive character of the South Oxfordshire district, its countryside and its villages, by general restraint on development. However, this objective has to be balanced against the needs of existing residents both now and in the future, and also the needs of the country as a whole.

Aspects of development

Many of the problems and issues in the rural area of South Oxfordshire are typical of rural areas generally, although the particular emphasis might be different.

(i) **Housing** All councils are required to ensure that there is a five year supply of land for house building. In South Oxfordshire this allocation is for 1250 houses, and a population of about 5000 people.

A common problem in rural areas is the lack of housing that is in the right location and price range for the local people. Because of the limited amount of housing in smaller settlements, young people leaving their parents' homes, or old people needing smaller accommodation than in the past, usually have to move to another area, possibly to a town. Many of the new houses being built in villages are larger and more expensive than the local residents want or can afford, so even if new housing is available it may not be suitable for local residents.

(ii) **Employment** As a consequence of the district's location in the south-east of the country, close to London and the M4 corridor, pressures for new office and industrial development are high. There is limited access to work within the rural district and three quarters of the economically active population have to travel daily outside the district for their employment. It is unlikely that the situation will change in the future.

(iii) **Shopping** Shopping patterns have changed, with the establishment of major food stores easily accessible to the car-borne shopper and the increased ownership of freezers. Village shops find it very hard to compete with superstores and supermarkets. While these changes do not cause problems for people who have access to a car, the closure of local shops can cause hardship to many rural residents who, in the past, depended on the local shop or post office.

(iv) **Transport** Public transport services have been cut back, a result partly of rising operating costs, particularly in the 1970s when oil prices rose dramatically, but also as car ownership increased. Subsidising public transport can reduce the effect of these trends, but the level of subsidies is very low and the public service remains inadequate for the small number who rely on it.

Because public transport is generally poor, travel to work can be a serious problem for the less well off, yet the widespread use of cars can give rise to considerable traffic congestion.

(iv) **Recreation and leisure** The Chiltern hills of South Oxfordshire offer a rich variety of recreational and leisure activities. However, the provision of facilities for large numbers of people may well destroy the resource that they come to enjoy.

Conservation issues

The designation of an AONB indicates that the landscape is of national significance, and not only of local or regional importance. The fundamental objective of planning policies in the AONBs is to preserve and enhance their natural beauty and landscape quality, while encouraging efficient agriculture and forestry. While every effort should be made to accommodate other interests, all must be subordinated to this theme. The Chiltern beechwoods are of outstanding importance to the AONB. One of the main aims might therefore be to retain this area as one of solitude and natural beauty (Fig. 12.6).

If provision is made for recreational car parking in the AONB it must be strictly limited. As part of its concern for the protection of the countryside of the district, the South Oxfordshire Council will consider the impact of development proposals on wild life.

Conservation areas can be designated under a special Act of Parliament. They are areas of special architectural or historic interest, the character and appearance of which it is desirable to preserve or enhance. These may be historic parks and country houses or village greens or town centres.

Social and demographic factors are leading to the creation of more smaller households. This is why new houses are needed despite the fact that the overall population of the district is not increasing significantly. However, smaller dwellings often mean high densities and in areas of spacious housing or in areas of particular attraction and character, higher density schemes are unlikely to be appropriate.

In accordance with nationally accepted policies, planning permission is not normally given for isolated development in the countryside, nor for new houses in hamlets or other small settlements. Similarly, permission is not normally given for a new development which would extend the limits of development of existing settlements into open countryside.

Figure 2.6 Aspects of the rural setting of South Oxfordshire

An essentially agricultural environment

Greys Court, a stately home owned by the National Trust

Narrow lanes

Student enquiry 12C

Development in the South Oxfordshire countryside

In this student enquiry we will look at the pressures on the South Oxfordshire region and at proposals to redevelop certain sites in particular. The proposals have been simplified and slightly altered for the purposes of this enquiry.

Circular 22/80 refers to the government's desire that small businesses should be encouraged and that planning policies and procedures should not generally hinder their development. At the same time the circular emphasises the government's continued commitment to the conservation of the countryside, to green belt policies and to the protection of AONBs.

1. Review the problems and issues listed so far in this chapter. Take each one separately and suggest a means of correcting the perceived problem. At this stage do not worry about the conflict that your solution may present with other solutions on your list.
2. Now make a matrix of the problems and solutions and find the areas where conflict will arise. Try to resolve these conflicts or explain why they cannot be resolved.
3. You should now put yourself in the role of the District Planning Department. The department has to follow the policy of protectionist measures outlined above. At the same time it has to resolve several pressures:
   (i) A scrap yard owner wants to develop his 10 hectare site for alternative use near Benson, east of Wallingford. The local community agrees that the present use is unsatisfactory, but the proposal is to develop a high tech site for industrial units. It is argued that this would result in an upgrading of the environment from the present use.
   (ii) The planning department has to allow the redevelopment of a disused hospital site at Peppard, next to Sonning Common. An international building firm and a property developer have jointly proposed this land be released for upmarket housing, to cater for the needs of the executive market who work on the M4 corridor. They argue that the quality of the proposed housing gives them a financial margin for landscaping and environmental improvement that would upgrade the site. They maintain that the 400 bed disused hospital is an eyesore.

   An alternative proposal is for the development of a country park, with a nature trail, organised horse and pony rides and other formal recreational opportunities. A further alternative is to create a small country zoo. The last alternative is to use the hospital as the basis of an open prison.
   (iii) An entrepreneur suggests that the future allocation of 1500 homes should all be amalgamated into a new village which could later expand into a new town and thus soak up all the population pressure from the Reading and Oxford areas in one contained node which could be provided with all required shopping services. It would relieve all pressure on other land and retain the essentially rural character of the rest of the district. It has provisionally been called Nuffield New Town, near the present hamlet of Nuffield, south-west of Wallingford.

Produce a detailed recommendation on each proposal in turn.

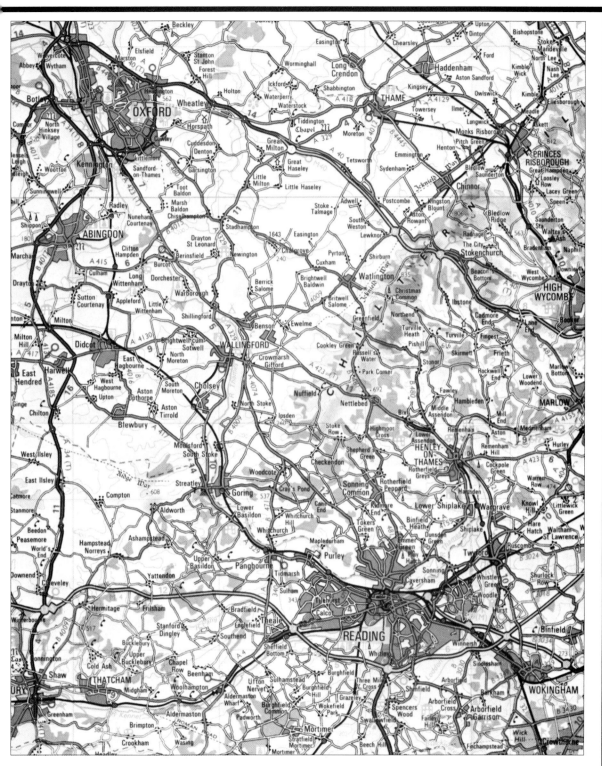

The South Oxfordshire region (Source: *Ordnance Survey*)

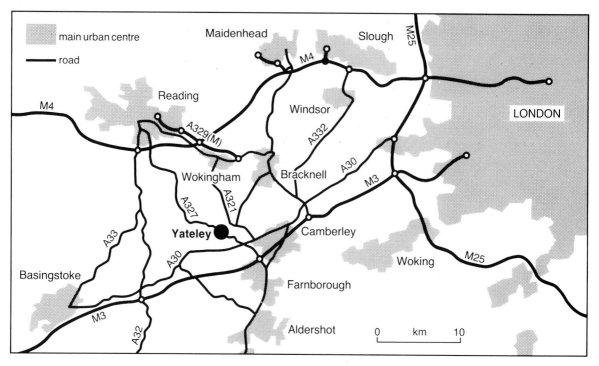

Figure 12.7 The location of Yateley

The effects of rapid rural growth: a case study of Yateley, Hampshire

This study follows on from student enquiry 12C. By now you will have been able to make some decisions about an area under pressure. Directly because of the restrictions to growth of the South Oxfordshire region, more development must occur in areas to the south of the M4. A prime location is between the M4 and M3 at Yateley (Fig. 12.7). This case study therefore shows how the countryside can become urbanised.

The parish of Yateley is in North Hampshire. In 1987 its population was 23 000 and had grown from a mere 2100 in 1931. Between 1961 and 1981 it was the fastest growing rural parish in England, and yet it was not part of a new town or other major structured development. However, Yateley is only 60 km from London, just off the M3 and A30 trunk road and within 20 km of the M4 growth corridor. Yateley does not have an industrial base of its own, rather it is a dormitory town for Reading, Bracknell and London.

Table 12.1 Yateley population growth

The development of Yateley

To the outsider, the prosperous village of Yateley would not seem a source of conflict. In Yateley people are living in their expensive new homes in the middle of the countryside.

There were two reasons for the rapid development of Yateley in the 1960s. First, the village had just had its main drainage network completed and none of the nearby villages had a proper drainage system. With a drainage infrastructure in place, buildings could be completed faster and at lower total cost than elsewhere. Secondly, planners allowed development at Yateley because they did not want expansion to spoil much prettier villages in the area. Within the area, conversion of farmland to building land was

Census Year	Population
1931	2100
1951	3157
1961	4461
1971	16 525
1981	20 464

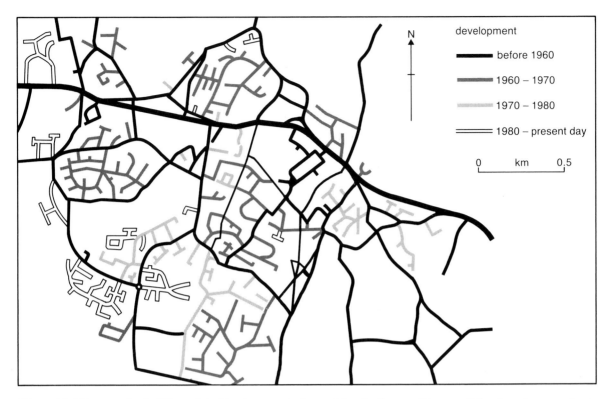

Figure12.8 Progressive infilling of the Yateley area is denoted by shading on this map. It has largely come about by piecemeal developments of unwanted land

obviously an attraction to land owners, since they stood to gain financially.

Growth of Yateley has been by infill of existing open spaces, progressively increasing the housing density (Fig. 12.8). Small housing developments have been allowed as owners wanted to sell off paddocks and other pieces of surplus 'amenity' land. However, the rather laissez-faire approach adopted by the planning authorities led to housing often being built on unsuitable sites and the demand for shopping and other central facilities outstripping their provision.

Yateley is now caught in an environmental trap. Having reached the present state of development, planning authorities see it as a preferable site for further development to adjacent areas which are:

    (i) the North Wessex Downs Area of Outstanding Natural Beauty;

    (ii) the Ministry of Defence land used by the military; and

    (iii) substantial tracts of undeveloped productive agricultural land.

Consequences of development

The Yateley area has a high water table, and large areas are prone to flooding. This has been made worse by builders directing the storm water drains into the sewerage system. One resident observed: 'It flooded so badly that people were able to canoe down the road . . . also the drain cover would float about 6 inches above the road.'

A local builder also confirms that many properties were constructed on land which was quite unstable: 'I am always getting phone calls from people who have subsidence and who want me to cure it.' In a survey of householders 17 per cent of homes reported subsidence problems.

Increase in traffic density is compounded by the fact that many homes were built without garage provision. Large numbers of cars are now left standing in streets, causing traffic hazards. Roads have not been upgraded to meet the demand and traffic jams within the village are commonplace in the morning rush hour.

The lack of provision of parking near to shopping areas has added a further problem to the village environment. Car parks are always full (Fig. 12.9).

The local police reported an increase in the amount of vandalism in the village. The change has come about because there are now sufficient people resident for large groups and gangs of young people to form. In 20 years the local police force has been increased to cope with this from 1 sergeant and 6 constables to 2 sergeants, 15 constables, 1 detective sergeant and 2 detective constables.

In a sample questionnaire survey of the residents of Yateley 50 per cent of the people complained that the rural environment that attracted them to move to the area has been eroded by further housing. This means that the reason people liked living in Yateley has been taken away (Table 12.2).

Figure 12.9 Shopping pressure on the car parks near the parade of shops in Yateley

Table 12.2 What people liked and disliked about Yateley (Source: John Tipton)

What people disliked most about Yateley when they first arrived	
Their house	16.7%
Lack of transport	16.7%
Shops	10.0%
Lack of facilities	10.0%
Others	46.6%

What people dislike most about living in Yateley now	
Lack of shops	9.5%
Lack of public transport	7.1%
Housing density and development too great	29.8%
Traffic congestion	16.7%
Lack of facilities	9.5%
Noise	3.6%
Lack of Parking	2.4%
Litter	4.8%
Others	16.7%

What people liked most about Yateley when they first arrived	
Rural location	30.8%
Village nature	30.8%
Quietness	15.4%
Church	5.1%
Other	17.9%

What people like most about living in Yateley now	
Location	25.0%
Accessibility to other places	13.2%
Local schools	8.8%
Quietness	5.9%
House they live in	8.8%
People in the area	19.1%
Others	19.1%

Student enquiry 12D

Developing the M4 corridor

The home counties to the west of London have experienced phenomenal growth as the development of 'Silicon Valley' has progressed along the M4 axis. While this has, as much as anything, been a phenomenon of redistribution of office based industry from London rather than high technology manufacturing, the pressure on land has been none the less real.

The structure plans have concentrated development into a selected number of regions. The Southern Oxfordshire region has been designated as an area of restricted development. Close to it the Eastern and Central Berkshire and North-East Hampshire districts have been earmarked for considerable growth.

1. From the articles calculate the number of new homes that Central Berkshire and North East Hampshire are expecting to make provisions for. Estimate the number of people involved.

2. Describe, in some detail, the provision that would have to be made if all these people were to be concentrated into a new town (see Chapter 11).
3. Some of the language used in the articles is highly emotive. Look particularly at the articles that describe what one local paper called 'The rape of Berkshire' and explain why such terms seem appropriate to the writers.
4. Yateley is one of the settlements to be affected. The Yateley Society (for the preservation of the village) maintains that the increase in population with less than adequate services and infrastructure is destroying the environment. This, they say, is resulting in a slackening in demand for further houses, such that any developments are unlikely to be filled.

   As a group suggest the strategies the Yateley Society might adopt if it cannot stop development entirely?

'Heseltown' battle reopens

The battle of 'Heseltown' reopens tomorrow with a new attempt by builders to get the strict curbs on further development in Berkshire removed. The county is fast becoming one of the most crowded in England.

'Heseltown' earned its sobriquet after Mr Michael Hesseltine, then Secretary of State for the Environment, told the Conservative-led county council in 1982 to allow for thousands of extra homes in its plans for the rest of the century.

Behind the present 'examination in public of the draft replacement structure plan for the county' lies fierce local determination to stem the county's growth in house building.

Even the Provost of Eton has joined the argument about whether the county can find more room for more homes.

The Berkshire battle dwarfs the controversy over builders efforts to build a new town in Essex countryside. Both are evidence of a widening clash between land-hungry builders and the conservation movement.

Berkshire County Council, supported by many residents and conservation groups, wants house building to be cut steadily from the present level of more than 6000 new homes a year to about 1000 a year in 10 years. Large building firms, many of which have bought land in the county, will tell tomorrow's public hearing that the council needs an extra 59 000 homes by 1996, and not the 37 000 proposed by the council.

Some open land is owned by Eton College, and agents for the Provost and fellows say in evidence to the hearing that they want to have 1200 houses built on college farmland between Slough and the M4 motorway, instead of the maximum of 900 recommended by the council

At the same time as the 'Heseltown' hearing another enquiry has been opened into the plans of a consortium, that includes Wates and Bovis, to develop 280 acres of land near Bracknell.

The Housebuilders' Federation says in evidence to the hearing that the county council is trying to 'export' housing pressure' and that building curbs will make it even harder for young families and workers new to the county to buy homes.

Pressure on open land in central Berkshire is acute since so much of the county is built up, while to the east and west it is protected by areas of special scenic value.

(Source: Hugh Clayton, *The Times*, 7 July 1986)

Student enquiry 12D concluded

County's plans blueprint is blown apart

The lines are drawn up, the gloves are off and the Battle for Berkshire is entering its final stage.

The fight is on for the future of the county. On the one side stands Secretary of State for the Environment, Nicholas Ridley, on the other 76 irate county councillors.

Mr Ridley announced today he wants to see an extra 43 000 houses in Berkshire by 1996 – 7000 more than councillors say the Royal county can absorb.

Sites earmarked for development include Bracknell, south Reading and Newbury, all areas bitterly opposed to more housing.

Shortage

The proposals are just part of a package of changes Mr Ridley wants to make to the council's structure plan which maps out the county's development until 1996.

He has also given the green light for extra shopping centres and thrown the council's plans for offices and warehouses into confusion.

While he approves their business policies, Mr Ridley wants the county to submit them all over again to fit new planning categories.

That could take until 1990. The structure was supposed to run from 1984 to 1986.

Mr Ridley believes his changes strike the right balance between pressures on the environment, roads and services and people's desire to live and work in Berkshire.

He argues the county council's original framework was unrealistic.

Its proposal to limit housing to 36 530 new homes would lead to a housing shortage in the 1990s.

Already the demand for homes in Berkshire exceeds the supply.

The regional planning group, SERPLAN, suggested cutting Berkshire building rates from 5000 a year to 2500.

The county council wanted to bring it down to 1000. Mr Ridley has settled on a gradual reduction to 3000 a year in the 1990s

Room must be found for an extra 7000 homes and below we pinpoint the areas where they must be.

(Source: Reading *Evening Post*, 29 Jan. 1988)

The Regional Guidelines for the 1990s

The new regional guidelines also recognise that much of the need for new housing in the 1990s is likely to result from social changes in the existing population. Accordingly, in addition to maximum housing provision in London, the strategy provides for housing needs to be met by development dispersed to existing settlements elsewhere in the region. Sensitive restraint is called for in areas subject to intensive growth pressures, notably to the west of London. The particular needs of South Hampshire, including Southampton and Portsmouth, the two largest cities in the region outside of London, are also recognised. The regional guideline for new housing in Hampshire in the 1990s is 63 000 dwellings, not including provision to replace those lost by demolition.

The County Strategy

Much of North-East Hampshire is either part of the Downlands or the Basingstoke/Blackwater gap. In addition much of the rest of the area is subject to strong countryside constraints and there are attractive towns and villages to be conserved. Opportunities for development in the east are limited by Ministry of Defence land ownership. The provision of some infrastructure has not kept pace with the rapid development of the last two decades. These factors together with the reduced need for new employment in the 1990s suggest the strategy (for North-East Hampshire) should be to slow the pace of development and limit the provision for new employment. Land should be made available for the development of about 14 100 dwellings between 1991 and 2001. Much of this land will be infilling within, and additions to, existing settlements. However, opportunities for such additions without breaching countryside constraints are limited. The development of a new community is being considered as an alternative to continued extensions of existing settlements.

(Source: *Extracts from the summary leaflet: Hampshire towards 2001*, Hampshire County Council)

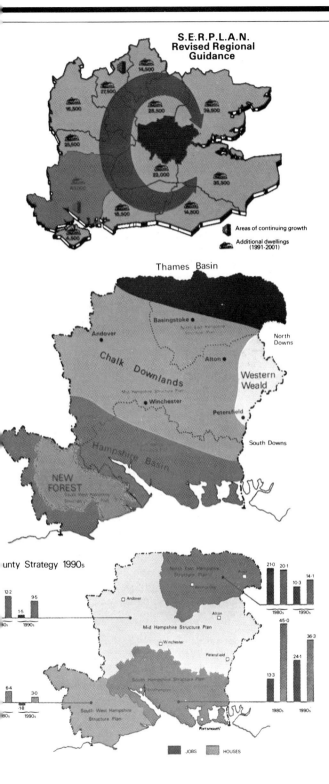

S.E.R.P.L.A.N.
Revised Regional
Guidance

Areas of continuing growth

Additional dwellings
(1991-2001)

Thames Basin

Basingstoke

Andover

North
Downs

Chalk Downlands

Alton

Western
Weald

Winchester

Petersfield

South Downs

Hampshire Basin

NEW
FOREST

unty Strategy 1990s

North East Hampshire Structure Plan

Andover

Mid Hampshire Structure Plan

Alton

210 20·1

14·1

10·3

1980s   1990s

Winchester

Petersfield

South Hampshire Structure Plan

45·0

36·3

24·1

13·3

1980s   1990s

South West Hampshire
Structure Plan

Portsmouth

JOBS   HOUSES

12·2   9·5

1·5

80s   1990s

6·4   3·0

·1·8

80s   1990s

The Structure plan by regions:

Hart District (1991-2001)

4600 new dwellings
12 hectares of industrial land
22 000 m² of new offices
15 000 m² of new shops

The County Council estimates that about 1200 of the suggested dwellings could be provided on sites within existing settlements. An allowance has been made for 14 000 m² of offices and 15 000 m² of new shops in Fleet town centre to recognise the continuing scope for improvements in the centre. Some 7 hectares of industrial land is proposed at Hook to allow for the extension of the land now being developed on the southern edge of the village.

If it is accepted that about 1200 dwellings could be provided by 'infilling', 3400 new dwellings would need to be provided by other forms of development. One alternative would be to disperse the new housing by further adding to existing towns and villages, including Fleet, Yateley, Hook and Hartley Wintney. Such sites would not be easy to find without breaching countryside constraints and would add to existing strains in towns and villages arising from recent rapid rates of development. The precise implications of a dispersal strategy cannot be measured at this stage as the distribution of new housing would need to be decided by Hart Council in a revised local plan. However, one major site that has been suggested for housing is land immediately to the north of Fleet at Railroad Heath, to the west of the existing golf course. New road connections to east and west would be necessary if this land were to be developed. The site could accommodate some 1700 dwellings. The dispersal strategy might also include an additional 8000 m of offices and 5 hectares of industrial land in or adjoining Fleet.

An alternative to continuing dispersed development would be the establishment of a new community in the northern part of the District. The whole of the 3400 new dwellings could be concentrated in a single location together with provision for new employment in offices (8000m²) and modern industry in a well landscaped parkland setting (5 hectares). A new shopping centre would also be required. Major road improvements would be required to link the area to the proposed new M3 motorway junction at Minley to the south, and to other major roads.

Figure 12.10 Disused gravel workings make an ideal site for a country park for both water and land based activities

Environmental pressure near to urban centres

Unique landscapes are, by definition, small in number, location and area. In practice they tend to be in upland or mountainous terrain, which in Britain means they are in the north and west of the country. Because most national parks have been designated for their 'wilderness' qualities, they lie mostly in relatively inaccessible locations. Thus, for example, the 15 million people in the London region must make at least a three hour journey to reach the nearest national park. National parks cannot, therefore, satisfy much of the recreational demand of a population and they must be complemented by more locally based semi-wilderness areas. Ideally these should be within easy reach of large populations, available to act as a safety valve for urban based people. Clearly it is not possible for most such areas to offer a great deal by way of landscape uniqueness, and their strategic location should mean that their prime objectives are different from national parks. With greater local catchments the opportunity should be taken to satisfy the greatest possible variety of need.

Most semi-wilderness facilities whose function (and often location) lie midway between urban parks and national parks are called **country parks**. In practice they occur in a wide variety of environments; some are in areas of heavy seasonal demand such as the Seven Sisters Country Park near Beachy Head at Eastbourne on the south coast; but most are near large urban centres, for example, the Lea Valley Country Park in East London or Cannock Chase near the Pottery towns of Staffordshire and the West Midlands conurbation. In many ways it is in the variety of the country parks that their appeal lies. But they are essentially places to 'walk the dog' rather than areas for major hiking; places for a Sunday picnic rather than for a week's holiday. Many are relatively small, and their location proximal to large centres of population makes them especially vulnerable to pressure. Some, like the country parks in London and Manchester, have been built up from virtual wastelands and represent the reclamation of old industrial sites and gravel pits. By contrast, others have been traditional beauty spots with their own wildscapes. It is these parks that are undergoing the greatest pressure from people on the environment.

Student enquiry 12E

The strategy for Cannock Chase 'Regional Nature Park'

Objective: Here you will be asked to suggest a management and development plan which sensitively balances recreational needs of the nearby urban population against conservation objectives in the Cannock Chase countryside. The strategy must be such that no needless restrictions are imposed upon the visitor, while securing a positive reversal of the environmental deterioration that has been in progress for a long time. Thus the objective is to produce a strategy which adopts the spirit of the words 'regional nature park'.

Background

Cannock Chase is an area of extensive and ancient woodlands and heaths (1200 hectares) situated between the pottery towns of Staffordshire and the northern outskirts of Birmingham. Three and a half million people live within 30 km of the Chase and thus it represents a convenient location to 'get away from it all'. The county structure plans required an additional 65 000 people and associated industry to be added to the fringes of the Chase between 1971 and 1991 and more are planned after this.

The upland location of the Chase provides more scenic opportunities than many other areas. In 1958, 66 km^2 were designated as an AONB and some areas further designated as **Sites of Special Scientific Interest** (SSSI) because of their wildlife and botanical interest. In 1973 large areas of the Chase were brought under the umbrella of country park so their future management could be planned in the light of increasing public pressure.

These three kinds of designation, and the fact that the area is shared by five planning authorities, emphasises the dilemma and raises the question: 'For how long can the area continue to function as a country playground, picnic spot and natural retreat for people from the urban areas without suffering permanent or unacceptable damage to the landscape and/or wildlife?'

You should write an answer to question 12; questions 1 to 11 will help provide some structure to the way you might approach the planning problem.

1. It is first important to set the regional scene. Using a regional map of scale 1:250 000 or similar, plot on a tracing overlay the location of Cannock Chase and the nearby major urban centres. Mark on a circle with effective radius 30 km which contains the 3.5 million people referred to above. Now draw on the major routes (motorways and trunk roads). From this suggest the likely pattern of access to the Chase and the locations most likely to experience heavy pressure if access is a major factor in people choosing a site for recreation.

2. Table 12E1 gives the result of a small spot questionnaire produced on a summer Sunday afternoon at about 3 pm near the visitor centre. Make these results up into some form of visual presentation, including a radial line diagram. Now compare the results of the questionnaire with your map of access. On a further overlay suggest the main directions of access to the Chase and the major source regions of the visitors.

3. Study the map of the Chase which shows the various land uses and roads. Some land uses (such as farmland) do not have unrestricted access. The main areas of public access and ownership are (i) Shoal Hill Common (70 hectares); (ii) Gentleshaw Common (80 hectares); (iii) Hednesford Hills Common (92 hectares); (iv) Sevens Road Picnic Area (5 hectares on reclaimed colliery site); (v) Shugborough (360 hectares of National Trust land, together with Shugborough Hall with its park).
   Suggest which of the areas are most likely to be heavily visited (**honeypots**) if ease of access is a prime consideration.

4. From other surveys taken on the Chase it is apparent that the main honeypots are Shugborough, Milford Common and Seven Roads. Can these main honeypots be explained merely by ease of access? If not, suggest some other factors that might be important.

Student enquiry 12E continued

5. Which areas of private and restricted access land might usefully be purchased and managed for public amenity?
6. The Forestry Commission has a policy of opening up areas of forest for public trails. Explain which areas might most usefully be opened up and which should be restricted to allow for wildlife preservation.
7. If a camping and caravaning site were to be allowed, where should it be?
8. The present visitor centre is near Seven Roads. If a new, enlarged visitor centre were to be built, complete with food and drink facilities, should it be on the same site and, if not, where should it be?

9. Car parking is a major requirement for the Chase. Explain the benefits and consequences of (i) a small number of large car parks with paved standing; and (ii) a larger number of small (max. 20 cars) unpaved car parks.
10. The following specialist activities need to be catered for. Examine each activity in turn and suggest how it can best be catered for within the basic strategy of the park: (i) orienteering; (ii) BMX bikes); (iii) model aircraft flying; (iv) organised festivals; and (v) golf.
11. It is proposed to set up a 'buffer zone' around the chase. Explain the use of a buffer zone and the kind of activities that could most usefully be directed to it.
12. **Activity objective**
    On a map of the Chase suggest a management and development plan which sensitively balances recreational needs against conservation objectives in Cannock Chase. The strategy must be such that no needless restrictions are imposed upon the visitor, while securing a positive reversal of the environmental deterioration that has been in progress for a long time. Thus the objective is to produce a strategy which adopts the spirit of the words 'regional nature park'. Produce a short report and visual illustration outlining the main principles of your strategy. The material should be in a form that could be posted up in the visitor centre.

Table 12E1 Origin of visitors in a small 'spot' survey

Wolverhampton	25
Birmingham	14
Walsall,Dudley	9
Stoke	9
Stafford	5
Cannock	11
Derby	4
London	2
Lichfield	2

Comments by some people who wrote to the planning authorities:
1. Main views: keep toilets and picnic sites away from the Chase; increasing visitors brings more vandalism, litter, fire damage, etc.
2. Main views: no caravan or camp sites should be allowed. Toilets are needed on some larger car parks. Provide more motorless zones – and control motorcycles. No refreshments (even ice cream vans) should be allowed. Information on the Chase is already adequate.
3. Keep the motor car to the perimeter; conserve the Chase.
4. Track barriers cause hardship to invalids and encourage poachers. Car drivers do not cause fires.

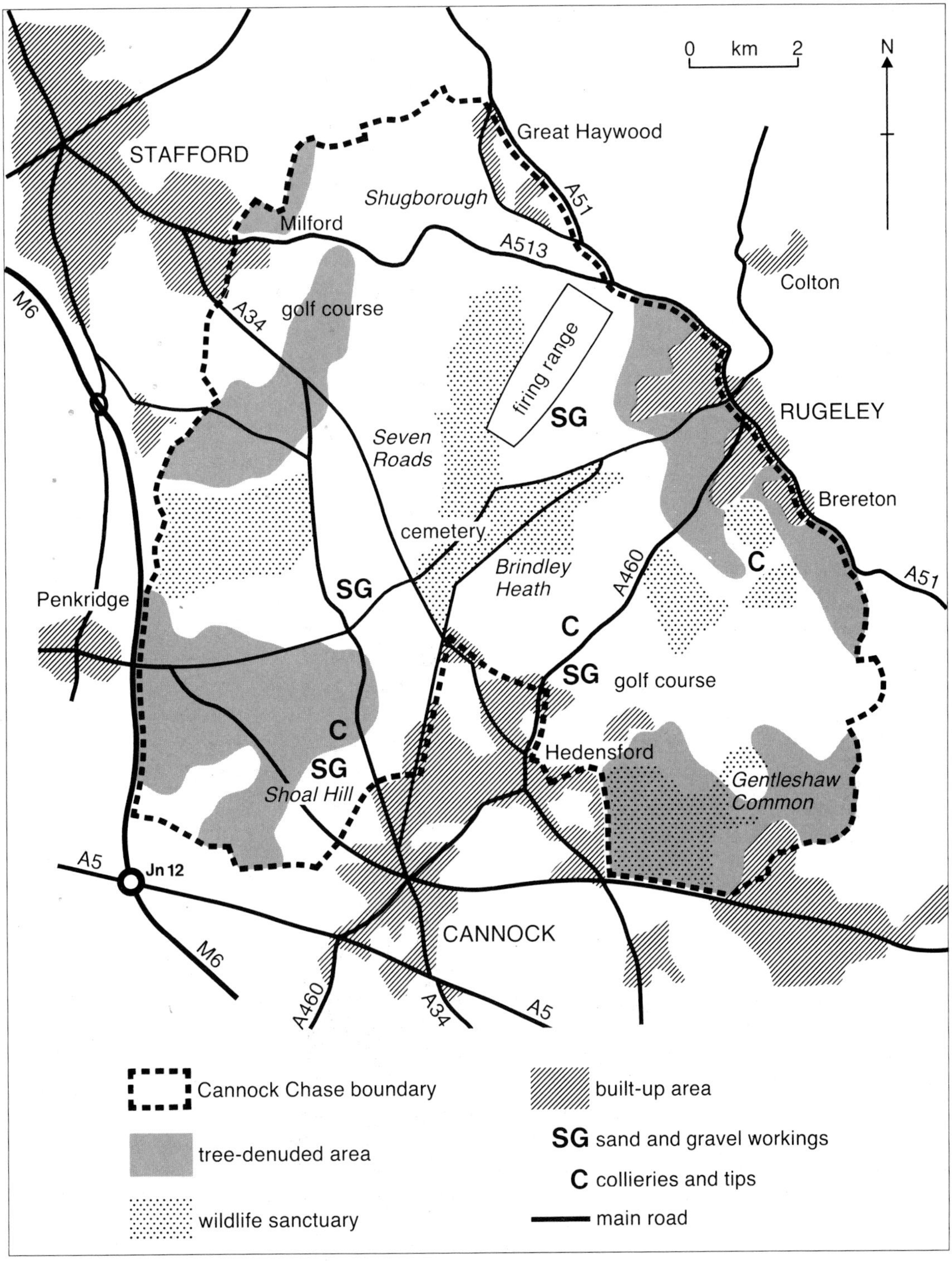
0 km 2
N
STAFFORD
Great Haywood
Shugborough
A51
Milford
A513
Colton
M6
A34
golf course
firing range
SG
RUGELEY
Seven
Roads
Brereton
cemetery
Brindley
Heath
A460
C
A51
SG
Penkridge
C
SG
golf course
C
SG
Hedensford
Shoal Hill
Gentleshaw
Common
A5
Jn 12
CANNOCK
M6
A460
A34
A5
Cannock Chase boundary
built-up area
SG sand and gravel workings
tree-denuded area
C collieries and tips
wildlife sanctuary
main road

12E2 Map of Cannock Chase

Student enquiry 12E concluded

site where questions asked	more access		wildlife value		quarries		urban development		car numbers	
	yes	no	high	low	resist	permit	permit	control	excessive	acceptable
Milford Common	85	12	94	6	57	30	55	39	45	24
Brereton	84	0	72	23	31	69	77	23	30	15
Seven Springs	89	11	94	6	50	44	83	17	50	11
Stafford Market Sq	72	28	84	14	45	50	61	33	60	16
Cannock Centre Car Park	83	16	83	5	66	33	72	27	38	44
Gentleshaw Common	66	26	80	20	66	19	66	33	53	13
Rugeley Market Sq	75	25	100	0	74	26	80	16	45	8
Shoal Hill	59	41	96	4	66	33	79	21	53	12
Average Chase answers	72	27	95	4	66	31	78	19	50	3
Average town answers	77	23	90	8	62	36	71	25	48	8

Notes

Many questionnaires were conducted and only a selection of sites is given above. The averages apply to all questionnaires conducted in and around the Chase, including those not specifically named above.

Questions tried to find out the preferences for a large number of options; only some are given here.

INDEX